TRADE ISSUES, POLICIES AND LAWS

TRENDS IN U. S. SERVICES TRADE

TRADE ISSUES, POLICIES AND LAWS

Additional books in this series can be found on Nova's website under the Series tab.

Additional E-books in this series can be found on Nova's website under the E-book tab.

AMERICA IN THE 21ST CENTURY: POLITICAL AND ECONOMIC ISSUES

Additional books in this series can be found on Nova's website under the Series tab.

Additional E-books in this series can be found on Nova's website under the E-book tab.

TRADE ISSUES, POLICIES AND LAWS

TRENDS IN U. S. SERVICES TRADE

CHARLES SCHNEIDER
AND
THOMAS G. HATCHET
EDITORS

Nova Science Publishers, Inc.
New York

Copyright © 2012 by Nova Science Publishers, Inc.

All rights reserved. No part of this book may be reproduced, stored in a retrieval system or transmitted in any form or by any means: electronic, electrostatic, magnetic, tape, mechanical photocopying, recording or otherwise without the written permission of the Publisher.

For permission to use material from this book please contact us:
Telephone 631-231-7269; Fax 631-231-8175
Web Site: http://www.novapublishers.com

NOTICE TO THE READER

The Publisher has taken reasonable care in the preparation of this book, but makes no expressed or implied warranty of any kind and assumes no responsibility for any errors or omissions. No liability is assumed for incidental or consequential damages in connection with or arising out of information contained in this book. The Publisher shall not be liable for any special, consequential, or exemplary damages resulting, in whole or in part, from the readers' use of, or reliance upon, this material. Any parts of this book based on government reports are so indicated and copyright is claimed for those parts to the extent applicable to compilations of such works.

Independent verification should be sought for any data, advice or recommendations contained in this book. In addition, no responsibility is assumed by the publisher for any injury and/or damage to persons or property arising from any methods, products, instructions, ideas or otherwise contained in this publication.

This publication is designed to provide accurate and authoritative information with regard to the subject matter covered herein. It is sold with the clear understanding that the Publisher is not engaged in rendering legal or any other professional services. If legal or any other expert assistance is required, the services of a competent person should be sought. FROM A DECLARATION OF PARTICIPANTS JOINTLY ADOPTED BY A COMMITTEE OF THE AMERICAN BAR ASSOCIATION AND A COMMITTEE OF PUBLISHERS.

Additional color graphics may be available in the e-book version of this book.

LIBRARY OF CONGRESS CATALOGING-IN-PUBLICATION DATA

Trends in U. S. services trade / editors: Charles Schneider and Thomas G. Hatchet.
 p. cm.
 Includes index.
 ISBN 978-1-62100-933-7 (hardcover)
 1. Service industries--Law and legislation--United States. 2. Foreign trade regulation--United States. 3. Service industries--Law and legislation. I. Schneider, Charles R. II. Hatchet, Thomas G. III. United States International Trade Commission.
 KF2041.T74 2011
 343.7307'8--dc23
   2011040392

Published by Nova Science Publishers, Inc. ✦ *New York*

CONTENTS

Preface vii

Chapter 1 Recent Trends in U. S. Services Trade: 2011 Annual Report 1
United States International Trade Commission

Chapter 2 U.S. Multinational Services Companies: Effects of Foreign
Affiliate Activity on U. S. Employment 133
United States International Trade Commission

Chapter Sources 195

Index 197

PREFACE

The United States is the world's largest service market and was the world's largest cross-border exporter and importer of services in 2009. Over the past three years, global trade in services has weakened in response to the downturn in the global economy, and new competitors have emerged. Despite these challenges, U. S. services providers remained highly competitive in 2009. This book provides an in-depth analyses of recent developments in the audiovisual services industry, which is highly influential both culturally and economically, as well as in four professional service industries - computer, education, healthcare, and legal services.

Chapter 1 – *Recent Trends in U. S. Services Trade: 2011 Annual Report* focuses principally on exports and imports of professional and other related services, including audiovisual, computer, education, healthcare, and legal services. This sector provides essential inputs to various goods and service industries, as well as specialized services directly to individual consumers. The largest professional service firms are located in developed countries and offer their services globally through cross-border trade and affiliate transactions. However, professional service firms in developing countries are becoming more competitive in the global market, and increasing demand for services in these countries continues to create new opportunities for expansion and investment by professional service firms both within and outside the United States. Professional service industries showed more resilience during the recent economic recession than infrastructure service industries such as telecommunications, banking, and logistics, with a smaller decline in employment and continued wage growth. As a result, the United States kept its surplus in cross-border trade in professional services in 2009, and remained competitive in the sales of services through foreign affiliates.

Chapter 2 – This working paper examines the effect that U. S. services firms' establishment abroad has on domestic employment. Whereas many papers have explored the employment effects of foreign direct investment in manufacturing, few have explored the effects of services investment. We find that services multinationals' activities abroad increase U. S. employment by promoting intrafirm exports from parent firms to their foreign affiliates. These exports support jobs at the parents' headquarters and throughout their U. S. supply chains. Our findings are principally based on economic research and econometric analysis performed by Commission staff, services trade and investment data published by the Bureau of Economic Analysis, and employment data collected by the Bureau of Labor Statistics. In the aggregate, we find that services activities abroad support nearly 700,000 U. S. jobs. Case studies of U. S. multinationals in the banking, computer, logistics, and retail industries provide the global dimensions of U. S. MNC operations and identify domestic employment effects associated with foreign affiliate activity in each industry.

In: Trends in U. S. Services Trade
Editors: Charles Schneider and Thomas G. Hatchet

ISBN 978-1-62100-933-7
© 2012 Nova Science Publishers, Inc.

Chapter 1

RECENT TRENDS IN U. S. SERVICES TRADE: 2011 ANNUAL REPORT

United States International Trade Commission

ABSTRACT

Recent Trends in U. S. Services Trade: 2011 Annual Report focuses principally on exports and imports of professional and other related services, including audiovisual, computer, education, healthcare, and legal services. This sector provides essential inputs to various goods and service industries, as well as specialized services directly to individual consumers. The largest professional service firms are located in developed countries and offer their services globally through cross-border trade and affiliate transactions. However, professional service firms in developing countries are becoming more competitive in the global market, and increasing demand for services in these countries continues to create new opportunities for expansion and investment by professional service firms both within and outside the United States.

Professional service industries showed more resilience during the recent economic recession than infrastructure service industries such as telecommunications, banking, and logistics, with a smaller decline in employment and continued wage growth. As a result, the United States kept its surplus in cross-border trade in professional services in 2009, and remained competitive in the sales of services through foreign affiliates.

ABBREVIATIONS AND ACRONYMS

ASEAN	Association of Southeast Asian Nations
BEA	Bureau of Economic Analysis
BLS	Bureau of Labor Statistics
CTS	Council for Trade in Services
EIU	Economist Intelligence Unit
FTE	Full-time Equivalent
GATS	General Agreement on Trade in Services
GDP	Gross Domestic Product

IT	Information Technology
ITU	International Telecommunications Union
IMF	International Monetary Fund
IPO	Initial Public Offering
MFN	Most-Favored-Nation
NHS	National Health Service
OECD	Organization for Economic Cooperation and Development
UN	United Nations
UNESCO	United Nations Educational, Scientific, and Cultural Organization
USDOC	U.S. Department of Commerce
USDOL	U.S. Department of Labor
USITC	U.S. International Trade Commission
USTR	Office of the United States Trade Representative
WHO	World Health Organization
WTO	World Trade Organization

EXECUTIVE SUMMARY

The United States is the world's largest service market and was the world's largest cross-border exporter and importer of services in 2009.[1] Over the past three years, global trade in services has weakened in response to the downturn in the global economy, and new competitors have emerged. Despite these challenges, U.S. services providers remained highly competitive in 2009.

Much of the United States' competitiveness in the global services market can be attributed to its professional service industries, which are the focus of this year's report.[2] Trade in many professional services was weakened by the economic downturn because these services are used as intermediate inputs for other industries, but overall, professional services proved more resilient than infrastructure services.

The *2011 Recent Trends in U.S. Services Trade* report provides in-depth analyses of recent developments in the audiovisual services industry, which is highly influential both culturally and economically, as well as in four professional service industries—computer, education, healthcare, and legal services. These industries provide critical services that contribute to the U.S. economy at home and abroad. For example, computer services enhance productivity and support business activities across all industries; education and healthcare services contribute to a knowledgeable, skilled, and healthy workforce, while meeting foreign demand for U.S. expertise; and legal services facilitate trade and investment by mitigating risk in business activity. The United States remained a world leader in these industries, recording a cross-border trade surplus in all but the computer services industry in 2009 (figure ES.1).[3]

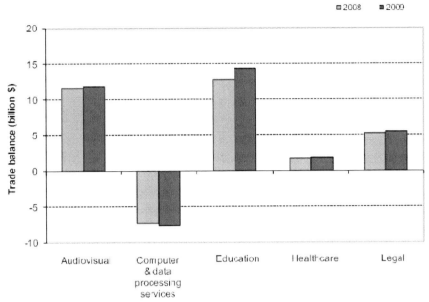

Source: USDOC, BEA, *Survey of Current Business*, October 2010, 36–37, tables 1 and 2.

Figure ES.1. Among the services discussed in this report, the United States recorded a cross-border trade surplus in all but the computer services industry in 2008 and 2009.

Leading firms in these industries have adapted to a number of economic challenges in markets at home and abroad, including shifting demand and changes in the way the industries operate. The recent economic downturn depressed demand for a number of these services, including computer, healthcare, and legal services. Reduced demand motivated suppliers in these and other service industries to cut costs. In industries inextricably related to government policy, such as education and healthcare, recent policy changes reflect government efforts to balance budgetary and social objectives. Demographic trends increased demand in mature audiovisual and healthcare services markets, and economic development in emerging markets stimulated demand in overseas markets for education and legal services and bolstered trade in computer services. Finally, innovations in technology-dependent industries, such as audiovisual and computer services, have reshaped these industries by enabling them to provide new services and use new methods of delivery.

Key Findings

Total U. S. Trade in Services

The United States Remained Highly Competitive in the Global Services Market in 2008-09

The United States remained the world's largest exporter and importer of services in 2009. In 2009, U. S. private service exports totaled $483.9 billion, or 14.1 percent of global services exports—twice the share of the next largest exporter—and U. S. service imports totaled

$334.9 billion, or 10.5 percent of global services imports. The United States' leading services trade partner was the United Kingdom ($51.0 billion of exports and $38.1 billion of imports), followed by Canada ($42.0 billion exports and $22.0 billion imports) and Japan ($40.9 billion exports and $20.8 billion imports). Travel services accounted for the largest single-industry share of U. S. services trade in 2009, accounting for 19.4 percent of exports and 21.9 percent of imports.

In 2008, the most recent year for which affiliate data are available, services supplied by foreign affiliates of U. S. firms (foreign affiliates) continued to exceed services supplied by U. S. affiliates of foreign firms (U.S. affiliates). Services supplied by foreign affiliates totaled $1.1 trillion in 2008, representing 12 percent growth over the previous year. Growth in services supplied by U. S. affiliates was slower that year, increasing 6 percent to $727.4 billion. As in cross-border services trade, the United Kingdom was the United States' largest market for affiliate transactions, accounting for 20 percent of services supplied by foreign affiliates and 18 percent of services supplied by U. S. affiliates.

The U. S. Cross-border Trade Surplus Declined in 2009, Largely Due to the Economic Downturn

The total U. S. cross-border trade surplus in 2009 shrank for the first time since 2003: it was $149.0 billion, down from $161.4 billion in 2008. As in most previous years, many individual U. S. service industries recorded trade surpluses in 2009; the largest surpluses among all services—infrastructure and professional—were in royalties and license fees ($64.6 billion) and financial services ($40.0 billion). The insurance industry again netted the largest cross-border trade deficit, which totaled $40.6 billion, largely due to payments by U. S. primary insurers to reinsurance firms in Europe and the Bahamas. Additionally, although service industries were more successful in weathering recent economic events than manufacturing industries, service industries with ties to goods industries netted cross-border services trade deficits owing in part to the indirect effects of the economic downturn. For example, the $6.2 billion trade deficit in transportation services largely reflects the U. S. trade deficit in manufactured goods. However, the recovery in global demand during 2010 has had a positive impact on service industries; trade data for the first three quarters of 2010 indicate an increase in both global merchandise trade and U. S. services trade.

Professional Services

Professional Services Account for a Large and Growing Share of the U. S. Economy

In 2009, professional services contributed $2.2 trillion, or 20 percent, to U. S. private sector GDP. Further, between 2004 and 2008, annual growth in professional services output of 3 percent surpassed output growth in infrastructure services (2.2 percent), as well as in the U. S. private sector as a whole (1.9 percent). Professional services employed 26 million persons, or 26 percent of U. S. private sector employment, in 2009. These workers are highly educated and highly skilled overall, and they earn higher wages, on average, than either infrastructure service providers or goods providers. Although wages vary widely among these industries, ranging from $40,785 for education service workers to $95,337 for computer systems design and related service employees, they have risen more rapidly than those for infrastructure services over the past five years.

Despite Wage Growth, Total Labor Productivity in Professional Services Weakened in 2009

Labor productivity for workers in all professional service sectors (calculated as industry value added or contribution to GDP per full-time equivalent employee) fell slightly, from $84,628 in 2008 to $84,042 in 2009. This drop represented the only decline among U. S. private sector industries; in that same year, labor productivity increased among goods manufacturers (4.9 percent) and infrastructure services providers (5.8 percent). The decline in productivity among professional services followed a period of slow growth: labor productivity increased less than 0.1 percent annually between 2004 and 2008. This creeping growth was due in part to rising employment. During 2004–08, full-time employment in professional services grew at an average rate of 3 percent per year, keeping pace with growth in professional services GDP. As a result, productivity gain was minimal.

However, not all professional service industries experienced productivity declines in 2010. The computer systems design and related services industry increased productivity by 4 percent in 2009. Providers of miscellaneous professional, scientific, and technical services increased productivity by 2 percent.

Regulation of Professional Services Balances Welfare Concerns and Economic Efficiency

Many professional services are subject to relatively heavy regulation, which is frequently enacted to protect consumer welfare or meet other non-market objectives. Research looking at the relationship between regulation and economic growth in OECD countries has suggested that such regulation may hinder labor productivity gains by reducing innovation and competition. However, many countries have prioritized social or other objectives over the potential economic benefits of deregulation.

Many Professional Services Are Outsourced to Offshore Firms

Professional services are increasingly outsourced to offshore locations as a result of firms' desire to contain labor costs and emphasize core competencies. Although this practice initially focused on low-skilled service jobs, more recently U. S. firms have moved certain high-skill jobs to developing countries. There is currently no consensus on the effect this trend will have on the U. S. professional services industry, as perspectives among researchers differ. Further, some studies on labor productivity suggest that the largest result of this trend may be to increase the productivity of the industries that consume professional services.

In 2008–09, Cross-border Trade in Professional Services Exceeded Sales through Affiliates

In 2009, professional services accounted for 20.2 percent of total U. S. cross-border services exports and 20.9 percent of total U. S. cross-border services imports. In that year, the United States recorded a cross-border trade surplus in professional services of $27 billion, as U. S. exports of professional services ($97.6 billion) substantially exceeded U. S. imports ($70.1 billion). Among the professional service industries, management and consulting services accounted for the largest share of U. S. professional service exports (28.9 percent) and imports (31.7 percent).

Cross-border trade in professional services slightly exceeded sales through affiliates. Nonetheless, in 2008, foreign affiliates of U. S. firms supplied no less than $91.8 billion in professional services, exceeding the $82.2 billion in professional services supplied by U. S. affiliates of foreign firms.

Audiovisual Services

Global Box Office Revenues, Led by the U. S. Industry, have Risen Steadily in Recent Years[4]

Global box office revenues reached an all-time high of $29.5 billion in 2009, an increase of just over 5 percent from the previous year ($28.0 billion). Notably, China ranked among the top 10 global markets in 2009 for the first time; in 2010, analysts predicted that by the end of the year China would have joined the world's billion-dollar box office markets, of which there were six in 2009. The U. S. market, with box office revenues of $9.7 billion, remained the world leader in 2009. U. S. cross-border exports of audiovisual services have consistently exceeded U. S. cross-border imports over the last decade. This trade surplus came to about $12 billion in 2009. Several factors underlie global growth, including increasing demand for and availability of more expensive 3-D and high-definition titles; the construction of more digital-ready movie theaters; higher movie ticket prices; and the proliferation of lower-cost digital distribution channels.

International Trade in the Audiovisual Industry Has Suffered from Serious Impediments

In several important markets, growing online intellectual property piracy has hampered industry growth in terms of both international trade and domestic sector development. Other lingering impediments include content quotas and foreign equity restrictions. In response, the industry is looking to implement more cost-effective production processes, increase film co-productions in rapidly growing markets such as China's, and diversify into more international market segments by taking advantage of the increasing use and overall availability of digital filmmaking and distribution technologies.

Computer Services

Despite the Downturn, the Global Computer Services Industry Grew during 2004–09

In response to the economic downturn, global spending on computer services contracted to $715.0 billion in 2009, following growth from $588.6 billion in 2004 to $745.0 billion in 2008 (representing average annual growth of 6.1 percent). Demand for computer services remained highest in Western Europe and North America, where most of the industry's leading firms are headquartered, but was most resilient to the downturn in the Asia-Pacific region, where several Indian companies have emerged as industry leaders. Sales dropped during the downturn due to the struggles of leading clients, notably financial firms, although persistent demand from government and healthcare firms helped offset the decline. Large computer hardware and software firms began to supply more computer services, especially over the

Internet (via "cloud computing"), often delivered across borders due to the rapid growth of broadband infrastructure.

U.S. Cross-border Trade in Computer and Data Processing Services Ran a Deficit Each Year during 2006–09

The United States' trade deficit in computer and data processing services grew by 8.1 percent during 2006–09, totaling $7.7 billion at the end of the period. India led the world in exports of these services, supplying one-third of U. S. imports in 2009. Sales by U. S. firms' foreign computer services affiliates far exceeded U. S. cross-border exports, and sales by foreign firms' computer services affiliates in the United States nearly doubled, from $10.8 billion in 2003 to $21.0 billion in 2008. While explicit barriers to trade and foreign investment in this sector are rare, the advent of cloud computing raised concerns about impediments to cross-border data flows. Forecasts suggest that demand for computer services, particularly those delivered over the Internet, will grow in the near future.

Education Services

International Trade in Education Services Continued to Expand

International trade in education services was influenced by diverse factors, including strong developing-country demand, especially from students in China and India; stricter regulations in several countries concerned about would-be immigrants posing as students; and government budget cuts. A growing number of universities are motivated to attract foreign students for financial reasons as well as to increase student body diversity. As competition among universities for foreign students—particularly the best-qualified students—intensifies, universities have sought to differentiate themselves from peer institutions by upgrading campus facilities and hiring foreign student recruitment firms, among other methods.

Worldwide, U. S. Universities Remained the Premier Destination for Foreign Students

The United States' cross-border trade surplus in education services expanded in 2009. Tuition increases and growing foreign student enrollments propelled U. S. export growth, whereas the increasing tendency of U. S. students to enroll in briefer, less costly study-abroad programs slowed import growth. Foreign students at U. S. universities mostly come from Asian countries, especially China, India, and Korea. By contrast, most U. S. students who attend foreign universities enroll in schools in the European Union, primarily in France, Italy, Spain, and the United Kingdom. International barriers to trade in education services largely involve restrictions on establishing campus facilities abroad and regulations governing the official acceptance of university degrees from other countries.

Healthcare Services

Global Spending on Healthcare Services has Steadily Risen since 2003

From 2003 through 2008, global healthcare spending rose at an average annual rate of roughly 9 percent to reach $5.9 trillion, or almost 10 percent of global GDP. The world's largest healthcare markets are still found in the United States and Europe. However, the fastest-growing markets are in developing countries, where private expenditures are rapidly increasing. Demand for privately financed care fell in developed markets, as people reduced spending following the economic downturn. However, the rising incidence of chronic illnesses has driven global demand for treatments to manage these conditions. Governments around the world have launched programs and reforms to meet the growing needs of their constituents and to address shortcomings in healthcare infrastructure and the supply of healthcare workers.

Despite Import Growth, High Quality Sustained the U. S. Cross-border Trade Surplus in Healthcare

The United States has maintained a trade surplus in healthcare services, which grew to $1.74 billion in 2009, largely due to exports to its neighbors in North America. In 2009, the U. S. exported $2.6 billion of healthcare services—triple the figure for U. S. imports, which totaled $879 million. U. S. exports maintained a competitive advantage based on the quality and expertise of U. S. providers, but a growing share of U. S. residents, particularly those without insurance, traveled to Mexico and other countries offering low- cost healthcare. Purchases from U. S. affiliates of foreign firms continued to exceed sales by foreign affiliates of U. S. firms, as the United States kept its position as the largest private healthcare market in the world.

Legal Services

Though Ascendant, U. S. and European Law Firms Lost Market Share to Providers in Developing Countries

In recent years, European and U. S. law firms have lost global market share to firms in the Asia-Pacific region. From 2005 to 2009, the Asia-Pacific share of the global legal services market doubled from 5.1 to 10.4 percent, while the shares accounted for by the Americas and Europe fell. During the global downturn, legal service providers in the Asia-Pacific fared better than in the United States or Europe, the traditional market drivers. Moreover, from 2005 through 2008, U. S. imports of legal services grew faster than exports, reflecting the growing competitiveness of foreign legal services providers. However, U. S. firms are taking advantage of commercial opportunities in developing countries. In 2009, direct investment abroad by U. S. law firms increased faster than in most other professional service industries, and although U. S. foreign affiliate sales remained concentrated in Europe, affiliates in the Middle East and Latin America are multiplying.

Despite the Global Legal Services Slowdown, U. S. Cross-border Trade and Affiliate Transactions Kept Growing

Although both U. S. exports and U. S. imports of legal services declined in 2009, exports declined more slowly; consequently, the U. S. legal services trade surplus grew to $5.5 billion in 2009. Further, growth in exports to Latin America and the Asia-Pacific region offset decreases in exports to Europe and Canada. Moreover, in 2008, the last year for which data are available, sales by foreign legal service affiliates of U. S. firms grew 8.6 percent to $3.4 billion and continued to exceed purchases from U. S. affiliates of foreign law firms, which totaled only $117 million. U. S. law firms managed costs during the slowdown by laying off employees and reducing other business costs, such as marketing.

RECENT USITC ROUNDTABLE DISCUSSION

The Commission hosted its fourth annual services roundtable on December 8, 2010. Participants from government, industry, and academia offered a range of perspectives on issues affecting services trade. This year's discussion topics included the effect of globalization on U. S. service jobs and wages, the net welfare effects of establishing service affiliates abroad, and the effects of technological advancements on the production and delivery of services. Roundtable participants emphasized the difficulties in understanding trade trends in the absence of comprehensive data, debated the significance of globalization on employment trends in U. S. service industries, and concluded with a discussion of challenges facing U. S. service industries—in particular, the need to develop a competitive, well-educated workforce.

1. INTRODUCTION

This annual report examines U. S. services trade, both in the aggregate and in selected industries; identifies important U. S. trading partners; and analyzes global competitive conditions in selected service industries. This year's report focuses on audiovisual services and the following professional services: computer, education, healthcare, and legal services.[5]

Data and Organization

The U. S. International Trade Commission (USITC) draws much of the services trade data used throughout this report from the U. S. Department of Commerce (USDOC), Bureau of Economic Analysis (BEA).[6] These data are supplemented with information from other sources, including individual service firms, trade associations, industry and academic journals and reports, electronic media, international organizations, and other government agencies.

The balance of this chapter examines cross-border trade in services from 2004 through 2009 and affiliate sales of services from 2005 through 2008;[7] compares the trade situation during the most recent year for which data are available to previous trends; and describes the nature and extent of cross-border trade and affiliate transactions. Chapter 2 discusses trends affecting professional service industries and examines the contribution of these industries in terms of economic output, employment, labor productivity,[8] and trade. Chapters 3 through 7 analyze the audiovisual, computer, education, healthcare, and legal service industries. These chapters provide an overview of global competitiveness, examine recent trends in cross-border trade and/or affiliate transactions, summarize trade impediments, and discuss industry-specific trends. Lastly, Chapter 8 summarizes the discussion of the fourth annual USITC services trade roundtable, hosted by the Commission in December 2010.

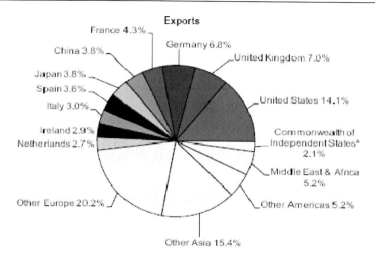

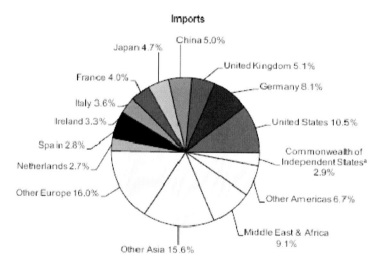

Source: WTO, *International Trade Statistics 2010, 2010*, 189–94, tables A8 and A9.
Notes: Excludes public-sector transactions. Geographic regions are shaded yellow.
[a] Includes Armenia, Azerbaijan, Belarus, Georgia, Kazakhstan, Kyrgyzstan, Moldova, Russia, Tajikistan, and Ukraine.

Figure 1.1. Global services: The United States led the world in cross-border exports and imports of services in 2009.

The U. S. Services Sector

Service industries account for an overwhelming majority of U. S. production and employment. In 2009, the U. S. services sector comprised 79 percent (or $8.9 trillion) of total

U. S. gross domestic product (GDP) and 81 percent (or 82.2 million) of U. S. full- time employees, compared to 21 percent and 19 percent, respectively, for the goods- producing sector. In that year, services sector workers earned an average salary of $49,285, which was slightly lower than the non-service sector worker's average salary of $55,505. Recent trends in the U. S. services sector have mirrored overall trends in the U. S. economy, as average annual increases in services sector GDP, employment, and wages were within 1 percent of the growth rates registered for the United States as a whole from 2004 through 2009.[9] A more detailed description of production and labor trends in U. S. professional service industries, which are the focus of this year's report, is given in Chapter 2.

Global Services Trade

Services trade, which has grown faster than trade in goods, is an important contributor to global GDP. In 2007, the volume of international trade in services (i.e., imports plus exports) amounted to roughly 12 percent of worldwide GDP—nearly double its share in 1990.[10] The United States is highly competitive in the global services market. As the world's top exporter of services, the United States accounted for $473.9 billion, or 14.1 percent, of global cross-border commercial services[11] exports in 2009 (figure 1.1). Other top single-country exporters included Germany and the United Kingdom (each accounting for approximately 7 percent). Although most of the world's top 10 services exporters in 2009 were developed countries, China tied Japan for fifth place among the largest services exporters. Overall, the top 10 exporting countries accounted for roughly 52 percent of global cross-border services exports in 2009.[12]

The United States was also the world's largest services importer in 2009, with $330.6 billion, or 10.5 percent, of global commercial services imports. In that year, Germany and the United Kingdom respectively accounted for 8.1 percent and 5.1 percent of such imports, while the top 10 importing countries together accounted for one-half of global commercial services imports. China, which was the fourth-largest importer of commercial services in 2009, was the only developing country to rank among the top 10 global importers.

The U. S. services trade surplus ($143.3 billion) in 2009 was the world's highest, followed by that of the United Kingdom ($72.4 billion). Saudi Arabia and China had the world's largest services trade deficits, with imports exceeding exports by $36.2 billion and $29.6 billion, respectively.[13]

U.S. Trade in Services

The BEA publishes data on both cross-border trade and affiliate transactions in services, which together account for a substantial portion of the services provided through all four modes of supply specified in the General Agreement on Trade in Services (GATS) (box 1.1). "Cross-border trade" occurs when suppliers in one country sell services to consumers in another country, with people, information, or money crossing national boundaries in the process. Such transactions appear explicitly as imports and exports in the balance of payments. Firms also provide services to foreign consumers through affiliates established in host (i.e., foreign) countries, with the income generated through "affiliate transactions" appearing as direct investment income in the balance of payments. The channel of delivery used by service providers depends primarily on the nature of the service.

Box 1.1. Services Trade under the General Agreement on Trade in Services

The GATS identifies four modes of supply through which services are traded between WTO members:

Mode 1 is cross-border supply. Data for this mode of supply do not completely overlap with BEA's data for cross-border trade (see discussion below). In this mode, a service is supplied by an individual or firm in one country to an individual or firm in another (i.e., the service crosses national borders).

Mode 2 is consumption abroad. In this mode, an individual from one country travels to another country and consumes a service in that country.

Mode 3 is commercial presence. In this mode, a firm based in one country establishes an affiliate in another country and supplies services from that locally established affiliate.

Mode 4 is the temporary presence of natural persons. In this mode, an individual service supplier from one country travels to another country on a short-term basis to supply a service there—for example, as a consultant, contract employee, or intracompany transferee at an affiliate in the host country.[a]

Cross-border trade and affiliate transactions data reported by the BEA do not correspond exactly to the channels of service delivery reflected in the GATS of the WTO.[b] The BEA notes that mode 1 and mode 2 transactions, as well as some mode 4 transactions, generally are grouped together in its data on cross-border trade, while mode 3 transactions are included, with some exceptions, in affiliate transactions data.

[a] USDOC, BEA, *Survey of Current Business*, October 2009, 40–43, tables 1 and 2.
[b] For more information on the four modes of supply under the GATS, see WTO, "Chapter 1: Basic Purpose and Concepts," n.d. (accessed April 7, 2009).

Box 1.2. The Rise of Affiliate Transactions

Since 1986, when the U. S. Department of Commerce began collecting statistics on U. S. services trade, the relative importance of cross-border trade and affiliate transactions has shifted significantly.[a] In each of the 10 years from 1986 through 1995, U. S. cross-border exports of services exceeded sales by majority-owned foreign affiliates of U. S. firms. Since 1996, however, sales by U. S. firms' foreign affiliates have exceeded cross-border services exports. In 2008, services supplied by U. S. firms' affiliates abroad ($1.1 trillion) were more than double the value of U. S. cross-border exports of services ($517.9 billion). Similarly, services supplied to U. S. citizens by foreign-owned affiliates have exceeded cross-border services imports since 1989. In 2008, services supplied to U. S. citizens by the U. S. affiliates of foreign companies ($727.4 billion) were nearly twice the value of U. S. services imports ($365.5 billion).[b]

The growing predominance of affiliate transactions largely reflects the global spread of service firms, facilitated by the liberalization of investment and services trade regimes. Liberalization first occurred in developed countries and has occurred more recently in a growing number of low- and middle-income countries.

[a] USDOC, BEA, *Survey of Current Business*, October 2006, 20–21.
[b] USDOC, BEA, *Survey of Current Business*, October 2010, 18.

For example, many services that require knowledge of and experience in the local market, such as advertising services, are supplied most effectively through affiliates located close to the consumer. Conversely, educational services to foreign consumers are predominantly provided through a form of cross-border trade known as consumption abroad, wherein a student from one country attends a university in another country. Affiliate transactions are the principal means of providing services to overseas customers, accounting for 66 percent of overall U. S. services trade volume in 2008 (box 1.2).

Cross-border Trade

According to the BEA, U. S. exports of private sector services totaled $483.9 billion in 2009, while U. S. imports totaled $334.9 billion, resulting in a $149.0 billion trade surplus (figure 1.2).[14] Professional services accounted for 20.2 percent of exports and 20.9 percent of imports (figure 1.3).[15] Travel services accounted for the largest single- industry share of U. S. services trade in 2009,[16] representing 19.4 percent of U. S. exports and 21.9 percent of U. S. imports.[17]

In 2009, U. S. cross-border services exports fell for the first time since 2003. According to BEA data on trade in private-sector services,[18] U. S. cross-border services exports decreased by 7 percent in 2009, following average annual growth of 12 percent during the five-year period beginning in 2004. This decline spread broadly across service industries, led by trade-related services (31 percent);[19] accounting, auditing, and bookkeeping services (27 percent); transportation services (19 percent);[20] travel services (15 percent); and financial services (9 percent). Although overall services exports decreased, several service industries had double-digit increases. These industries include, sports and performing arts services (47 percent); mining services (31 percent); services related to the installation, maintenance, and repair of equipment (18 percent); and education services (11 percent). The impact of the global economic downturn on services trade is examined in box 1.3.

The value of U. S. services imports fell by 8 percent in 2009, following average annual growth of 12 percent from 2004 through 2008. Imports fell in over half of the reported service industries, with the largest decrease in transportation services (23 percent). U. S. imports in several other categories also dropped significantly, including passenger fares (20 percent), finance (18 percent), and legal services (15 percent).

As in most previous years, the majority of U. S. service industries registered cross-border trade surpluses in 2009. Royalties and license fees achieved the largest surplus in 2009 ($64.6 billion), followed by financial services ($40.0 billion), [21] travel services ($20.7 billion), education services ($14.3 billion), and audiovisual services ($11.9 billion). Service industries that netted cross-border trade deficits in 2009 include insurance services ($40.6 billion), transportation services ($6.2 billion), and computer and data processing services ($7.7 billion). The deficit in insurance services principally reflects U. S. primary insurers' payments to European and Bermudian reinsurers in return for their assuming a portion of large risks. The deficit in transportation services (i.e., freight transport and port fees) largely reflects the U. S. deficit in manufactured goods trade and the way in which U. S. imports of freight transportation services are measured. For example, Chinese shipments of manufactured goods to the United States typically exceed U. S. shipments of goods to China, and payments to Chinese or other foreign shippers for the transport of U. S. merchandise imports are recorded by BEA as U. S. imports of transportation services. Lastly, the deficit in computer and data processing services largely reflects the outsourcing by U. S. firms of many of these services to Indian providers.[22]

A small number of developed countries account for a substantial share of U. S. cross-border services trade. Canada, Japan, and the United Kingdom collectively accounted for 28 percent of total U. S. cross-border services exports in 2009. The United Kingdom (11 percent), Canada (9 percent), Japan (8 percent), and Ireland and Germany (5 percent each) accounted for the largest single-country shares of U. S. services imports in 2009. The EU accounted for 36 percent each of U. S. services exports and imports in 2009.[23]

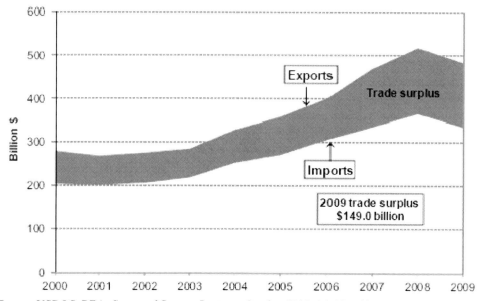

Source: USDOC, BEA, *Survey of Current Business*, October 2010, 36–37, table 1.

Figure 1.2. U. S. services: U. S. cross-border trade in private-sector services resulted in a U. S. trade surplus each year during 2000–2009.

Box 1.3. Effects of the Economic Recession on Global Trade Flows and Their Impact on the Service Sector

The worldwide economic recession substantially reduced global trade flows in 2009. According to the WTO, the volume of global merchandise trade declined by more than 12 percent among all countries during that year, with the most pronounced decline—15 percent—occurring among countries in the developed world.[a] In the United States, exports and imports of manufactured goods fell 12 percent by value between 2008 and 2009.[b] By contrast, U. S. trade in services exhibited more resilience, declining by only half that amount, or 6 percent, during the same period.[c]

Nonetheless, many U. S. service sectors experienced a decrease in exports or imports in 2009. Industries that registered the largest declines were those inextricably linked to merchandise trade:[d] trade-related services;[e] transportation services;[f] financial services; and accounting, auditing, and bookkeeping services. Financial, accounting, and trade-related services were most likely affected by the overall drop in merchandise shipments, as fewer businesses sought—or were able to access—credit from banks; inventory levels declined; and financially strapped consumers made fewer overseas purchases, whether online or through intermediaries.[g]

Trade in transportation services—especially maritime freight transport—was particularly hard hit by the recession. A decline in consumer and industrial spending reduced the demand for cross-border shipments of manufactured goods. Maritime freight prices fell precipitously and this, together with the smaller volume of goods shipped, decreased the value of maritime trade flows. For example, U. S. maritime freight exports to Europe contracted by 60 percent in 2009 from the previous year, while U. S. exports to Asia fell by 12 percent.[h] Trade in air freight services was similarly affected by the recession in 2009: U. S. airlines transported 15 percent fewer goods by volume to foreign countries than in 2008, leading to a 32 percent decrease in the value of U. S. exports of air freight and port services combined.[g]

2010 brought a reversal in the downward trend. In the first half of that year, global merchandise trade increased as GDP grew in major economies such as Europe, Japan, the United States, and China. As a result, by the end of 2010, global merchandise trade rose an estimated 14 percent over the previous year.[a] Such growth has had a positive impact on U. S. services trade: data from BEA for the first three quarters of 2010 show an overall increase in U. S. exports and imports of services over 2009, led principally by transportation services (see figure below).

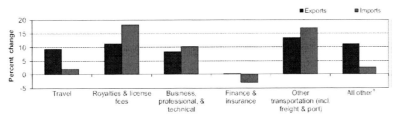

Source: USDOC, BEA, "Table 3a," December 16, 2010.
[a] Includes passenger fares, education, insurance services, telecommunications, and other services.

U.S. trade in private services increased during the first three quarters of 2010 compared to the whole of 2009.

[a] WTO, "Trade Likely to Grow by 13.5% in 2010," September 20, 2010.
[b] USDOC, BEA, *Survey of Current Business*, October 2010, table F.1.
[c] Borchert and Mattoo, "The Crisis-Resilience of Services Trade," April 2009, 2–5. In a 2009 World Bank study examining the effects of the global economic recession on services trade, the authors found that, in general, U. S. services exports, as well as those from other countries, were less affected by the recession than exports of manufactured goods.
[d] As noted, U. S. exports of passenger fares and travel services also decreased in 2009.
[e] See footnote 15.
[f] Not including passenger fares.
[g] JP Morgan, "Global Trade," n.d. (accessed November 5, 2010).
[h] Federal Maritime Commission, *48th Annual Report for Fiscal Year 2009*, 2009, 19, 29.

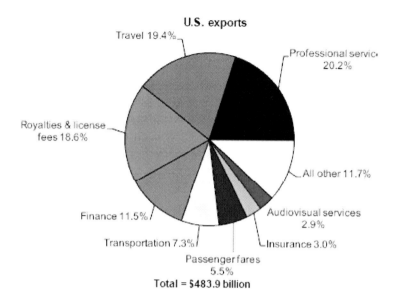

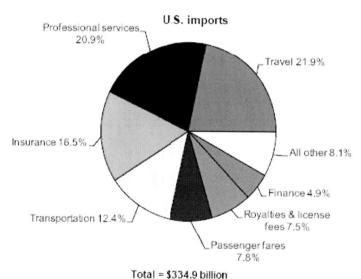

Source: USDOC, BEA, *Survey of Current Business*, October 2010, 36–37, table 1.
Note: Trade data exclude public sector transactions.

Figure 1.3. U. S. services: Professional services accounted for a large share of U. S. cross-border exports and imports of services in 2009.

In 2009, the United States maintained large bilateral services trade surpluses with Japan ($20.1 billion), Canada ($20.0 billion), the United Kingdom ($12.9 billion), Mexico ($8.3 billion), and China ($7.5 billion), as well as with the EU ($50.5 billion). In that year, the United States registered its largest bilateral services trade deficit with Bermuda ($14.1 billion), which primarily reflected payments for insurance and reinsurance services to affiliates of U. S. and foreign firms with operations in that country.[24]

Affiliate Transactions

In 2008, services supplied by U. S.-owned foreign affiliates[25] increased by 12 percent to $1.1 trillion, similar to the 13 percent average annual growth rate registered from 2005 through 2007.[26] Professional services accounted for roughly 8 percent[27] of services supplied by U. S.-owned foreign affiliates in 2008 (figure 1.4). By contrast, wholesale services accounted for approximately 21 percent of total services supplied by U. S.-owned foreign affiliates. The largest host-country markets for services supplied by U. S.-owned affiliates were the United Kingdom (20 percent of U. S.-owned affiliates services), Canada (10 percent), and Ireland and Japan (6 percent each). The EU accounted for 49 percent of total services supplied by U. S.-owned affiliates in 2008.[28]

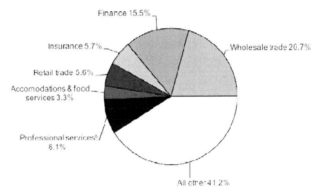

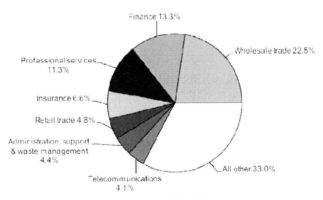

Source: USDOC, BEA, *Survey of Current Business*, October 2010, 58, 60, tables 9.2 and 10.2.
Note: Trade data exclude public sector transactions.
[a] Services supplied by majority-owned foreign affiliates of U. S. parent firms.
[b] Data are underreported due to suppression of data by the BEA.
[c] Services supplied by majority-owned U. S. affiliates of foreign parent firms.

Figure 1.4. U. S. services: Wholesale trade and finance led services transactions by affiliates in 2008; professional services ranked third.

Services supplied by foreign-owned affiliates in the United States increased by 6 percent to $727.4 billion in 2008, slower than the 9 percent average annual growth rate of 2005 through 2007. Professional services supplied by foreign-owned U. S. affiliates accounted for 11 percent of the total services supplied by such affiliates in 2008.[29] By comparison, wholesale services accounted for more than twice that proportion at 23 percent, making it the largest single service industry represented by foreign-owned affiliates in the United States. By country, the United Kingdom accounted for the biggest share of services supplied by foreign-owned affiliates in 2008 (18 percent) followed by Japan (14 percent) and Germany (13 percent). France and Canada rounded out the top five with 10 percent and 9 percent, respectively. Overall, 54 percent of services supplied by foreign-owned affiliates were from affiliates of EU-parent firms.

2. PROFESSIONAL SERVICES OVERVIEW

Professional services represent a diverse group of industries—from education and healthcare to computer, engineering, legal, and accounting services—and employ a large proportion of highly educated and highly skilled workers.[30] A number of characteristics distinguish professional services from infrastructure services such as energy and transportation. Professional services are labor rather than capital-intensive; tend to be more regulated, especially through requirements to license and certify service providers; and are at the center of a growing trend for firms to outsource noncore functions to entities located abroad.[31] Moreover, professional services have withstood some ill effects of the economic recession better than infrastructure services; for example, wages among professional service workers continued to grow during 2008–09 (albeit slowly), while wages among workers in infrastructure services declined. This chapter discusses current trends in professional services, including the impact of the economic recession on the industry, and reviews key economic and trade data for the sector.

Impact of the Economic Recession on Employment in Professional Services

During the recession of 2008–09, employment in professional services proved more resilient than those in infrastructure services. The sector was nonetheless far from immune to the recession's effects. According to the BEA, the number of full-time equivalent (FTE) employees in professional services, excluding those in the education and healthcare industries, decreased by 4 percent in 2008–09. At the same time, the average length of unemployment among professional service workers increased from 9.8 weeks in 2008 to 15.7 weeks in 2009.[32] Not surprisingly, the 1.2 percent decrease in the value of professional services GDP in 2008–09 contrasted sharply with the 3.0 percent average annual increase during 2004–08.

Of course, some job loss is normal in this sector during a downturn: because nearly 80 percent of services in this sector are used as intermediate inputs (i.e., they are used in the production of other goods and services),[33] demand for these services generally decreases as the health of the economy declines. This is particularly true of business services, such as legal and accounting work. Owing to the severity of the 2008–09 recession, however, even white-collar professional service workers—including lawyers and computer software engineers—suffered layoffs.[34] Moreover, employment growth slowed in professional service industries seldom affected by economic downturns, such as education and healthcare.[35] Finally, the recession's severity translated into unusually long periods of unemployment among many laid-off professionals, who risked having their skills erode as a result.[36]

Regulation

Regulation of professional services is principally intended to correct for asymmetry of information between service providers and consumers, as the latter often have too little knowledge to judge the quality of the service they are purchasing.[37] In addition to protecting consumer welfare, regulations can also be designed to promote social, developmental, demographic, and cultural objectives. Some research suggests that regulation hinders labor productivity growth within professional services: highly regulated industries face less competition and therefore have less incentive to implement the types of innovative technology and management practices that raise productivity.[38] Where deregulation among service industries has already occurred—most notably among certain infrastructure services, such as air transport and telecommunications—prices have dropped and less efficient providers have exited the market.[39] Despite the potential economic benefits of deregulation, however, many countries have chosen to prioritize social or other objectives over economic efficiency, hoping to strike the optimal balance for their particular circumstances. In addition, incumbents' opposition may hinder reform, as many fear that regulatory capacity is insufficient to achieve reforms' desired objectives.[40]

Offshore Outsourcing

The production of professional services is increasingly outsourced to firms located abroad.[41] This activity, known as offshore outsourcing (or "offshoring"), is largely the result of firms' desire to reduce labor costs and to focus on their core competencies.[42] Some have suggested that "tradable" service industries, and the occupations associated with them, have the greatest potential to be moved offshore (box 2.1).[43] Jobs in professional services, including architecture, engineering, law, and computer programming, are among the primary examples of tradable occupations.[44]

The debate as to whether the offshoring of services by U. S. firms is good or bad for the domestic economy is evolving. Early in the discussion, when "offshoring" referred to the transfer abroad of low-skill service jobs (e.g., those related to data processing and call center operation), it was argued that such activity made room for higher-skilled, higher-wage jobs at home.

Box 2.1. Impact of U. S. Trade in Services on U. S. Service Sector Employment

In a 2005 paper, J. Bradford Jensen and Lori Kletzer classified service industries and occupations as tradable or non-tradable based on the extent to which they were geographically concentrated within the United States. The rationale for this approach is that services that are highly concentrated in a particular region are more likely to be sold outside of that region than services that are more evenly distributed in proportion to the population. For example, services that were found to be more geographically concentrated and thus identified as tradable include architecture and engineering services, computer services, financial services, and legal services. The authors then examined employment growth and job displacement rates in these industries and occupations. For the period 1998–2002, they found that employment in the average tradable service industry grew by about 8 percent—about the same as in non-tradable services. Nonetheless, among service *occupations*, average employment growth was higher in tradable as opposed to non-tradable ones over the 1999–2003 period. The authors found that tradable service occupations in the U. S. service sector were jobs of higher wage and higher skill (e.g., those in professional services), and that workers in these occupations were potentially more vulnerable to job displacement through offshoring than workers in nontradable occupations. However, the authors also concluded that because tradable occupations in the U. S. service sector are those in which the United States has comparative advantage, these occupations are not necessarily destined to be moved offshore; in fact, it is possible that continued liberalization of global services trade, "would directly benefit workers and firms in the United States."[a]

[a] Jensen and Kletzer, "Tradable Services," September 2005; also published in Brainard and Collins, *Brookings Trade Forum: 2005*, 2006.

Box 2.2. Effects of U. S. Offshore Outsourcing and Inshoring on Employment of U. S. White-Collar Workers

In 2008, Runjuan Liu and Daniel Trefler examined the effects on workers of U. S. purchases of services from unaffiliated parties in low-wage countries ("offshore outsourcing") and U. S. sales of services to unaffiliated parties in those same markets ("inshoring"). In particular, they investigated the likelihood of workers switching occupation or industry as a result of either offshore outsourcing or insourcing and the effect on their employment and earnings. They used trade data from 1995–2005 and census data from 1996–2006 across a number of service industries and occupations, including business, professional, and technical services. Liu and Trefler found that the net effect of inshoring and offshore outsourcing across employment outcomes was small but positive. That is, if offshore outsourcing of business, professional, and technical services were to continue at the 1995–2005 rate for nine additional years, the cumulative effects on workers in occupations exposed to outsourcing would be a 2 percent *decline* in the likelihood of occupational switching, a 0.1 percent *decrease* in the time spent unemployed as a share of weeks in the labor force, and an *increase* in earnings of 1.5 percent. The authors of the study also found that in cases where offshore outsourcing produced a small yet adverse impact on the employment of certain workers, these workers tended to be the less educated and less skilled.[a]

[a] Liu and Trefler, "Much Ado about Nothing," June 2008.

More recently, however, U. S. firms have also moved certain high- skill jobs—such as software development and medical diagnostic services—to developing countries, where they are performed by workers of increasing education and ability.[45] Some view this new trend as evidence of the emerging vulnerability of U. S. professional service workers.[46] Nonetheless, current research is unclear as to whether there is a direct cause-and-effect relationship between the offshoring of U. S. high-skill jobs and the displacement of white-collar workers in the U. S. economy (box 2.2), although perspectives on this issue differ.[47] In addition, some researchers suggest that whether certain intermediate services are produced at home or abroad is less important than the fact that these services may increase the productivity of the industries that consume them. If such productivity-enhancing services can be provided at lower cost to domestic industries, this will boost aggregate productivity growth in the domestic economy, in turn stimulating higher economic growth overall.[48]

Table 2.1. Full-time equivalent (FTE) employees, wage and salary accruals, gross domestic product, and labor productivity, by goods and service industries, 2004–09

	2004	2008	2009	Average annual growth, 2004–08 (%)	Percent change, 2008–09 (%)
Full-time equivalent employees (FTEs) (thousands)					
Private sector	103,318	108,037	101,331	1.1	(6.2)
Goods	22,642	22,123	19,169	(0.6)	(13.4)
Manufacturing	14,024	13,149	11,529	(1.6)	(12.3)
Nonmanufacturing	8,618	8,974	7,640	1.0	(14.9)
Services	80,676	85,914	82,162	1.6	(4.4)
Professional services	23,597	26,567	26,444	3.0	(0.5)
Infrastructure services	31,668	32,488	30,573	0.6	(5.9)
Other services	25,410	26,858	25,147	1.4	(6.4)
Wage and salary accruals ($ per FTE)					
Private sector	43,207	50,144	50,462	3.8	0.6
Goods	46,436	54,587	55,505	4.1	1.7
Manufacturing	49,423	56,373	57,374	3.3	1.8
Nonmanufacturing	41,577	51,972	52,686	5.7	1.4
Services	42,300	49,000	49,285	3.7	0.6
Professional services	50,424	59,102	59,436	4.0	0.6
Infrastructure services	47,298	54,088	53,756	3.4	(0.6)
Other services	28,529	32,854	33,172	3.6	1.0
Gross domestic product[a] (billion $)					
Private sector	10,714	11,546	11,198	1.9	(3.0)
Goods	2,482	2,472	2,314	(0.1)	(6.4)
Manufacturing	1,518	1,609	1,470	1.5	(8.6)
Nonmanufacturing	964	864	845	(2.7)	(2.2)
Services	8,233	9,076	8,887	2.5	(2.1)
Professional services	1,996	2,248	2,222	3.0	(1.2)
Infrastructure services	3,539	3,864	3,847	2.2	(0.4)
Other services	2,701	2,965	2,827	2.4	(4.7)

Table 2.1. Continued

	2004	2008	2009	Average annual growth, 2004–08 (%)	Percent change, 2008–09 (%)
Labor productivity[b] ($ per FTE)					
Private sector	103,697	106,874	110,505	0.8	3.4
Goods	109,964	111,861	120,851	0.4	8.0
Manufacturing	108,236	122,336	127,479	3.1	4.2
Nonmanufacturing	112,776	96,512	110,851	(3.8)	14.9
Services	102,054	105,643	108,156	0.9	2.4
Professional services	84,587	84,628	84,042	0.0	(0.7)
Infrastructure services	111,747	118,927	125,833	1.6	5.8
Other services	106,289	110,407	112,435	1.0	1.8

Sources: USDOC, BEA, "Full-Time Equivalent Employees by Industry," December 14, 2010; USDOC, BEA, "Table 6.6D," August 5, 2010; USDOC, BEA, "Table 6.3D," August 5, 2010; USDOC, BEA, "Real Value Added by Industry," December 14, 2010.

Note: Totals may not add due to rounding.

[a] Real value added by industry using 2005 chained dollars.

[b] Labor productivity, calculated by USITC staff, is GDP by industry divided by FTEs.

Gross Domestic Product (GDP), Employment, Salaries, and Labor Productivity

Professional services continue to represent a large and growing contribution to GDP[49] in the private sector (table 2.1). In 2009, professional services GDP reached $2.2 trillion, accounting for nearly 20 percent of total U. S. private sector GDP and approximately 25 percent of total U. S. service sector GDP. From 2004 through 2008, professional services GDP grew at an average annual rate of 3.0 percent, surpassing GDP growth in both infrastructure services (2.2 percent) and the private sector as a whole (1.9 percent). During 2004–08, computer systems design and related services accounted for the largest share of GDP growth in professional services, increasing at an average annual rate of 10 percent (table 2.2). This was followed by average annual GDP growth in miscellaneous professional, scientific, and technical services (4 percent) and healthcare services (3 percent). Overall, healthcare services represented the largest segment of professional services GDP in 2009 (41.9 percent)—a trend that remained unchanged from previous years (figure 2.1).[50]

Employment in professional service industries made up a significant share of total private sector employment in 2009. In that year, the number of FTE employees in professional services stood at 26 million, comprising roughly 26 percent of total U. S. private sector employment. Healthcare services accounted for slightly more than half of total professional services employment in 2009 at 15 million workers (figure 2.2). Between 2004 and 2008, professional services employment grew at a robust average annual rate of 3.0 percent, five times the rate of employment growth in infrastructure services (0.6 percent) and more than twice the rate of employment growth in the private sector overall (1.1 percent). During the recession of 2008–09, employment in professional services fell 0.5 percent. However, this decrease was modest compared to that recorded in infrastructure services (5.9 percent) and in goods-producing industries (13.4 percent).

Average wages among U. S. professional service workers increased by 0.6 percent in 2009, much slower than the 4.0 percent average annual growth rate for this category during 2004–08. Average wages among professional service workers varied widely in 2009—from a high of $95,337 for computer system design and related services employees to a low of $40,785 for education service employees. Average wages among U. S. infrastructure service workers were dispersed throughout a similar range, although such wages grew at a slightly lower rate (3.4 percent) during the 2004–08 period than in professional services.[51]

Table 2.2. Full-time equivalent (FTE) employees, wage and salary accruals, gross domestic product, and labor productivity, by selected service industries, 2004–09

	2004	2008	2009	Average annual growth, 2004–08	Change, 2008–09
				%	
Full-time equivalent employees (FTEs) (thousands)					
Computer systems design and related services	1,091	1,379	1,343	6.0	(2.6)
Educational services	2,510	2,782	2,807	2.6	0.9
Healthcare and social assistance	12,907	14,431	14,662	2.8	1.6
Legal services	1,113	1,123	1,083	0.2	(3.6)
Management of companies and enterprises	1,669	1,816	1,797	2.1	(1.0)
Miscellaneous professional, scientific, and technical services	4,307	5,037	4,752	4.0	(5.7)
Wage and salary accruals ($ per FTE)					
Computer systems design and related services	83,311	94,733	95,337	3.3	0.6
Educational services	33,854	39,221	40,785	3.7	4.0
Healthcare and social assistance	41,080	47,071	48,354	3.5	2.7
Legal services	71,991	85,387	85,752	4.4	0.4
Management of companies and enterprises	82,418	101,450	96,586	5.3	(4.8)
Miscellaneous professional, scientific, and technical services	61,785	73,667	74,470	4.5	1.1
Gross domestic product[a] (billion $)					
Computer systems design and related services	116.2	171.3	173.5	10.2	1.3
Educational services	123.5	123.9	122.1	0.1	(1.5)
Healthcare and social assistance	813.9	918.8	932.5	3.1	1.5
Legal services	191.3	188.6	176.5	(0.4)	(6.4)
Management of companies and enterprises	221.1	222.0	217.3	0.1	(2.1)
Miscellaneous professional, scientific, and technical services	530.3	625.7	604.0	4.2	(3.5)

Table 2.2. Continued

	2004	2008	2009	Average annual growth, 2004–08	Change, 2008–09
				%	
Labor productivity[b] ($ per FTE)					
Computer systems design and related services	106,508	124,220	129,188	3.9	4.0
Educational services	49,203	44,536	43,498	(2.5)	(2.3)
Healthcare and social assistance	63,059	63,668	63,600	0.2	(0.1)
Legal services	171,878	167,943	162,973	(0.6)	(3.0)
Management of companies and enterprises	132,475	122,247	120,924	(2.0)	(1.1)
Miscellaneous professional, scientific, and technical services	123,125	124,221	127,104	0.2	2.3

Sources: USDOC, BEA, "Full-Time Equivalent Employees by Industry," December 14, 2010; USDOC, BEA, "Table 6.6D," August 5, 2010; USDOC, BEA, "Table 6.3D," August 5, 2010; USDOC, BEA, "Real Value Added by Industry," December 14, 2010.

[a] Real value added by industry using 2005 chained dollars.

[b] Labor productivity, calculated by USITC staff, is GDP by industry divided by full-time equivalent employees.

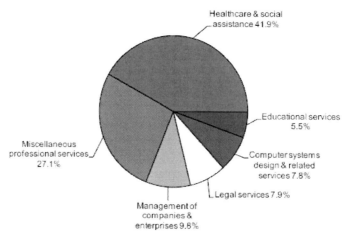

Source: USDOC, BEA, "Real Value Added by Industry," December 14, 2010.

Figure 2.1. U. S. professional services: Healthcare and social assistance services had the largest contribution to GDP in 2009.

Despite the growth in wages among U. S. professional service workers in 2009, labor productivity among professional services industries fell by 0.7 percent that year—the only productivity decline recorded among all private sector industries (see table 2.1).[52] By comparison, labor productivity within the manufacturing sector grew by 4.2 percent in 2009, and in infrastructure services, by 5.8 percent. During 2004–08, labor productivity in professional services increased by less than 0.1 percent annually, significantly lower than the

0.8 percent average annual increase registered by the private sector as a whole. As noted, employment in professional services has grown rapidly in recent years, and that growth has diluted gains in professional services productivity. Nonetheless, certain professional service industries have experienced productivity growth: namely, computer systems design and related services, where productivity grew by 4 percent in 2009, equal to the industry's average annual productivity increase during 2004–08; and miscellaneous professional, scientific and technical services, where productivity grew by 2 percent in 2009 (see table 2.2). In contrast, education, healthcare, and legal services experienced either zero productivity growth or a decrease in labor productivity during the years 2004 through 2009.[53]

U.S. Trade in Professional Services

In 2009, professional services accounted for 20.2 percent of total U. S. cross-border services exports and 20.9 percent of U. S. cross-border services imports. The United States posted a cross-border trade surplus in professional services in 2009, with U. S. exports of such services ($97.6 billion) substantially exceeding U. S. imports ($70.1 billion). Management and consulting services represented the largest share of U. S. professional services exports (28.9 percent) and imports (31.7 percent) in 2009 (figure 2.3). By country, the United Kingdom accounted for approximately 9 percent of U. S. professional services exports in 2009, followed by Ireland (7 percent), Canada and Japan (6 percent each), and China (5 percent). The United Kingdom also supplied the largest share (15 percent) of U. S. professional services imports in 2009; a substantial portion of these were imports of management, consulting, and public relations services (table 2.3).[54] Other significant suppliers of U. S. professional services imports that year were India (11 percent), Canada (10 percent), Germany (7 percent), and Japan (5 percent).[55]

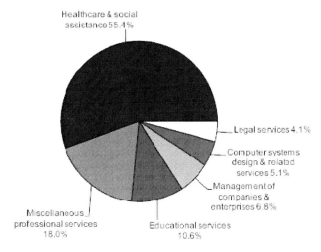

Source: USDOC, BEA, "Full-Time Equivalent Employees by Industry,"August 5, 2010.

Figure 2.2. U. S. professional services: Healthcare and social assistance accounted for the largest share of professional services employment, by industry, in 2009.

Table 2.3. U. S. professional services: Top five export and import markets and leading industries, 2009

Rank	Country	Top export to country
1	United Kingdom	Management, consulting, and public relations services
2	Ireland	Management, consulting, and public relations services
3	Canada	Management, consulting, and public relations services
4	Japan	RandD and testing services
5	China	Education services
Rank	**Country**	**Top import from country**
1	United Kingdom	Management, consulting, and public relations services
2	India	Computer and data processing services
3	Canada	Computer and data processing services
4	Germany	Management, consulting, and public relations services
5	Japan	Education services

Source: USDOC, BEA, *Survey of Current Business*, October 2010, 54–55, table 7.2.

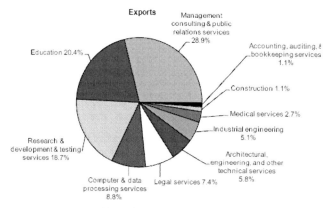

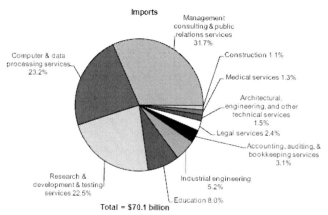

Source: USDOC, BEA, *Survey of Current Business*, October 2010, 36–37, table 1.
Note: Trade data exclude public-sector transactions.

Figure 2.3. U. S. professional services: Management consulting and public relations led U. S. cross-border exports and imports of professional services in 2009.

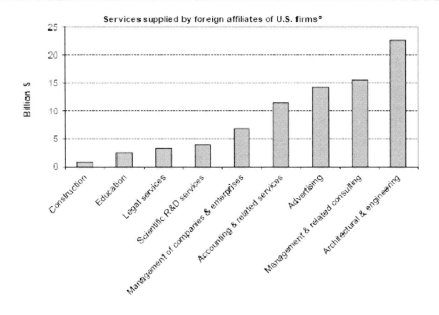

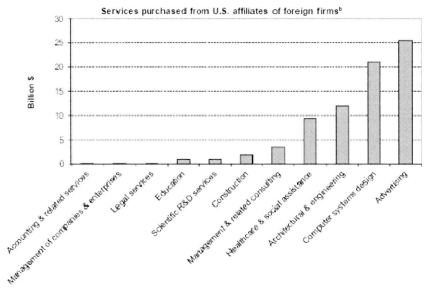

Source: USDOC, BEA, *Survey of Current Business*, October 2010, 58, 60, tables 9.2 and 10.2.
Note: Trade data exclude public sector transactions.
[a] Services supplied by majority-owned foreign affiliates of U. S. parent firms.
[b] Services supplied by majority-owned U. S. affiliates of foreign parent firms.

Figure 2.4. U. S. professional services: In 2008, architectural and engineering services led transactions by foreign affiliates of U. S. firms; advertising services led transactions by U. S. affiliates of foreign firms.

The United States remains competitive in the provision of professional services through foreign affiliates. Professional services supplied by U. S.-owned foreign affiliates equaled no less than $91.8 billion in 2008.[56] This surpassed the $82.2 billion of professional services supplied by foreign-owned U. S. affiliates. Overall, however, professional services represented a small portion of total U. S. affiliate services transactions, accounting for 8 percent of services supplied by U. S. -owned foreign affiliates and 11 percent of services supplied by foreign-owned U. S. affiliates in 2008. In that year, architectural, engineering, and related services accounted for the single largest category of professional services supplied by foreign affiliates of U. S. firms ($22.6 billion), whereas advertising services accounted for the highest amount ($25.4 billion) of services supplied from U. S. affiliates of foreign firms (figure 2.4).

3. AUDIOVISUAL SERVICES

SUMMARY

The recent global economic downturn has depressed overall movie production levels, as investment in small to medium-sized movie producers and developing national film industries dropped considerably. However, overall box office revenues, both globally and in the United States, have risen steadily in recent years. Several factors underlie this growth, including increasing demand for and availability of 3-D and high-definition titles; the construction of more digital-ready movie theaters; higher movie ticket prices; and the proliferation of lower-cost digital distribution channels. U. S. cross- border exports of audiovisual services have consistently exceeded U. S. cross- border imports over the last decade. This trade surplus came to about $12 billion in 2009.

Nonetheless, in several important markets, growing online intellectual property piracy has hampered industry growth in terms of both international trade and domestic sector development. Other lingering impediments include content quotas and foreign equity restrictions. In response, the industry is looking to implement more cost-effective production processes, increase film co-productions in rapidly growing markets such as China, and diversify into more international market segments by taking advantage of the increasing use and overall availability of digital filmmaking and distribution technologies.

INTRODUCTION

Providers of audiovisual services[57] collect royalties, rental fees, license fees, and sales revenue in return for granting rights to display, broadcast, reproduce, or distribute audiovisual works. The U. S. motion picture industry[58] serves as a major supplier of entertainment and information to the world by producing videos, television programs, and movies that can be seen in more than 100 countries.[59]

Government policies (by way of trade impediments) often play a significant role in the production and distribution abroad of audiovisual services since the sector can, in some cases, influence audiences through its content and messaging. Hence, important policy issues can include the promotion of cultural values, restrictions on illicit content, protection of intellectual property rights, the regulation of advertising practices, and the provision of investment and tax incentives.[60]

Table 3.1. Audiovisual services: Top 10 countries, by estimated global box office revenue, 2009

Rank	Country	Estimated revenue (million $)	Share of global revenues (%)
1	United States	9,740	33
2	Japan	2,199	8
3	France	1,731	6
4	United Kingdom	1,478	5
5	India	1,417	5
6	Germany	1,360	5
7	Spain	935	3
8	China	906	3
9	Korea	906	3
10	Canada	885	3

Source: *Screen Digest*, "Global Box Office Hits New High," November 2010, 339.

Table 3.2. Audiovisual services: Top 10 film producers, by estimated global feature film production (including co-productions), 2009

Rank	Country	Number of films	Share of global production (%)
1	India	1,288	24
2	United States	677	13
3	China	456	9
4	Japan	448	8
5	France	230	4
6	Spain	186	4
7	Germany	150	3
8	Korea	139	3
9	Italy	131	2
10	United Kingdom	126	2

Source: *Screen Digest*, "World Film Production Drops Again," August 2010, 4–5.
Note: Nigeria has been excluded from this list due to lack of reliable and timely data (See box 3.1).

Competitive Conditions in the Global Audiovisual Services Market

Global box office revenue has increased by almost $12.0 billion in the last decade (it was valued at $17.6 billion in 1999).[61] Despite the global economic downturn, this revenue reached an all-time high of $29.5 billion in 2009, about a 5 percent increase from the previous year ($28.0 billion). Vogel (2004) theorized that when an economy enters a recessionary phase, the leisure-time spending preferences of consumers shift more toward lower-cost, closer-to-home entertainment activities than when economic growth is strong. Hence, this would explain why ticket sales often remain steady or rise during the earlyto-middle stages of a recession, faltering only near the recession's end, when budgets are reserved for essential goods and services.[62]

Although all world regions reported revenue growth from the previous year, in 2009 growth was less robust for emerging markets in Central and Eastern Europe and Asia, largely due to currency fluctuations (particularly for the Russian ruble)[63] and to box office declines in India.[64] Latin America, by contrast, recorded the largest gains, thanks to rapid movie screen construction throughout the region.[65] Japan was the second largest international box office market (behind the United States), followed by France, the United Kingdom, and India, respectively (table 3.1).[66] Notably, China ranked among the top 10 global markets in 2009 for the first time, accounting for over $906 million in box office receipts. In recent years, China has become a significant box office market in Asia largely because of the rapid construction of new cinemas and rising ticket prices. By the end of 2010, China is forecast to join the ranks of the six (as of 2009) billion-dollar box office markets.[67] Overall, the top 10 box office markets accounted for about 73 percent of global box office dollars, with much of the growth being buoyed by an influx of titles available in digital 3-D.[68]

The worldwide volume of film production, by contrast, dropped about 2 percent to 5,360 films in 2009, making it the second consecutive annual decline since reaching an all-time production high of 5,560 films in 2007. About 100 fewer feature films were produced year-over-year since 2007. This decline is largely due to the economic downturn's negative effect on advertising revenue and private and public financing, which are of particular importance to "indie" film producers[69] and developing film markets, such as those in Central and Eastern Europe and Southeast Asia.[70]

Overall, only 12 countries can be reliably stated to have produced more than 100 feature films in 2009. Films from these countries accounted for over 75 percent of the global feature film volume that year, which is consistent with previous years.[71] India, the United States, China, Japan, and France were the top five film-producing countries by volume in 2009 (table 3.2). China surpassed Japan for the first time, with an output of 456 feature films. Russia, a major film producer within its region, dropped out of the top 10 film producing-nations due to a dearth of available international financing. However, despite rapid theater construction and increasing cooperation with international co-productions, many Chinese films do not receive a theatrical release largely due to a lack of modern screens, which causes a logjam in distribution. Consequently, a large number of these films instead go straight into a DVD market that has been plagued by piracy.[72] Often overlooked due to a lack of consistent and reliable data, the Nigerian film industry, referred to as "Nollywood," is reportedly the second largest producer of films[73] behind India and ahead of the United States, according to a 2009 UNESCO study (box 3.1).

The global motion picture industry is dominated by a handful of large U. S. -based movie studios, which account for about 60 percent of total global box office receipts (table 3.3). U. S. movies earn a significant portion of their total revenue from international audiences: for example, Avatar (Fox), the world's top-grossing movie of 2009, generated $2.8 billion in global box office revenue that year, of which 73 percent came from foreign markets.[74] Further, according to a European Audiovisual Observatory report,[75] in 2008, U. S. movies accounted for the lion's share of the box office market share in countries such as Canada (88 percent), Australia (84 percent), Russia (75 percent), Germany (73 percent), Spain (72 percent), Italy (71 percent), and the United Kingdom (65 percent). Outside the United States, only in India, Egypt,[76] China, and Japan did domestically produced films account for more than 50 percent of total box office receipts. (Foreign films accounted for only 8 percent of U. S. domestic box revenue).[77]

Box 3.1. The Nigerian Film Industry: Nollywood's Growing Influence in Africa

In 2006, Nollywood was estimated to have the second-largest film industry in the world. Its output included 872 films in video format (with more than half produced in English), which was roughly 400 more than Hollywood produced that year.[a] Nigeria's approach to film production and distribution is significantly different from Western models: producers primarily use handheld video camcorders; production costs are much more limited (on average, about $20,000); the videos are not viewed in theaters; production is typically domestically owned; and the videos are distributed informally, with illegal piracy being the most common method of transmission across borders.[b]

Despite the official figures documented in the UNESCO study, it is reported on the ground that Nollywood produces, on average, more than 50 full-length features a week, with most being shown in airports, hotels, public buses, and restaurants all across Africa. With DVDs usually selling for $1 or less, slow Internet connections, and little competition from poorly run state television broadcasts, Nigerian films have continued to proliferate on the continent. Other factors such as the declining price of digital cameras, a rise in average incomes, the use of English in most films, diverse casting, and clever plot lines have made the films even more ubiquitous.[c]

The popularity of Nigerian films on the continent has grown so much that certain governments have enacted trade barriers in order to stem the "Nigerianization" of Africa. For example, Ghana has imposed fees of $1,000 on visiting actors and $5,000 on producers and directors, and the Democratic Republic of Congo has tried to ban the import of all Nigerian-produced films in an effort to limit their cultural influence on the Congolese.[d]

Arguably the most important player in Nollywood's pan-African success has been the distribution network set up by copyright pirates. Sources report that it takes copyright pirates only about two weeks to distribute a Nollywood film all across the continent after its initial release. Consequently, legitimate merchants have about a fortnight to make as much profit as they can before the pirates commoditize the films (this two-week time period is locally referred to as the "mating season"). By the end of the two weeks, most Nollywood filmmakers are usually already in the process of planning their next production.[e]

Despite the rampant piracy, Western film producers have begun teaming up with Nollywood directors to co-produce movies, and several Nollywood films have been shown in international film festivals such as Sundance and at exhibitions in London through the British Film Institute.[f] Nollywood's success has also spurred other African countries to develop their own film industries. For example, Cameroon, South Africa, and Tanzania are now producing hundreds of films a year, Kenyan films are beating Nollywood films at Nigerian award ceremonies, and Ghana and Liberia have already dubbed their nascent film industries "Ghallywood" and "Lolliwood."[g]

---

[a] United Nations Education, Scientific, and Cultural Organization (UNESCO), Institute for Statistics (UIS), *Analysis of the UIS International Survey of Feature Film Statistics*, March 3, 2010.
[b] WTO, "Audiovisual Services: Background Note by the Secretariat," January 12, 2010, 8; Ryan, "Nollywood Comes of Age," October 1, 2010.
[c] *Economist*, "Nollywood," December 16, 2010. Many of the films' plots revolve around the travails of new arrivals in big cities, an experience many Africans can relate to.
[d] Ibid.
[e] Ibid.
[f] Ibid.; Ryan, "Nollywood Comes of Age," October 1, 2010.
[g] *Economist*, "Nollywood," December 16, 2010.

U.S. movie studios also lead the world in terms of budget, access to technology, and skilled labor.[78] Despite declining production levels overall, films produced in the United States had higher production budgets, on average, than other major film-producing markets. When all movie studios, large and small, are considered, a U. S. film production investment averaged about $20 million in 2009, versus about $12 million in the United Kingdom, $9 million in Australia, $1.5 million in China, and $150,000 in India (table 3.4).[79] Larger U. S. production budgets allow greater use of special effects technologies, such as 3-D, high-definition, or digital graphics, and computer-generated imagery, as well as access to the most well-known and marketable talent. Moreover, with the predominance of English as an international language, U. S. movies are distributed globally at lower cost than non-English films, since dubbing is unnecessary in many cases.[80]

Table 3.3. Audiovisual services: Top 10 movie studios, by estimated global gross box office revenue and market share, 2009

Company	Country	Estimated revenue (million $)	Estimated market share (%)
Warner Brothers	U.S.	4,307	16.1
Twentieth Century Fox	U.S./Australia	3,964	14.8
Buena Vista (Disney)	U.S.	2,683	10.0
Sony Pictures	Japan	2,554	9.5
Universal Pictures	U.S.	2,001	7.5
Paramount Pictures	U.S.	1,191	4.4
Toho	Japan	763	2.8
PPI (Philips)	U.S.	671	2.5
Lion's Gate	U.S.	554	2.1
Paramount/Dreamworks	U.S.	519	1.9
Top 10 total		19,207	71.7
All others		7,580	28.3
Grand total		26,787	100.0

Source: ShowBizData.com, "Worldwide Global Theatrical Market Shares for 2009," n.d. (accessed October 20, 2010).

Note: Gross box office revenue figures at the company level may not precisely match *Screen Digest*'s estimates due to slight differences in collection methods and data availability.

Table 3.4. Audiovisual services: Top 10 countries, by average investment per film production (million $), 2009

Rank	Country	Estimated investment
1	United States	19.6
2	United Kingdom	12.0
3	Australia	8.9
4	Germany	7.7
5	Estonia	7.5
6	France	6.7
7	Latvia	5.9
8	Japan	5.8
9	Belgium	4.9
10	Ireland	4.5

Source: *Screen Digest*, "World Film Production Drops Again," August 2010, 7.

The top six major U. S. movie studios[81] produce most of the content seen on U. S. television and movie theaters. Since the economic downturn, smaller, independent filmmakers have found it more difficult to finance new productions or pay for a film's distribution, which is the primary driver behind the decline in overall film production levels in recent years.[82]

Although thousands of movies are produced each year, only a small number of them account for the majority of box office receipts. Unlike blockbusters like *Avatar*, which reportedly cost Fox about $387 million to film and promote[83] (and earned about $750 million in U. S. box office receipts alone),[84] the majority of films do not make a full return on their investment from domestic box office revenue alone. Instead, filmmakers rely on profits from foreign markets and other distribution channels such as broadcast, cable, and satellite television, DVD/Blu-ray sales, and the Internet.[85] However, in the United States, cumulative sales from DVDs, Blu-ray discs, and digital copies of films have fallen by 8 percent since 2005. According to industry sources, DVD sales of new films fell by 17 percent between 2008 and 2009 alone. These sales drops have largely been attributed to the emergence of inexpensive and convenient rental services such as Netflix and Redbox. Internationally, although drops in sales have been less steep, foreign consumers have never been major purchasers of legal DVDs compared to U. S. consumers.[86]

Consequently, in response to the uncertainty of movie revenues, co-productions have been a way for movie studios to spread their financial risk.[87] In particular, international co-productions have been an important feature of the audiovisual services industry for many years. Most commonly, U. S. studios have cooperated in the production of motion pictures with companies in Canada, the United Kingdom, continental Europe, Australia, New Zealand, and Japan.[88] Often, these co-productions are based on investment treaties that provide incentives to partnering countries in the form of tax credits or other cost rebates if certain budgetary and employment limits are reached during a film's production, a factor that will be discussed in further detail later in the chapter. European- based production companies, in particular, have been most active in the making of co- productions, either with U. S. studios or with other production companies within Europe. On average, between one-third and one-half of the movies produced in the top European filming nations (e.g., France, Germany, Italy, Spain, and the United Kingdom) have been co-productions.[89]

Demand and Supply Factors

Changing Demographics Shift Demand for Movies

The demand for entertainment and leisure services—in this case, motion picture viewing—has been significantly affected by changes in the relative growth of different age groups.[90] Younger, more technology-savvy consumers have driven box office growth in the motion picture industry due to their increasing demand for 3-D films. In the United States, for example, the broad demographic shifts most important to the entertainment industry include an increase in the number of 18- to 34-year olds in the early 2000s; there were approximately 4.8 million more in this age group in 2010 than in 2000.[91] According to industry surveys, people under the age of 39 tend to be the most avid moviegoers overall, and those under 35 tend to be the most frequent viewers of 3-D films.[92] Hence, the recent gains in box office revenue have largely been driven by these younger audiences.[93] The largest U. S. -based movie studios have met much of this demand due to their near monopoly on 3-D titles.[94] In

North America alone, 3-D films drove almost all of the growth in box office receipts in 2009, generating gross box office earnings of about $1.1 billion that year with the release of 20 3-D films. By comparison, total North American gross box office earnings from 3-D films amounted to approximately $240 million from 2005 through 2008.[95]

Although younger audiences account for a large part of 3-D movie going in Europe, particularly in Eastern European markets,[96] the EU's overall age demographic is expected to "gray" at a much faster rate than in the United States. According to estimates, the median age in the United States in 2050 is expected to be 35.4, only a very slight increase from what it was in the early 2000s. In Europe, by contrast, it is expected to rise from 37.7 to 52.3.[97] Nonetheless, the rapid growth of 3-D screens allowed 3-D movies such as *Ice Age 3* (Fox), *Up* (Disney), and *Avatar* to sell about 86 million more tickets throughout the European Union in 2009, helping to boost EU movie admission levels by 6 percent over the previous year. Moreover, premium pricing for 3-D screenings drove up average global ticket prices by $1 to $3 or more, further bolstering box office revenue figures.[98]

Although at the forefront of the digital rollout in its early years, Asia has lagged behind North America and Europe in the last few years with regard to 3-D technology. This in large part has been due to a lack of theaters that support such technology (China and India), the predominance of domestically produced non-3-D films (China, India, and Japan), and cultural differences.[99] Japan also faces demographic challenges. Japanese aged 60–65 represent the country's largest population segment, and people over 65 already make up 23 percent of Japan's population—the world's highest such percentage. That figure is forecast to jump to about 40 percent by 2050, according to government data.[100]

Infrastructure Investment and Digital Technology Streamline the Industry

Technological advances have made it easier, in terms of cost, quality, and time, to transmit a greater amount of content across borders; enabled content to be distributed on a variety of platforms and devices by diverse operators; and granted greater control to consumers over what, when, where, and how they watch audiovisual content. Investment in digital-ready theaters and the implementation of uniform transmission standards has become a major priority for many governments and national film associations in order to realize the efficiencies offered by digital technology. The adoption of digital technology makes it possible to distribute movies to theaters through the use of satellite or fiber-optic cable. Bulky metal film canisters can be replaced by easy-to-transport hard drives. Moreover, by establishing a common set of content requirements, distributors, studios, exhibitors, digital cinema manufacturers, and vendors can be assured of interoperability and compatibility. In the United States and Europe, for example, major investments have been made by both the private and public sectors to accelerate the digitization process through the acceptance of Digital Cinema Initiatives[101] as the international standard for digital film formatting and through the development and promotion of the Virtual Print Free (VPF) model, by which distributors contribute, through third-party investors, to financing the digitization of cinemas.[102]

To illustrate the growing importance of digital and 3-D technology in the movie industry, the number of screens served by digital projectors worldwide rose from about 3,000 to 16,400 between 2006 and 2009.[103] In 2009, the number of digital 3-D screens worldwide more than tripled from the previous year, rising from 2,543 to 8,989, with most of the increases seen in North America and Europe.[104]

Tighter Budgets, Digital Technology, and Government Incentives Drive Production Abroad

Digital technology and computer-generated imaging have started to transform the industry's production strategies by allowing content to be transmitted across borders more efficiently and at lower cost. As a result, more movie producers are moving certain production or post-production activities (e.g., special effects, animation, editing) abroad. In an environment of sluggish economic growth, MGM's bankruptcy filing in November 2010, and Universal and Disney's poor return on investments in 2009 (e.g., *G-Force*, *Confessions of a Shopaholic*), all of the major Hollywood studios have committed to becoming more cost-conscious in their film budgeting.[105] Hence, movies are increasingly being shot in foreign sites, which often compete to attract large-budget productions through tax breaks and other cost or labor incentive s.[106]

As a consequence, all but seven U. S. states and territories and 24 other countries now offer or are preparing to offer rebates, grants, or tax credits that cut 20–40 percent off the cost of filming a movie.[107] Industry sources note that producers often first compare the incentives offered by the different locations and only then look at their scripts to see which of the places on the list make sense. The phenomenon of "runaway production" has been a major issue in California since 1998, when Canada began to attract producers and their crews away from Los Angeles with tax breaks.[108] California's world share of studio films (i.e., those made by the six largest studios) dropped from 66 percent in 2003 to 34 percent in 2008.[109] Competition for movie productions has been fierce because such projects can provide the location with almost immediate economic benefits. A U. S. industry source estimates that the average big-budget feature film costing about $32 million leads directly to 141 jobs, from caterers to make-up artists, and indirectly to another 425 jobs. Such a production can generate up to $4.1 million in sales and income tax revenue.[110] Some of the most popular foreign filming sites for U. S. -based studios include Australia, Canada, Ireland, New Zealand, the United Kingdom, and various countries in Eastern Europe.[111]

Moreover, making changes to a picture is much easier using digital techniques. Backgrounds can be inserted after the actors perform on a sound stage, or locations can be digitally modified to reflect the script. Even actors can be created digitally.[112] Since these technologies have increased the divisibility of production tasks, more firms have taken advantage of offshoring or outsourcing opportunities in developing countries or with lower-cost foreign firms that specialize in certain activities. In 2004–05,[113] Lucasfilm opened its first overseas special effects studio in Singapore, making Lucasfilm the first major production studio to set up shop in Asia.[114] The Singapore studio's less experienced artists required lower salaries than their California counterparts, proved easier to hire abroad since the company didn't have to navigate U. S. immigration laws, and used the 16-hour time difference between Singapore and San Francisco to essentially double Lucasfilms' productive capability. Currently, more than 90 percent of the animation for American films and television shows is processed in Asia, mainly in Japan and Korea. However, the $100 billion animation industry is rushing to tap the deep pools of young, well-trained, and relatively inexpensive artists in countries such as China, India, the Philippines, and Singapore.[115]

Technological Advances Further Challenge Intellectual Property Rights

Advances in technology have made the regulation and protection of intellectual property rights more difficult for audiovisual service providers, national governments, and industry associations.[116] According to an industry source, the sale and distribution of illicit content have reportedly cost the movie industry several billion dollars in lost revenue in recent years, making the production and distribution of films even more expensive for legitimate producers operating in a highly leveraged market.[117] The Motion Picture Association of America, which represents the six largest movie studios in Hollywood, mentions illegal camcording in theaters, the expanding network of peer-to-peer file sharing and illicit video streaming, and user-generated content sites on the Internet as some of the primary threats to their industry.[118] They also note that Internet piracy has become a growing problem in key markets such as China, Europe, Korea, North America, South Africa, and Taiwan.[119]

Consequently, new technologies are emerging in order to better identify and root out pirated materials online.[120] Current methods of protection, such as digital "watermarking," are insufficient, since they only recognize and flag duplicates. Movies that are illegally camcorded from theaters can easily sidestep these online interventions. These new systems offer two benefits: they automate what is currently a manual procedure for checking whether an uploaded video on the Internet is pirated or not, and they would better detect whether a work is authentic, even if it has been illicitly filmed or digitally altered in any way.[121]

Trade Trends

Cross-Border Trade

U.S. exports substantially exceeded imports of audiovisual services in 2009 (box 3.2). U. S. cross-border exports of audiovisual services amounted to $13.8 billion, reflecting a growth rate of about 3 percent over 2008 (figure 3.1). This was below the growth trend from 2004 through 2007, when U. S. exports increased by close to 7 percent annually on average. The decline in exports observed in 2008 is likely related to several factors during that period, including slow growth in demand in several developing economies, financial constraints on movie production due to the economic downturn, and a dearth of strong feature films from Hollywood and other major film industries.[122] By a wide margin, the United Kingdom was the largest U. S. export market for audiovisual services in 2009, accounting for revenues of $3.7 billion (27 percent). Other important export markets included Canada ($1.3 billion), Germany ($1.2 billion), Japan ($1.1 billion), and France ($829 million). Europe, by far the most significant regional consumer of U. S. audiovisual services exports, accounted for about 63 percent of such exports in 2009 (figure 3.2).[123] U. S. films have long dominated most European markets,[124] for reasons that include the widespread use of English in the region, the popularity of A-list American actors and actresses throughout most of Europe, the predominance of U. S.-made films in European film festivals such as Cannes and Venice, and the multicultural make-up of most U. S. films (largely due to the United States' diverse ethnic and cultural population).[125]

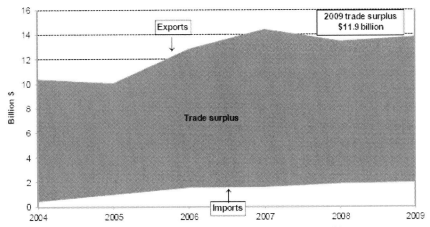

Source: USDOC, BEA, *Survey of Current Business*, October 2010, 36–37, table 1.
[a] Cross-border trade data measure films and television tape rentals.

Figure 3.1. Audiovisual services:[a] U. S. cross-border trade in private-sector services resulted in a U. S. trade surplus each year during 2004–09.

Box 3.2. Understanding Available Trade Data in Audiovisual Services

Overall, publicly available data on motion picture trade flows are of limited quality and quantity. The UN Comtrade database reports trade in motion pictures in terms of the value of "cinematographic film exposed or developed," which is a commodity rather than a service.

Available Balance of Payments data significantly understate global trade in this sector, as many WTO members do not collect statistics at this level of disaggregation.[a] Data used in the trade discussion below are prepared by the Bureau of Economic Analysis (BEA) of the U. S. Department of Commerce (USDOC).

BEA data on cross-border trade in audiovisual services reflect payments for rights to display, reproduce, or distribute motion pictures and television programs.[b] In other words, cross-border trade data reflect the exchange of limited intellectual property rights. BEA's statistics, however, do not reflect global box office receipts, which broadly measure demand for movie-going and, in turn, affect cross-border trade.[c]

Data on affiliate transactions reflect sales to foreign consumers of motion pictures, television tapes, and films by U. S. - owned production and distribution affiliates, as well as purchases by U. S. consumers from foreign-owned motion picture affiliates located in the United States.[d] The data presented by the BEA provide a limited view of bilateral trade flows for the film industry, as most of the numbers are suppressed to avoid disclosure of data of individual companies. As a result, U. S. affiliate transactions are not included in this trade discussion.[e]

[a] WTO, "Audiovisual Services: Background Note by the Secretariat," January 12, 2010, 4.
[b] USDOC, BEA, *Survey of Current Business*, October 2010, 46–49.
[c] Specific box office revenue data are not analyzed in the "Trade Trends" discussion.
[d] USDOC, BEA, *Survey of Current Business*, October 2010, 46–49.
[e] Hanson and Xiang, "International Trade in Motion Picture Services," January 2008, 3–9.

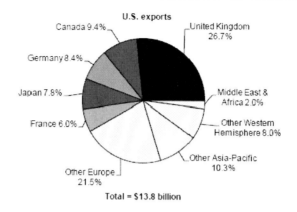

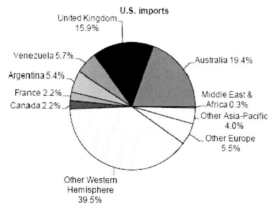

Source: USDOC, BEA, *Survey of Current Business*, October 2010, 48–49, table 5.2.
Note: Geographic regions are shaded in yellow.
[a] Cross-border trade data measures films and television tape rentals.

Figure 3.2. Audiovisual services:[a] Europe was the largest market for audiovisual services exports, while Latin America and Other Western Hemisphere countries were the largest exporters of audiovisual services to the U. S. market in 2009.

Imports of foreign films and television programs have continued to capture an increasing share of the U. S. market, though it is still relatively small. Cross-border imports in 2009 totaled about $1.9 billion, a 6 percent increase over the previous year. By comparison, imports grew at an average annual rate of 44 percent from 2004 through 2008. Such growth can be attributed to increasing imports from Latin America.[126] Venezuela, in particular, has been a major source of audiovisual services imports in recent years. This influx can largely be attributed to the Venezuelan government's concerted efforts to boost this sector by building up its infrastructure to support its state distribution company, Amazonia Films.[127] Australia accounted for $377 million, or 19 percent, of U. S. audiovisual services imports in 2009, while imports from the United Kingdom and Venezuela totaled $308 million (16 percent) and $110 million (6 percent), respectively. In contrast to its high importance as a regional market for U. S. exports, Europe supplied only about 24 percent of U. S. imports of audiovisual services in 2009.[128]

Multilateral Negotiations, Liberalization, and Remaining Barriers

Audiovisual services is among the services sectors with the lowest number of WTO members with commitments (30, as of January 31, 2010), although many of the most important producing countries have some commitments. The sector is also characterized by a high number of exemptions to most-favored-nation (MFN) or nondiscriminatory treatment, which largely focus on concessions allowed for international film coproductions.[129]

Following the Hong Kong Ministerial Declaration of December 2005, a group of developing and developed country members prepared a plurilateral request for audiovisual services. Essentially, the request seeks more commitments on cross-border supply (mode 1) and consumption abroad (mode 2). For commercial presence (mode 3), the request noted important lingering barriers to trade in the sector, particularly content quotas, foreign equity restrictions, limits on the number of suppliers, discriminatory taxes, and other trade-inhibiting requirements.[130] The request also sought to reduce the scope and content of MFN exemptions in the sector.[131] Although negotiations have stalled at the multilateral level, these barriers to trade remain important topics for discussion, particularly within pending bilateral trade agreements such as the U.S-Korea Free Trade Agreement.[132] Nonetheless, in most trade negotiations (both bilateral and multilateral), many governments continue to incorporate special carve-out measures, such as those mentioned above, for the provision of audiovisual services, since the importation of foreign movies and other content can have (perhaps unintended) cultural and societal influences. Hence, the effects of trade liberalization in this sector are not solely economic in nature.[133]

Outlook

Box office revenue for 2010–11 is forecast to be lower than previous years due to increasing market saturation in developed markets and the proliferation of inexpensive entertainment options such as Netflix and Redbox rental services, video on demand, hand-held tablet devices, and video game systems. However, the emergence of MGM Studios from bankruptcy with $500 million in new financing indicates some renewed interest in the highly leveraged movie industry.[134] Major U. S. -based movie studios will likely increase content available in 3-D and high-definition Blu-ray discs and will look to shorten the release window between the time a film debuts theatrically and when it becomes available for home viewing in order to take fuller advantage of lower-cost digital distribution options.[135]

Weakness in consumer spending on discretionary services, such as audiovisual services, is expected to continue in key markets in Europe and Asia due to relatively flat-tonegative forecast economic growth.[136] However, China's spending and production will likely continue to grow rapidly, according to SARFT,[137] China's state film agency. SARFT estimated that 1.65 new cinema screens were built every day in China during 2009, and there are no signs this rapid pace will slow any time soon. In the first six months of 2010, total box office revenue had already reached 4.6 billion yuan (about $697 million), surpassing the total for the entire year of 2008.[138] As mentioned previously, China is on track to break into the select group of countries with over $1.0 billion in annual box office revenue. In addition, China has been linked to co-production deals with film companies in France, India, New Zealand, and the United Kingdom, further bolstering its future movie production potential.[139]

4. COMPUTER SERVICES

SUMMARY

Despite the 2008–09 economic downturn, the global computer services industry grew during much of the past decade. Demand remained highest in Western Europe and North America, where most of the industry's leading firms are headquartered, but showed the most resistance to the effects of the downturn in the Asia-Pacific region, where several Indian companies have emerged as industry leaders. Sales dropped during the downturn due to the struggles of leading clients, notably financial firms, although resilient demand from government and healthcare firms helped offset the decline. Large computer hardware and software firms began to supply more computer services, especially over the Internet (via "cloud computing"), often delivered across borders due to the rapid growth of broadband infrastructure.

The United States' trade deficit in computer and data processing services grew during 2006–09, totaling $7.7 billion at the end of the period. India led the world in exports of these services, supplying one-third of U. S. imports of them in 2009. Sales by U. S. firms' foreign computer services affiliates far exceeded cross-border exports, and sales by foreign firms' computer services affiliates in the United States nearly doubled, from $10.8 billion in 2003 to $21.0 billion in 2008. While explicit barriers to trade and foreign investment in this sector were rare, the advent of cloud computing raised concerns about impediments to cross-border data flows. Forecasts suggested that demand for computer services, particularly those delivered over the Internet, would grow significantly in the near future.

INTRODUCTION

The computer services industry is growing rapidly in many countries, including the United States.[140] Between 1994 and 2009, the share of U. S. economic output from computer systems design and related services[141] rose from 0.6 percent to 1.2 percent,[142] while employment in that industry segment grew from 505,000 to 1.4 million.[143] Trade in computer services has also increased markedly: between 2006 and 2009, U. S. trade (imports plus exports) in computer and data processing services increased at a compound annual rate of 10.2 percent.[144] The industry's principal activities include design, installation, and management of computer systems; development of customized software; delivery of noncustomized software over the Internet; Web page development and hosting; data processing and hosting; and computer consultancy.[145]

Competitive Conditions in the Global Computer Services Market

The computer services industry grew rapidly during much of the past decade due to steadily increasing demand in North America and Western Europe and even stronger demand growth in emerging markets. Global spending on computer services grew at an average annual rate of 6.1 percent between 2004 and 2008, from $588.6 billion to $745.0 billion. It then contracted to $715.0 billion in 2009, as the economic downturn caused demand to slump in North America and Western Europe and to stagnate in much of the Middle East, Africa, and Latin America. However, spending continued to grow in the Asia-Pacific region in 2009—notably in China, where the economy continued to grow rapidly, as well as in Japan, where spending on computer services grew strongly despite a weak economy. As a result, Asia-Pacific's share of the industry's global spending rose from 15.5 percent in 2005 to 18.1 percent in 2009, while North America's share fell from 49.6 percent to 46.8 percent (figure 4.1).[146]

Table 4.1. Computer services: Top 10 computer systems design and related services companies, 2009[a]

Rank	Company	Country	Services revenue (billion $)	Services' share of total revenue (%)
1	International Business Machines Corporation (IBM)	U.S.	55.0	58
2	Hewlett-Packard Company (HP)[b]	U.S.	34.7	30
3	Computer Sciences Corporation (CSC)[c]	U.S.	16.1	100
4	NTT Data Corporation[d]	Japan	12.3	100
5	Capgemini	France	11.7	100
6	Science Applications International Corporation (SAIC)[e]	U.S.	10.8	100
7	Cisco Systems Inc.[f]	U.S.	7.6	19
8	Atos Origin	France	7.2	100
9	Tata Consultancy Services Limited (TCS)[d]	India	6.4	75
10	Logica PLC	UK	5.8	100

Source: Bureau van Dijk, Orbis Companies Database (accessed December 27, 2010); company Web sites, annual reports, and SEC filings.

[a] Includes only firms for which Orbis reported computer systems design and related services as a primary industry. Ranking based on revenues from services.
[b] Revenues for the 12 months ending on October 31, 2009.
[c] Revenues for the 12 months ending April 2, 2010. May include some revenues from software licensing fees.
[d] Revenues for the 12 months ending March 31, 2010.
[e] Revenues for the 12 months ending January 31, 2010.
[f] Revenues for the 12 months ending July 31, 2010.

Table 4.1 lists the 10 largest global firms in the computer systems design and related services industry segment. The table captures two of the most important trends among computer services companies. First, computer hardware is or once was the chief source of revenue for 3 of the top 10 companies—IBM, Hewlett-Packard (HP), and Cisco. Like many firms whose original specialty was software or hardware, these firms saw services as a promising area for growth. Second, while the top 10 is dominated by companies from the United States and Europe, the presence of an Indian firm, Tata Consultancy Services, points to India's emergence as a leading producer of computer services.[147] The leading Indian firms offer high-quality services with lower labor costs than their counterparts in the United States and Europe.[148]

Western firms have responded to the competition by establishing their own facilities in India and other developing countries, such as Malaysia and Egypt. For example, Electronic Data Systems (EDS)—one of the largest computer services firms before its acquisition by HP in 2008—had 41,000 workers outside the United States at the end of 2007 (including 27,000 in India). Its non-U.S. workfrce numbered 32,000 (18,000 in India) a year earlier.[149]

Numerous companies whose primary activity is not computer systems design and related services are also leading players in the industry. For example, U. S. management consulting firms Accenture, Booz Allen Hamilton, and Deloitte were among the global leaders in terms of information technology (IT) consulting revenues in 2008.[150] These firms seek to advise and assist clients across the full range of business operations, including computing.

Large and small firms play different roles in the computer services industry. A select cadre of very large firms, such as those named above, compete for multiyear "outsourcing" contracts to undertake computing-related tasks, such as management of data centers, remote data processing,[151] and software programming and maintenance, for large clients. For example, in November 2010, IBM was awarded a contract to manage the IT operations of the Bank of Ireland, including its data centers, desktop computers, servers, mainframes, and service center.[152]

Most computer services firms in the United States are small. For example, in the computer systems design and related services industry segment, 72 percent of firms were nonemployers in 2007.[153] Small firms are also important providers of computer services in the EU[154] and India.[155] Small computer services companies often offer specialized services, such as virus protection and database construction, to smaller corporate clients. Competition among these firms tends to be high because barriers to entry are low. There are few regulatory obstacles to entry in most countries,[156] and the capital requirements for start-up are minimal. Recruitment of staff is the primary constraint to supply.[157]

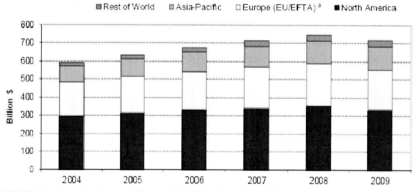

Source: IHS Global Insight, *Digital Planet 2010*, October 2010, 26.

[a] EU is the European Union. EFTA is the European Free Trade Association. It includes Iceland, Liechtenstein, Norway, and Switzerland.

Figure 4.1. Computer services: North America accounted for nearly half of all computer services spending in 2009.

Computer services firms deliver their services via three channels: in person, remotely via information and communication technologies, and combinations of the two. International "multimodal" service delivery is common. For example, a company might establish a commercial presence in a country (mode 3), source selected tasks through cross-border supply (mode 1), and arrange periodic visits by staff from headquarters (mode 4).[158] In-person consultations are particularly important for high-value-added service s,[159] such as design and management of complex software systems. For example, in March 2009, Infineon, a German manufacturer of semiconductors, awarded a multiyear contract to India-based TCS to operate and maintain software for supply chain management, marketing, and sales. To manage this complex system, TCS placed four employees at Infineon's headquarters, supported by an additional 30 TCS employees located outside Germany.[160]

Demand and Supply Factors

Demand for Computer Services Weakens as Key Clients Struggle
Computer services firms' success is tightly linked to that of their clients, making them vulnerable to the economic turbulence of recent times. For example, financial services firms in the United States and Western Europe are among the most important consumers of computer services.[161] The financial industry's struggles in 2008 and 2009, along with the broader economic downturn in the United States and Europe, weakened demand for computer services. However, relatively robust demand in several other sectors, such as government and health care, partially offset the decline among financial clients.[162]

Diverse factors explain this resilient demand. Demand from governments was buoyed by major economic stimulus programs, such as the United States' American Recovery and Reinvestment Act of 2009.[163] Demand from healthcare firms in developed countries for services such as claims processing and management of patient records remained relatively strong due to long-term trends (such as aging populations) and governments' reluctance to cut healthcare expenditures too deeply.[164] By late 2009, there were signs that demand for computer services from North American financial services firms was recovering.[165]

Large Hardware and Software Firms Move Increasingly into Services
Provision of services has become increasingly important for large companies that once drew (or still draw) the bulk of their revenues from hardware or packaged software. IBM is the foremost exemplar of this trend: it drew 57 percent ($55 billion) of its total revenues from services in 2009,[166] compared to 16 percent (about $11 billion) in 1 990.[167] Other large hardware companies followed in IBM's footsteps by acquiring leading services providers: HP acquired EDS in 2008, Dell Inc. purchased Perot Systems in 2009, and Xerox Corporation bought Affiliated Computer Services in 2009. Companies that traditionally sold packaged software have also moved into services. For example, Microsoft's services include a consulting arm[168] and software delivered over the Internet, such as Office 365.[169]

These firms have focused more on services for several reasons. First, during the past decade, much hardware (and some software) became "commoditized." Consumers came to view many products as homogenous, forcing their manufacturers to compete more aggressively on price. For example, HP lowered the prices of its desktop printers in the early 2000s in order to compete with lower-cost competitors that were gaining market share.[170] Hardware and software firms have seen services as a way to recapture higher margins.

Secondly, the recession highlighted the advantages of multiyear service contracts, which offer more predictable streams of revenue than one-time sales of hardware and software. Finally, firms have sought to capitalize on businesses' growing interest in cloud computing (see discussion, next section).[171]

Cloud Computing Expands the Range and Volume of Activities Delivered as Services

Cloud computing is "a standardized IT capability delivered via the Internet in a pay-per-use and self-service way" that is altering the supply of computer services.[172] It enables users to replace capital expenditures on hardware and packaged software with services paid for on a subscription or utility basis (i.e., fees that vary based on the amount of computing power used).[173] Cloud computing comprises IT infrastructure services, such as data processing and storage; platforms for designing and hosting Web applications;[174] and Internet-delivered software (box 4.1).

While Internet-based delivery of computer services is not new,[175] it is growing. By one estimate, cloud computing revenues totaled $58.6 billion in 2009.[176] Many companies whose IT budgets were squeezed during the recession saw cloud services as cost-effective alternatives to hardware and packaged software. IT suppliers, in turn, expanded their cloud offerings.[177] Cloud computing has, however, raised concerns about data privacy[178] and spurred new debates about how to regulate cross-border data flows (see "Multilateral Negotiations, Liberalization, and Remaining Barriers" below).[179]

Box 4.1. Cloud Computing Helps Businesses Improve Performance and Reduce Costs

Cloud computing is transforming how businesses invest in and benefit from IT. The three types of cloud computing services—Infrastructure as a Service, Platform as a Service, and Software as a Service—enable users to perform vital computing functions without large investments in hardware or packaged software.

Infrastructure as a Service (IaaS) allows businesses to purchase computing capacity and data storage space on an as-needed basis.[a] IaaS providers include Amazon Web Services (AWS) and VMware vCloud Express. One representative of an online marketing firm explained how his firm uses IaaS. The firm built and managed a Web site for a company selling nutrition bars. One of its promotions attracted an unusually high number of Web site visitors, causing the site to crash. The marketing firm bought time on "virtual machines" from AWS in order to manage the data generated by the additional traffic. When traffic to the site declined, the marketing firm simply stopped paying for the virtual machines. AWS allowed the firm to solve its problem rapidly without investing in hardware that would be redundant in normal circumstances.[b]

Platform as a Service (PaaS) lets software developers create computer applications without investing in the hardware they would otherwise need.[c] Examples of PaaS include Google's App Engine and Microsoft's Windows Azure. The City of Miami used Windows Azure to create an online application for Miami 311, a service that allows citizens to report nonemergency problems (such as potholes) and track progress on resolving them.

Windows Azure gave the city's IT Department the capacity to complete all stages of development and process the data required to run Miami 311.[d]

Software as a Service (SaaS) refers to software delivered to customers over a network (most commonly the Internet).[e] It includes software oriented to business users, such as Salesforce, and products for individual consumers, such as Google's Gmail e-mail service and its Docs word processor. SaaS eliminates the need to procure packaged software and install it on users' individual machines. It also makes it easier to connect users. For example, Restoration Hardware, a distributor of home furnishings, adopted Salesforce for a sales program targeting "trade" customers, such as property developers, hotels, and interior designers. Restoration used Salesforce to create a centralized database of these customers and to build a portal through which staff in Restoration's stores can forward leads to a specialized sales team. The software improved staff collaboration, customer service, and conversion of leads into sales.[f]

[a] Amazon, "What is AWS?"
[b] Industry representative, interview by USITC staff, December 30, 2010.
[c] Gray, "Cloud Computing," October 21, 2010.
[d] Microsoft, "City of Miami," February 24, 2010, 5.
[e] Gray, "Cloud Computing," October 21, 2010.
[f] Salesforce, "Restoration Hardware," n.d. (accessed January 4, 2011).

Broadband Internet Facilitates Trade in Computer Services

Cross-border trade in computer services has grown rapidly since the mid-1990s. Among Organization for Economic Cooperation and Development (OECD) countries, imports of computer services nearly quadrupled from 1996 to 2005, and exports quintupled.[180] The rapid expansion of the global broadband Internet[181] infrastructure has facilitated this growth in trade.[182] In India, for example, the total number of fixed broadband subscriptions grew from 180,000 in 2004 to over 7.7 million in 2009, while the country's computer services exports nearly tripled and its imports nearly quintupled.[183] Over this same period, Malaysia's broadband subscribership grew by 58 percent[184] and its computer services exports and imports quadrupled.[185] Broadband connections facilitate trade by allowing computer service providers and their clients to exchange large amounts of data quickly. This is particularly important for many cloud computing services.[186] Broadband connections are costly and unreliable in many lower-income countries, which limits their ability to competitively produce computer services for export.[187] In 2009, the average cost of a monthly broadband subscription was $322 in sub-Saharan Africa and $96 in Latin America and the Caribbean, compared to $6 in India.[188]

Trade Trends

Cross-border Trade[189]

In 2009, U. S. cross-border exports of computer and data processing services (box 4.2) totaled $8.6 billion and cross-border imports totaled $16.3 billion, producing a trade deficit of $7.7 billion (figure 4.2). The United States ran a deficit in cross-border trade in computer and data processing services every year from 2006 through 2009.[190] The deficit grew by 5.0 percent from 2008 to 2009, a steeper annual increase than in the two previous years.

Box 4.2. Understanding Data on Trade in Computer Services

This chapter's data on cross-border trade were prepared by the Bureau of Economic Analysis (BEA) of the U. S. Department of Commerce (USDOC). In analyzing cross-border trade, the chapter focuses on "computer and data processing services" as defined by BEA, which include data entry; computer systems design; custom software and programming; hardware and software integration; and other computer services, such as maintenance and Web site management. Fees for database services and software usage are classified separately.[a]

BEA records cross-border trade data by type of service. A single firm may report imports and exports of a variety of services, and each service may be produced by firms in multiple industries. For example, if a manufacturing firm designed custom software for a foreign affiliate, the transaction would be counted as an export of computer and data processing services.

The data on affiliate transactions also come from BEA. It collects these data through surveys of U. S. direct investment abroad and of foreign investment in the United States. However, BEA compiles these data differently, classifying them by primary industry of the affiliate rather than by the type of service. For example, if an affiliate whose primary industry was computer systems design also sold other services, BEA would record all of the affiliate's sales under computer systems design. Computer services supplied by affiliates in other industries, such as computer manufacturing, software publishing, or wholesale trade, are captured separately in the BEA data.[b]

For this reason, the data on affiliate sales cannot be directly compared with those on cross-border trade. The analysis of affiliate transactions in this chapter therefore focuses on firms whose primary industry is "computer systems design and related services" as defined in the NAICS (see footnote 2).

The computer services trade data are described by BEA as reflecting "services supplied"; for computer systems design and related services, services supplied correspond to sales. The two terms are used interchangeably below.

[a] USDOC, BEA, "Quarterly Survey of Transactions," January 2010, 16; USDOC, BEA, "International Services Surveys," January 2010, 9.
[b] USDOC, BEA, "Where Can I Find Information?" November 3, 2010.

U.S. exports of computer and data processing services grew by 1.4 percent in 2009, compared to an average annual rate of 21.4 percent during 2006–08. The slowdown was due largely to weaker demand in Europe in response to the economic downturn. During the 2006–09 period, affiliated (intra-firm) exports grew faster than unaffiliated ones. Intra-firm exports by U. S. -owned companies grew fastest (figure 4.3). Most exporters of computer and data processing services to affiliated parties were not firms whose primary industry was computer services.[191] Thus, exports grew fastest among firms in other industries providing computer services to their affiliates.

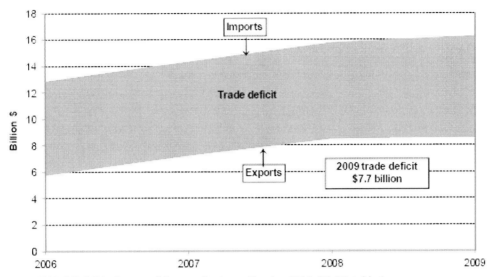

Source: USDOC, BEA, *Survey of Current Business*, October 2010, 36–37, table 1.

Figure 4.2. Computer services: U. S. cross-border trade in private-sector services resulted in a U. S. trade deficit each year during 2006–09.

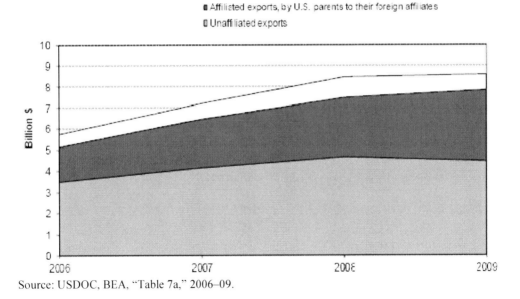

Source: USDOC, BEA, "Table 7a," 2006–09.

Figure 4.3. Computer services: Cross-border exports of computer and data processing services from U. S. parents to their foreign affiliates grew faster than both unaffiliated exports and exports from U. S. affiliates to their foreign parents during 2006–09.

Over half of U. S. exports of computer and data processing services were destined for Europe from 2006 through 2009. The United Kingdom was the most important single export market in each of these years, while Germany was consistently among the top five. However, in 2009, exports to Europe contracted while those to the Asia-Pacific region grew. As a result, Europe's share of exports declined from 58.9 percent in 2008 to 52.9 percent in 2009, while Asia-Pacific's share grew from 18.5 percent to 22.1 percent (figure 4.4).

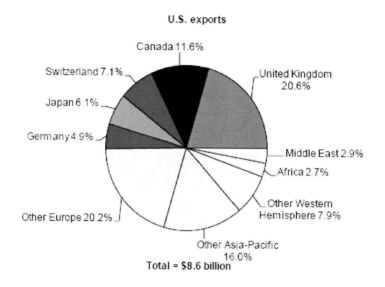

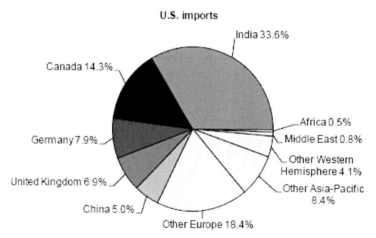

Source: USDOC, BEA, *Survey of Current Business*, October 2010, 54–55, table 7.2.
Note: Geographic regions are shaded in yellow.

Figure 4.4. Computer services: The United Kingdom and India, respectively, were the top markets for U. S. exports and imports of computer and data processing services in 2009.

Growth of imports of computer and data processing services into the United States also slowed in 2009, falling to 3.1 percent compared to average annual growth of 10.8 percent during 2006–08. The slowdown in import growth reflected the decline in U. S. demand for computer services during the economic downturn. Over three-quarters of all imports during this period were intra-firm.[192] Most affiliated imports involved firms whose primary industry was computer services. This suggests that multinational computer services firms operating in the United States often combine imported inputs with locally produced ones.[193]

India accounted for 33.6 percent of U. S. imports of computer and data processing services in 2009. It has been the leading source of imports since at least 2006, and its lead over its competitors widened steadily through 2009. U. S. imports from India in 2009 were more than twice those from the second-largest source, Canada, and more than those from all of Europe combined (see figure 4.4). Factors that have contributed to India's emergence as a premier computer services exporter include a large pool of skilled, English-speaking workers; competitive wages well below those in developed countries; government incentives favorable to the industry's growth; a liberal environment for domestic and foreign investment; and low telecommunications costs.[194] Additional factors that have favored India's success in exporting to the United States include similar political and legal institutions and a time zone differential between the two countries that fosters "round-the-clock" service provision.[195]

Affiliate Transactions[196]

U.S. firms' sales of computer services through foreign affiliates[197] tend to be larger than cross-border exports, reflecting the importance of having a local presence when delivering these services.[198] In 2006, sales by U. S. -owned foreign affiliates whose primary industry was computer systems design and related services totaled $52.5 billion—over nine times the value of U. S. cross-border exports of computer and data processing services.[199] The top six countries for these sales included the five leading markets for cross-border exports (the United Kingdom, Canada, Germany, Australia, and Japan).[200] Recent literature suggests that cross-border trade and affiliate sales of computer services are complements.[201] This may explain why the lists of leading destinations for exports and affiliate sales are similar.

Sales by foreign-owned U. S. affiliates in the computer systems design and related services industry totaled $21.0 billion in 2008, an increase of 22.2 percent over 2007 and nearly double their sales of $10.8 billion in 2003 (figure 4.5).[202] Growth of sales by foreign parents' U. S. affiliates outpaced the growth of cross-border imports in 2007 and 2008, suggesting that the importance of commercial presence for delivery of computer services to clients in the United States may be increasing vis-à-vis other modes. In part, this may reflect the recent expansion of a number of the leading Indian computer services companies within the United States. One example is Wipro, which established a large service center in Atlanta, Georgia, in 2008. It has expanded within the United States to make it easier to work on complex projects that require more face-to-face interaction with customers, and to attract clients that may not allow their data to cross U. S. borders, such as government agencies and defense contractors.[203]

Multilateral Negotiations, Liberalization, and Remaining Barriers

International trade agreements rarely contain explicit barriers to trade and investment in computer services. Ninety-four World Trade Organization (WTO) members have made commitments on computer and related services under the General Agreement on Trade in Services (GATS), and few have included sector-specific limitations to market access and national treatment within those commitments.[204] However, members' limits on the entry of temporary workers can seriously hinder industry operations. For example, after Switzerland lowered its quota of foreign workers in December 2009, Google, IBM, and Accenture announced that they might move projects out of the country because they could not bring in enough foreign IT specialists.[205]

The advent of cloud computing has introduced a host of new concerns related to the flow of data across borders. Because cloud services providers store and transmit clients' data across multiple locations, it is not always clear which country's regulations apply with respect to issues such as data privacy and protection of intellectual property. Moreover, countries' policies may conflict. For example, one country's law enforcement officials might request access to data, but that access could violate the data owner's privacy rights under another country's laws.[206] Companies have voiced particular concern about the heterogeneity of regulations among members of the European Union. While certain EUwide statutes exist, such as the Data Protection Directive, member countries do not always implement the statutes consistently.[207] In some cases, a company that wants to send data across the territories of multiple members must get separate authorizations from each country.[208]

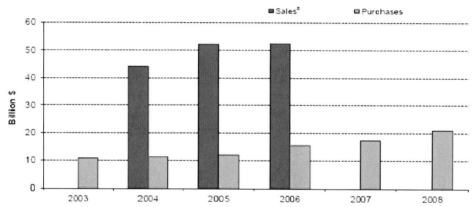

Source: USDOC, BEA, *Survey of Current Business*, various issues.

[a] BEA reports "services supplied" by foreign affiliates. In the computer systems design and related services industry, services supplied correspond to sales. Data were suppressed in 2003, 2007, and 2008 to avoid disclosure of individual company data.

Figure 4.5. Computer services: Purchases of computer system design and related services from U. S. affiliates of foreign firms showed a marked increase in 2008 from 2007, while the latest data show sales by foreign affiliates of U. S. firms remained steady.

Countries are trying to ensure that international agreements keep up with the rapid pace of change in the computer services industry. At the WTO, a number of members, including the United States, have sought to clarify the coverage of computer services under the United Nations Provisional Central Product Classification, which is used by many WTO members for scheduling GATS commitments.[209] The European Commission announced its intention to revise its data protection regulations in 2011;[210] it and the United States agreed on a set of "Trade Principles for Information and Communication Technology Services" in April of that year.[211] Similarly, the proposed U.S-Korea Free Trade Agreement calls for the parties to avoid creating unnecessary barriers to cross- border data flows.[212]

Outlook

Numerous observers have predicted that demand for computer services will continue to grow in the coming years. Forrester, a technology market research firm, forecast robust growth of demand for software and services in 2011, notably IT consulting and system integration. Forrester noted that hardware led IT spending growth in 2010, as companies made investments that they deferred during the recession, but that software and services were likely to be the drivers moving forward.[213] The forecasting firm IHS Global Insight largely concurred: it predicted that global computer services spending would grow at an average annual rate of 8.1 percent during 2010–13, and that services would grow more than hardware or software.[214]

The IT consultancy Gartner predicted that cloud computing services would continue to grow rapidly due to increasing interest from business consumers and an "explosion of supply-side activity." Gartner forecast that global spending on cloud services would increase from $58.6 billion in 2009 to $148.8 billion in 2014. It predicted that firms in the United States and Western Europe would remain the most important consumers of these services, but that other regions would also experience growth.[215]

5. EDUCATION SERVICES

SUMMARY

International trade in education services continues to expand, as an increasing number of students study outside their home country each year. U. S. universities are highly regarded around the world and, as a result, host more foreign students than the institutions of any other country. A growing number of universities are motivated to attract foreign students for financial reasons as well as to increase student body diversity. As competition among universities for foreign students—particularly the best-qualified students—intensifies, universities have sought to differentiate themselves from peer institutions by upgrading campus facilities and hiring foreign student recruitment firms, among other methods. Leading factors driving international trade in education services include strong developing-country demand, especially from students in China and India; stricter immigration regulations in several countries; and government budget cuts.

The United States' cross-border trade surplus in education services expanded in 2009, although this figure may be somewhat overstated due to data limitations. Tuition increases and growing foreign student enrollments propelled U. S. export growth, whereas enrollment in briefer, less costly study- abroad programs by U. S. students slowed import growth. Foreign students at U. S. universities mostly come from Asian countries, especially China, India, and Korea. By contrast, most U. S. students attend universities in the European Union, primarily in France, Italy, Spain, and the United Kingdom. International barriers to trade in education services largely involve restrictions on setting up campus facilities abroad and regulations governing the official acceptance of university degrees from other countries.

INTRODUCTION

Education services include formal academic instruction at primary, secondary, and tertiary (higher education) institutions, as well as instructional services offered by libraries and vocational, correspondence, language, and special education schools. This chapter presents information on the pursuit of instruction at universities and colleges (hereafter referred to as universities) by students from other countries. University studies are the only education services for which data on cross-border trade are reported. Cross-border trade is the primary means of providing education services to foreign students. Such trade consists of expenditures for tuition, fees, and living expenses of students who study in institutions abroad. Although comparable worldwide estimates are not available, industry sources estimate that foreign students contributed $18.8 billion to the U. S. economy in 2010, a $1.2 billion (6 percent) increase from the previous year.[216]

Competitive Conditions in the Global Education Services Market

The United States is recognized around the world as having an extensive and top-quality system of higher education. For example, rankings developed by the Institute for International Education at Jiao Tong University in China placed U. S. universities in 13 of the top 20 spots worldwide (table 5.1). U. S. universities owe this position to several interrelated factors, including highly regarded professors, world-class academic facilities, cutting-edge research on a variety of subjects, and decades of substantial funding from both public and private sources.

Universities in many countries seek to attract foreign students. One of their most important aims is to increase the international flavor of their campuses, a process that not only broadens the experience of domestic students but also heightens academic competition, often leading to higher academic performance by both domestic and foreign students.[217] However, one of the most notable trends in higher education is that universities increasingly seek to enroll foreign students for financial reasons as well (see below).[218] Globally, competition among universities for foreign students is intense, with many actively taking steps to differentiate themselves from peer institutions. Moreover, the world's best universities—so-called "super-league" institutions like Harvard University and the University of Cambridge—compete fiercely for the world's best students.[219]

One of the most important distinguishing factors among universities is an institution's reputation, which is often based on a subjective assessment of factors including name recognition, perceptions of academic quality and students' post-graduation job prospects, and even a school's history and heritage.[220] In recent years, competitive pressures for highly qualified students—both domestic and foreign—have led universities to redesign curricula, upgrade campus facilities, install state-of-the-art communications networks, and enhance campus amenities. Universities attract top students by providing financial aid as well, including low-interest loans, tuition grants, scholarships, and on-campus employment. Universities' efforts to attract foreign students also include active marketing and recruitment campaigns, such as extensive informational Web sites aimed at foreign students, foreign "road shows," and the use of specialized international student recruiting consultants.[221]

Table 5.1. Education services: Institute for International Education's world university rankings, 2010

Rank	University	Country
1	University of Cambridge	UK
2	Harvard University	U.S.
3	Yale University	U.S.
4	UCL (University College London)	UK
5	Massachusetts Institute of Technology	U.S.
6	University of Oxford	UK
7	Imperial College London	UK
8	University of Chicago	U.S.
9	California Institute of Technology (Caltech)	U.S.
10	Princeton University	U.S.
11	Columbia University	U.S.
12	University of Pennsylvania	U.S.
13	Stanford University	U.S.
14	Duke University	U.S.
15	University of Michigan	U.S.
16	Cornell University	U.S.
17	Johns Hopkins University	U.S.
18	ETH Zurich (Swiss Federal Institute of Technology)	Switzerland
19	McGill University	Canada
20	Australian National University	Australia
21	King's College London (University of London)	UK
22	University of Edinburgh	UK
23	University of Hong Kong	Hong Kong
24	University of Tokyo	Japan
25	Kyoto University	Japan

Source: Top Universities, "World University Rankings 2010."

Due to the reputation of U. S. universities and to the sheer number of options available, the United States was the most common destination for foreign students in 2008, hosting approximately 21 percent of all students studying abroad. Nevertheless, international competition has increased over the past few decades, and U. S. universities' share of all foreign students studying abroad has consistently declined, from approximately 37 percent in 1970 to 21 percent in 2008. In 2008, other important host countries included the United Kingdom (12 percent), France (8 percent), Australia (8 percent), and Germany (6 percent) (figure 5.1).

Demand and Supply Factors

Foreign Demand for U. S. Education Services Surges

From 2007 through 2010, the number of foreign students enrolled in U. S. universities surged to new heights. During 2008 and 2009, the number of foreign students rose by 7 percent and 8 percent respectively, the fastest annual growth rates in nearly 30 years.

Although annual growth slowed to 3 percent in 2010, a record 691,000 foreign university students were studying in the United States by the end of the year (figure 5.2). Over the past several years, the largest number of foreign students studying in the United States came from mainland China, India, and Korea (table 5.2), with China taking the number one slot in 2010 as a result of 30 percent growth during the 2009/10 academic year.

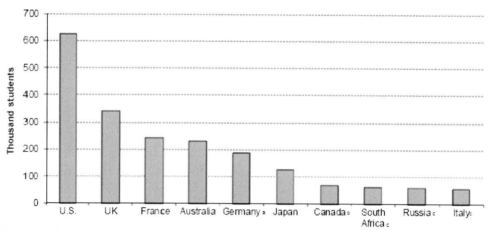

Source: United Nations Education, Scientific, and Cultural Organization (UNESCO), Institute for Statistics (UIS), *Global Education Digest 2010*, 2010, 172, 174, table 9.

[a] Data reported are incomplete.

[b] Data are for 2006, the latest year available, and data reported are incomplete.

[c] Data are for 2007, the latest year available.

Figure 5.1. Education services: United States led as host to foreign students in 2008.

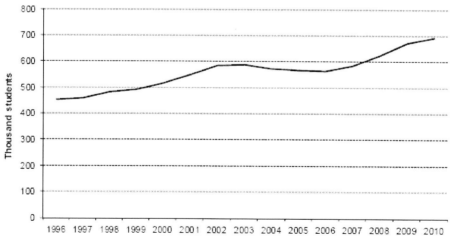

Source: Institute of International Education (IIE), "Open Doors 2010 Fast Facts," 2010; Koh Chin, ed., *Open Doors 2003*, 2003, 3.

Figure 5.2. Education services: Growth in number of foreign students in U. S. universities tapered off in 2010.

China's position as the number one source of foreign students enrolled at U. S. universities was driven in large part by enrollments at the undergraduate level. Although historically the majority of Chinese students studying at U. S. universities focused on graduate-level programs, the number enrolled in undergraduate programs has grown very rapidly over the past couple of years, increasing by 65 percent in 2008 and 60 percent in 2009. In contrast, enrollment by Chinese students in graduate programs increased by 15 percent in 2008 and 10 percent in 2009. In part, the surge in undergraduates from China is attributable to the expanded use, both by Chinese students' families and by U. S. universities, of firms that recruit foreign students into undergraduate programs.[222]

Table 5.2. Education services: Top 10 countries of permanent residence among foreign students at U. S. universities, 2008–09 and 2009–10

Rank	Country of origin	2008–09	2009–10	2009–10, share of total (%)	Percent change, 2008/09–2009/10 (%)
1	China	98,235	127,628	18.5	29.9
2	India	103,260	104,897	15.2	1.6
3	Korea	75,065	72,153	10.4	(3.9)
4	Canada	29,697	28,145	4.1	(5.2)
5	Taiwan	28,065	26,685	3.9	(4.9)
6	Japan	29,264	24,842	3.6	(15.1)
7	Saudi Arabia	12,661	15,810	2.3	24.9
8	Mexico	14,850	13,450	1.9	(9.4)
9	Vietnam	12,823	13,112	1.9	2.3
10	Turkey	12,148	12,397	1.8	2.0
11	Nepal	11,581	11,233	1.6	(3.0)
12	Germany	9,679	9,548	1.4	(1.4)
13	UK	8,701	8,861	1.3	1.8
14	Brazil	8,767	8,786	1.3	0.2
15	Thailand	8,736	8,531	1.2	(2.3)
	World total	671,616	690,923		2.9

Source: IIE, "Open Doors 2010 Fast Facts," November 15, 2010.

Changing Visa Requirements in Australia and the United Kingdom May Divert Demand for Education Services

The legislatures of two English-speaking countries that are important suppliers of education services—Australia and the United Kingdom—recently made (or proposed) student visa policy changes that may lead to a decrease in the number of foreign students attending universities in those countries. In both cases, the governments were responding to foreigners' increased use of student visas to obtain permanent residency and/or employment, as opposed to temporary residence while pursuing a degree.[223]

For example, many foreign students who choose to study in Australia are partly motivated by the long-term prospect of permanent residency. Until recently, many students could reasonably expect to remain in Australia after graduation. However, a surge of immigrants into Australia in recent years, partly through the student visa system, led the

Australian government to strengthen regulations on universities and other international education providers in 2009 and 2010. The government also amended requirements pertaining to student visa and skilled migration programs, increasing its scrutiny of visa applications and toughening student visa qualifications.[224] Some Australian university officials predicted that these changes would lead to a decline in the number of Chinese students attending Australian universities.[225] These fears/predictions appear to have been well founded. In 2010, the number of student visas issued by the Australian government declined for the first time in at least 25 years,[226] prompting the government to launch a strategic review of the current student visa program and relax documentation requirements on visa applications by students from China, India, and other countries of particular importance to Australia's education services exports.[227]

The UK government is also taking steps to crack down on the abusive use of student visas to obtain residency and/or work permits. Fueled by an estimate that at least 40 percent of UK student visa holders failed to enroll in classes in 2009, the government proposed legislation in November 2010 that would significantly tighten student visa requirements, with the intention of issuing student visas to fewer, but more qualified, degree-seeking students.[228] If passed, one likely consequence would be the diversion of legitimate degree-seeking students to universities in other countries, particularly to English-speaking universities in the United States and Canada.

Budget Cuts Force Universities to Look Abroad

The economic downturn has placed financial pressure on universities around the world, particularly institutions in developed countries. In the United States, the downturn has undermined state governments' financial support for universities,[229] largely due to a decline in tax receipts, which are estimated to have fallen 12 percent (adjusted for inflation) over the last three years.[230] Accordingly, more than 40 state governments cut financial support to public universities, where at least 70 percent of U.S. students are enrolled, in the fiscal years ending in 2009 and 2010.[231] Such funding shortfalls have led the governing boards of many state universities to authorize reductions in student financial aid, tuition increases of 10 percent or more, staff furloughs and layoffs, expanded class sizes, the consolidation or termination of degree programs, and reductions in student and academic support services, among other measures.[232] Though less dependent on public financial assistance, U.S. private universities are also facing funding problems, with approximately 15 percent reporting decreased revenues in 2010 and the same percentage anticipating flat or declining revenues during 2011.[233]

The economic downturn and associated decline in government support is also impacting universities in Europe and Asia. For example, in 2010, the UK government announced a 40 percent reduction in funds for university instruction.[234] To cover the decline in financial support, the Parliament voted to increase the maximum allowable amount that British universities can charge for annual tuition to $15,000, three times the previous cap.[235] This move prompted massive student street protests in London. Similarly, in 2010, the government of Japan reduced subsidies to universities and salaries to faculty and staff.[236]

One potential effect of declining governmental financial assistance may be increased international trade in education services, as cash-strapped universities increasingly pursue foreign students as a means to offset funding shortfalls. Foreign students are often courted by universities because foreign students usually pay full tuition rates, typically from personal resources.[237] For example, U. S. universities, motivated partly by the need to develop new sources of revenue, are aggressively pursuing measures to expand and diversify foreign student enrollments, with methods ranging from recruiting trips in foreign countries to hiring overseas agencies that recruit students for a per-student commission.[238] Similarly, in the United Kingdom, the revenues derived from foreign students are often an essential source of funding for universities,[239] with schools ranging from the London School of Economics to Middlesex University to the University of Oxford actively calibrating foreign student numbers as a means of funding operations and research programs.[240]

A number of universities have also opened campuses abroad. U. S. universities, for example, maintain 78 campuses in foreign countries, while Australian universities operate campuses in Malaysia, Singapore, and the United Arab Emirates. Although less international than their American and Australian peers, British universities are also opening campuses abroad, including campuses in Malaysia and Qatar operated by the University of Nottingham and University College London, respectively.[241]

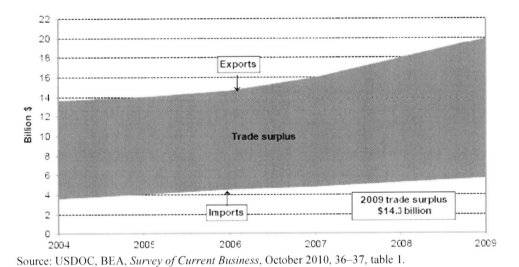

Source: USDOC, BEA, *Survey of Current Business*, October 2010, 36–37, table 1.

Figure 5.3. Education services: U. S. cross-border trade in private-sector services resulted in a U. S. trade surplus each year during 2004–09.

Trade Trends

Cross-Border Trade

In 2009, the value of U. S. cross-border exports of education services (box 5.1) increased by 11 percent to $19.9 billion, exceeding the average annual growth rate of 7 percent recorded from 2004 through 2008 (figure 5.3) and reflecting a 13 percent tuition increase as well as a growth in enrollment of foreign students (see above). U. S. imports of education services increased by 8 percent in 2009, which was somewhat slower than the 10 percent average annual growth rate reported from 2004 through 2008. The slower growth rate is attributable to the increasing tendency of U. S. students to choose brief study-abroad programs as well as the tighter budgets of many such study-abroad programs, especially at public universities. The latter development has prompted many universities to introduce less expensive destinations among study-abroad options. As a result of these trends, the U. S. trade surplus in education services in 2009 widened by 12 percent to $14.3 billion, double the 6 percent average annual increase from 2004 through 2008. In 2009, the principal markets for U. S. exports of education services were the same as in 2004, except that Canada (ranked fourth after India, China, and Korea) surpassed Japan in 2009. In 2009, exports to the United States' top three education services markets—China, India, and Korea—accounted for 42 percent of total education services exports, up from 36 percent in 2007 and 26 percent in 2002.[242] By region, students from Asia accounted for more than three-fifths of U. S. exports in 2009 (figure 5.4), followed by students from the European Union (9 percent), with other European countries providing an additional 5 percent of receipts.

Box 5.1. An Explanation of BEA Data on Cross-border Trade in Education Services and Transactions by Education Affiliates

U.S. cross-border exports of education services reflect estimated tuition (including fees) and living expenses of foreign residents (which exclude U. S. citizens, immigrants, or refugees) enrolled in U. S. colleges and universities. Cross-border imports of education services represent the same expenses for U. S. residents studying abroad.[a]

Data on U. S. imports of education services are estimated by the BEA based on two pathways by which U. S. permanent residents study in a foreign country. In the first, U. S. residents receive academic credit for study abroad from accredited U. S. colleges and universities, whether or not the U. S. residents also receive academic credit from the foreign institution. The BEA does not include the tuition and living expenses of students whose academic credits for study abroad do not transfer to U. S. institutions (with three country exceptions, as explained below), or who study abroad on an informal basis. The second pathway—from 2002 onward—supplements U. S. import data on education services by also including estimated tuition and living expenses for U. S. permanent residents who enroll in a degree program at a university in Australia, Canada, or the United Kingdom and reside temporarily in these countries in order to pursue their education. Because only formal study for credit toward a degree is included in estimates of tuition and living expenses that account for U. S. imports of education services, the full extent of studying abroad by U. S. students is understated in the trade data and, accordingly, the U. S. trade surplus in education services is overstated.

Data on education affiliate transactions are limited, especially data concerning transactions by education affiliates located in the United States but owned by a foreign firm. Because transaction data from education affiliates cover a wide range of education providers other than the higher education segment, which is the focus of this chapter, education affiliate transaction data are not presented herein.

Sources: BEA representative, e-mail to USITC staff, December 7, 2010, and February 9–10, 2009; Koh Chin, ed., *Open Doors 2004*, 2004, 92.

[a] Estimates for cross-border online instruction are included in "Other business, professional, and technical services" in the balance of payments, rather than the education services category.

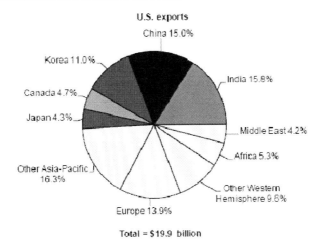

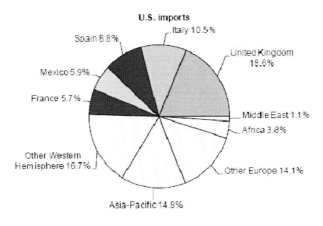

Source: USDOC, BEA, *Survey of Current Business*, October 2010, 48–49, table 5.2.
Note: Geographic regions are shaded in yellow.

Figure 5.4. Education services: The Asia-Pacific region was the leading destination for U. S. education services exports in 2009, while the leading sources of U. S. education imports were in Europe.

As with exports, the five leading sources for U. S. imports of education services were the same in both 2004 and 2009, with expenditures flowing primarily to the United Kingdom, followed by Italy and Spain (by Spain and Italy in 2004), respectively, Mexico, and France. By region, the European Union received 55 percent of U. S. payments for study abroad by U. S. students in 2009 (down 5 percentage points from 2004), followed by countries in the Western Hemisphere, which received 23 percent.

Multilateral Negotiations, Liberalization, and Remaining Barriers

Services supplied in the exercise of governmental authority, such as public education services provided without charge to a country's citizens, are excluded from the scope of the

General Agreement on Trade in Services (GATS).[243] Other education services are included in the GATS. However, only about 30 percent of signatories have made commitments to any portion of the education services sector under the GATS. A 2008 World Trade Organization report stated that some (unnamed) governments were prepared to make new commitments in the Doha Round of multilateral negotiations on private education services, removing existing provisions that discriminate against foreign providers. Several governments signaled their intention to seek additional commitments on private education services.[244] Some governments proposed that negotiations should take into account changes in the delivery of certain education services and the emergence of new education providers that are outside the traditional education system, while continuing to uphold governments' responsibility to maintain and improve service quality and to establish education-related regulatory measures based on policy objectives.

Few countries impose trade barriers expressly limiting the movement of students or the movement of personal funds to obtain higher education services across borders. More commonly, barriers take the form of restrictions on the establishment of campus facilities. For example, universities of another country are not allowed to establish branch campus universities in India for the purpose of awarding degrees recognized in India, although they may establish offices in India for other purposes, such as student recruitment or engagement in partnerships, research collaborations, or dual-degree programs with Indian universities. National regulations limiting the official acceptance of degrees or course credits from foreign universities, or of academic credentials of faculty seeking to cross borders, also may inhibit education services trade.

In recent years, governments and education industry stakeholders within and between regions have collaborated to increase the comparability, accessibility, and transparency of higher education systems while sustaining universities' autonomy. An important goal of these collaborations is to achieve greater ease of movement between countries for faculty, researchers, and students, starting with countries within a single region. For example, the European Higher Education Area officially began in March 2010, following a 10-year reform process that encouraged the development of credit-transfer policies, quality assurance mechanisms, commonality in university degrees, and measurement standards for higher education learning outcomes. A similar process begun by the Association of Southeast Asian Nations (ASEAN) in 2005 is targeted for completion in 2015. Other related activities in Asia include (1) a dialogue on these subjects between members of ASEAN, China, and Australia, motivated by mutual interests in developing skilled workforces and advancing economic growth, and (2) a project begun in 2010 to increase foreign student mobility at universities in Korea, Japan, and China.

Dialogues in other regions and between regions, such as the EU, Latin America, and North Africa, have recently gained momentum. In the United States, some of the reforms undertaken in Europe have begun to be adopted, such as the acceptance by some U. S. graduate programs of three-year undergraduate degrees from European universities, as well as the introduction of accelerated three-year undergraduate degrees at certain U. S. universities to complement traditional four-year undergraduate degrees.[245]

Outlook

The trends and issues discussed above will likely continue to drive international trade in education services over the next several years. Demand for education services should continue to grow as students from China, India, and other developing countries seek to study abroad.[246]

Additionally, fiscal constraints faced by many developed-country governments are expected to continue to cut into funds available for university operations.[247] As a result, a growing number of universities around the world will likely be forced to offset declining revenues by raising annual tuition levels and by stepping up efforts to recruit and enroll foreign students, particularly full-paying students.[248] The market share of one important segment—foreign university students being educated in English—that is held by universities in Australia, the United Kingdom, and the United States will likely shrink as universities located in countries such as Canada, Germany, and Malaysia offer increasing competition in the form of growing reputations and English-language curricula.[249]

6. HEALTHCARE SERVICES

SUMMARY

Since 2003, global spending on healthcare has steadily risen. The world's largest markets are still found predominantly in the United States and Europe. However, the fastest-growing markets are in developing countries, where private expenditures are rapidly growing. Demand for privately financed care has fallen in developed markets, as people have reduced spending following the economic downturn. Nonetheless, the rising incidence of chronic illnesses has driven global demand for treatments to manage these conditions. Governments around the world have launched programs and reforms to meet the growing needs of their constituents and address shortcomings in healthcare infrastructure and the supply of healthcare workers.

The United States has maintained a trade surplus in healthcare services, which grew to $1.74 billion in 2009, largely due to exports to its neighbors in North America. U. S. exporters maintained a competitive advantage based on the quality and expertise of U. S. providers, but a growing share of U. S. residents, particularly those without health insurance, imported care from Mexico and other lower-cost providers. Purchases from U. S. affiliates of foreign firms continued to exceed sales for foreign affiliates of U. S. firms, as the United States kept its position as the largest private healthcare market in the world. Measures that impede trade remain in place, such as policies and procedures related to healthcare financing and reimbursement. However, rapidly rising demand and growing public sector budget concerns have led to increased integration of public and private healthcare sectors.

INTRODUCTION

Healthcare is a fundamental service, demanded by almost everyone and provided in every market around the world.[250] Providing such services requires cooperation among a number of different parties, including public and private providers, financers, and regulators. Governments take an interest in the healthcare industry due to its critical role in economic growth[251] and development.[252] Further, in many countries, access to healthcare is considered a constitutional right, requiring these governments to play a larger role in the healthcare industry. However, medical advances, growing demand that is exceeding the capacity of public systems, and steadily rising healthcare prices all create profitable opportunities for private firms, particularly healthcare providers and insurers. Hence, most healthcare systems comprise a mix of public and private providers, financed by a combination of public and private sources.

Competitive Conditions in the Global Healthcare Services Market

Robust growth in global healthcare expenditure since 2003 has largely been driven by public spending, which grew more rapidly than private spending and accounted for an increasing share of overall expenditure.[253] From 2003 through 2008, global healthcare spending rose at an average annual rate of roughly 9 percent to reach $5.9 trillion dollars, or nearly 10 percent of global GDP.[254] Although public and private healthcare spending maintained steady growth, public spending grew more rapidly, rising at an average annual rate of 10 percent from 2003 through 2007, compared to 8.5 percent average growth in private spending. This disparity was further magnified in 2008, as advanced economies began to feel the effects of the economic downturn: growth in private spending slowed to 6.7 percent, while public spending rose 10.3 percent (figure 6.1). The slowdown in global private expenditure in 2008 is largely attributed to lagging growth in the U. S. market,[255] which slowed from an average annual rate of 5.9 percent during 2003– 07, to 2.6 percent in 2008, primarily due to the decline in employer-sponsored health insurance.[256] As a result, between 2003 and 2008, the share of global expenditure attributed to public spending increased from 58.3 percent to 60.4 percent.

During 2003 through 2008, spending by developed countries rose, though growth in private expenditure slowed during 2008. Global healthcare spending is driven by trends in healthcare spending in developed countries, particularly in the United States and Europe, where the bulk of healthcare expenditure occurs. The United States is the world's largest market, spending an estimated $2.3 trillion on healthcare in 2008 (table 6.1). By comparison, in that same year, total European healthcare expenditure was estimated at $2 trillion. High levels of spending in these countries are driven by a combination of factors, including higher incomes, lower mortality rates, a higher incidence of chronic diseases,[257] and higher patient expectations due to the availability of expensive new treatments and advanced technologies.[258] However, as these advanced economies began to feel the effects of the economic downturn in 2008, private spending fell, although public spending remained steady. The decline in private spending was most pronounced in the United States, where private expenditure accounts for the majority of the market, while growth in public spending occurred in Europe, where governments play a large role in the healthcare industry.[259]

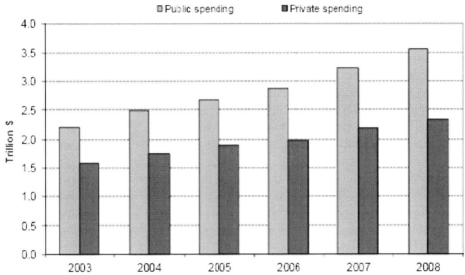

Source: USITC staff calculations based on data from WHO, GHO Database and World Bank, World dataBank Database.

Figure 6.1. Healthcare services: Global spending on healthcare rose steadily during 2003–08, largely driven by public spending.

Table 6.1. Healthcare services: Top 10 global healthcare markets, 2008

Rank	Country	Total expenditure (billion $)	Share of total expenditure from private expenditure (%)	Private expenditure (billion $)	Share of private spending from out-of-pocket expenditure (%)
1	United States	2,299.1	54	1,230.0	23
2	Japan	395.8	19	75.6	81
3	Germany	380.2	23	88.2	57
4	France	316.8	21	66.5	33
5	United Kingdom	239.6	17	41.2	63
6	Italy	206.7	23	46.7	86
7	China	194.9	53	103.9	92
8	Canada	154.4	30	46.6	50
9	Spain	138.7	27	37.7	75
10	Brazil	137.6	56	77.1	59

Source: USITC staff calculations based on data from WHO, GHO Database and World Bank, World dataBank Database.

In contrast, demand for high-quality services drove rapid growth in healthcare expenditure, particularly private expenditure, in developing countries during 2003 through 2008. Healthcare spending in Africa more than doubled between 2003 and 2008. Similarly, spending in the Asia-Pacific region increased 14.7 percent in 2008, following average annual growth of 7.9 percent from 2003–07. Growth in these markets is largely attributable to a rapid rise in private healthcare spending. In Brazil, private expenditure tripled, from $24 billion in 2003 to over $77 billion in 2008; similar growth was seen in Africa and the Middle East during that period, although outlays remained low relative to developed economies.[260] This growth is often driven by a rising middle class that demands higher-quality services. For example, in China, urban middle class consumers have demonstrated a growing preference for private hospitals over China's nonprofit public facilities.[261] As a result, China and Brazil were among the top 10 global healthcare markets in 2008 (see table 6.1), but are the second- and fourth-largest private healthcare markets (figure 6.2).

The world's largest healthcare providers are located in the United States, and most are private; in other countries, the largest providers are frequently public organizations. The global healthcare market is largely fragmented along national lines. Although many healthcare facilities treat foreign patients who either travel specifically seeking foreign care or require emergency treatment while traveling, very few operate in multiple markets. Firms that do expand into foreign markets often operate only a few facilities. To illustrate, of the 10 largest healthcare systems[262] in the United States (table 6.2), only 1— HCA—has foreign operations. HCA operates 6 hospitals and 4 outpatient centers in London; in the United States, it operates over 150 hospitals and over 100 outpatient centers.[263] Few health firms establish foreign operations because doing so requires complying with a host of new regulations,[264] understanding new market systems,[265] and, for markets with universal health coverage, entering into government reimbursement networks, among other things—all of which add time and expense to new investments.

Governments intervene in healthcare markets[266] to address distortions caused by information asymmetry and the presence of insurers or other third-party payers.[267] Information asymmetry exists because healthcare providers have more information about procedures and costs than patients. Patients generally seek a given service only once, as treatment for a particular malady, leaving them unfamiliar with the procedure.[268] Additionally, healthcare services are highly specialized due to the discipline's inherent complexity and each patient's unique characteristics and history, making it difficult for patients to evaluate the quality or cost of care received. The participation of third-party payers also distorts the market by insulating patients from the true cost of healthcare services, resulting in higher demand for services and less comparison shopping. In the United States, which is also the largest third-party payer market in the world, the prevalence of employer-sponsored health insurance further distorts the market, because employers rather than employees choose the array of services offered and thus consumed.[269]

In response to these market failures, governments frequently provide, finance, or regulate the industry. National markets differ in the degree of government participation in these activities. To illustrate, in some countries, such as China, Spain, and the United Kingdom, the government both finances and provides health services; in other countries, such as France and Japan, the government finances care provided by a mix of public and private facilities. In the United States, the government generally does not provide healthcare services directly,[270] but instead finances care for at-risk populations through the Medicare and Medicaid programs.[271]

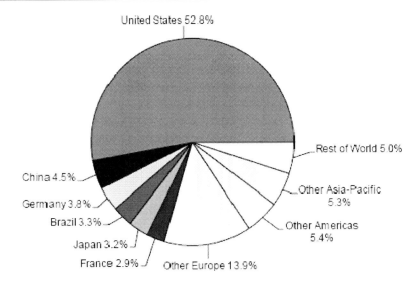

Source: USITC staff calculations based on WHO, GHO Database and World Bank, World dataBank Database.
Note: Geographic regions are shaded in yellow.

Figure 6.2. Healthcare services: The United States remained the world leader in private spending on health in 2008.

Table 6.2. Healthcare services: 10 largest U. S. healthcare systems, ranked by net patient revenue (million $), 2009

Rank	Company	Net patient revenue
1	U.S. Veterans Affairs Department	46,545
2	HCA	30,052
3	Ascension Health	13,628
4	Community Health Systems	12,108
5	Catholic Healthcare West	8,719
6	Tenet Healthcare Corp	8,672
7	New York-Presbyterian Healthcare System	8,533
8	Catholic Health Initiatives	8,258
9	Sutter Health	7,410
10	Mayo Clinic	6,474

Source: *Modern Healthcare*, "10 Largest Healthcare Systems, By Revenue," June 7, 2010 and company Web sites.

In almost all markets, including those with public provision of care, healthcare systems comprise a mix of public and private providers and a combination of public and private financing. For example, China and the United Kingdom both have universal health coverage, but individuals can elect to pay out of pocket for private healthcare providers.[272] In 2008, private spending in the United Kingdom was less than 20 percent of total health spending, due

To the public's satisfaction with the public provider, the National Health Service (NHS);[273] in contrast, China's growing middle class population was largely unsatisfied with public hospitals, driving private expenditures upward to over 50 percent of total spending.[274]

Government participation and the system of healthcare financing in a national healthcare market play a large role in determining how much a country participates in international trade and investment in healthcare services. Traditionally, government policies in these areas have led most of a country's healthcare industry to focus inward on domestic provision of services. However, rising costs, growing demand, and supply limitations have motivated governments and private payers alike to access healthcare resources outside domestic markets. Consequently, the international healthcare market has expanded over the past decade, though data on its size and growth are limited. The following discussion focuses on broad trends in the global healthcare industry, paying special attention to how they relate to trade and the international healthcare market.

Demand and Supply Factors

Healthcare Demand Falls in Developed Markets due to the Economic Downturn

The financial crisis and the ensuing economic downturn during 2008–09 resulted in sharply rising unemployment rates across Europe and North America, which reduced individuals' ability to pay for healthcare services; however, the degree to which demand fell depended on each country's system of healthcare financing.[275] Demand for healthcare services is inversely related to the direct or out-of-pocket cost borne by individuals. However, healthcare financing, specifically third-party payers, can shift demand for healthcare services by reducing or eliminating the direct cost to patients, as illustrated by a survey of medical care usage in developed countries following the economic downturn. In countries where national health insurance requires individuals to share the cost of physician services and inpatient care, such as France and Germany, more individuals reported forgoing medical care since the financial crisis, whereas in countries with universal health coverage, such as the United Kingdom and Canada, demand for healthcare remained robust, with fewer individuals reporting forgoing care.[276]

The U. S. market was hit especially hard by rising unemployment due to its system of employer-sponsored health insurance, which covered the majority of the population. Between 2007 and 2009, the number of U. S. residents covered by employer-sponsored health insurance fell by 8.3 million, or 5 percent, as unemployment rates rose and workers shifted from full-time to part-time positions.[277] In the survey of medical care usage following the downturn, U. S. respondents reported the greatest fall in demand for healthcare—26.5 percent of U. S. respondents said they had reduced their use of medical care since the onset of the financial crisis.[278] Although Congress passed legislation[279] to subsidize insurance premiums for the newly unemployed, many still could not afford to keep their health insurance, and the growth rate of U. S. healthcare spending in 2009 was the slowest in 50 years.[280]

Faced with high healthcare costs and a troubled economy, some individuals in developed countries sought affordable care outside their home market. Generally, individuals who travel for care are self-financed and do so within the geographic region of their home country.[281] For example, Mexico has reported treating growing numbers of U. S. patients in recent years.[282] U. S. demand for healthcare services from Mexico has likely grown due not only to the growing number of uninsured U. S. residents (box 6.1), but also to the inability of some U. S.

patients to pay for elective surgeries in more distant medical travel destinations, such as India or Thailand.[283] Common procedures chosen by U. S. residents include services not covered by insurance, such as dental care and weight-loss surgeries.[284] Exceptions to this rule included many European patients, who traveled to the United States to receive elective procedures in late 2007 and 2008. Reportedly, a weak dollar made the price of cosmetic surgeries performed in the United States up to 25 percent less than that of comparable services in the United Kingdom.[285] In addition, U. S. providers marketed specifically to European patients, fueling demand for such services by patients from the United Kingdom, Germany, Spain, and France.[286]

Patients with Chronic Diseases Demand More Healthcare to Manage their Conditions

The number of individuals with chronic diseases, such as cardiovascular disease, diabetes, and cancer, has risen worldwide, and these conditions have become the leading cause of global mortality, accounting for 60 percent of deaths in 2005.[287] People with chronic conditions demand more medical services than the healthy population. For example, a study of diabetes in the United States found that diabetic individuals use healthcare facilities much more than nondiabetics, and make up to 3.5 times as many physician visits annually.[288] Higher utilization of facilities often reflects the introduction of new treatments to prevent complications or the worsening of a condition, allowing individuals to manage chronic illnesses over time.[289]

The rise in the incidence of chronic conditions can be attributed to two trends. First, mortality rates from chronic conditions have fallen as medical advances, such as the availability of new drugs or surgical procedures, allow earlier diagnosis and a better quality of life afterward. To illustrate, U. S. mortality rates from cardiovascular disease have fallen over the past 30 years[290] while incidence rates have remained steady, suggesting that while death is delayed, a growing number of patients return home with this disease as a chronic condition.[291] In 2005, 133 million people in the United States, or close to 50 percent of adults, were living with at least one chronic illness.[292] The decline in mortality rate has largely been achieved in developed countries, where advanced treatments are more widely available. At the same time, however, the incidence of risk factors for chronic diseases[293] has been rising in developing countries. For example, it is currently estimated that, worldwide, 1 in every 10 adults is obese—a condition which is linked to a number of chronic diseases.[294] As a result, many developing countries, such as India and China, have joined the United States and Europe in facing the burden of longterm conditions.[295]

In response to the rise in incidence of chronic illnesses, governments in developing countries have begun to improve access to and quality of care. Currently, 80 percent of global mortality resulting from chronic diseases occurs in developing countries.[296] However, recent government programs in these markets have allowed earlier diagnosis and more treatment options for people with chronic conditions. For example, in 2005, Chile implemented a healthcare reform that expanded insurance coverage to include many chronic conditions.[297] Since the reform went into effect, data show earlier detection of cancer and increased demand from individuals with other chronic diseases; treatment for type 2 diabetes and hypertension has increased 30 percent.[298]

Box 6.1. Lack of Health Insurance Drives U. S. Imports of Healthcare along the U. S. Border with Mexico

Studies of U. S. cities and regions along the U. S. border with Mexico have consistently found that the low rate of health insurance among these populations has driven imports of healthcare services from Mexico. Incomes in the four southwest border states[a] are lower than the U. S. average, and residents who may be offered insurance through their employers frequently cannot afford the premiums.[b] In 2005, these four states accounted for 30 percent of the U. S. uninsured population.[c] As a result, border residents often see healthcare in Mexico as an affordable alternative to expensive care in the United States.

Comprehensive data on U. S. residents who travel to Mexico seeking care and treatment are currently unavailable;[d] however, estimates suggest that most U. S. imports are demanded by U. S. residents living along the U. S. -Mexican border. One study of the U. S. border region around El Paso, Texas, and Ciudad Juárez, Mexico, reported 32.5 percent of respondents had crossed the border for healthcare in the past two years. Of these, 27.1 percent reported seeking healthcare services and 63.2 percent reported seeking dental services.[e] A 2010 report estimated annual expenditure by residents of the four border states on healthcare-related products and services in Mexico to be roughly $191–350 million, approximately half of which paid for medical services.[f] Older Americans living near the Mexican border have long crossed the border for prescriptions and dental care—two areas Medicare does not completely cover.[g] Mexico's private healthcare sector enjoys a cost advantage over U. S. facilities, and many Mexican clinics, particularly those near the border, advertise in the U. S. market, offer bilingual personnel, and in some cases offer transportation across the border.[h]

The majority of U. S. residents who seek care in Mexico finance such services out of pocket.[i] However, growing awareness of the number of patients seeking care in Mexico has driven some advances in portable financing options. In 1999, California approved cross-border health insurance, allowing individuals enrolled in such plans to seek care in either the United States or Mexico. Currently, a number of insurers offer or are developing such plans, including Blue Cross Blue Shield, Aetna, and United Health.[j]

---

[a] The four southwestern states on the U. S. -Mexico border are California, Arizona, New Mexico, and Texas.

[b] Institute for Population Health Policy, "Use of Health Care in the US-Mexico Border," February 2009; Peng, "Ultimate Outsourcing," November 19, 2008.

[c] Bastida, Brown, and Pagán, "Health Insurance Coverage," 2007, 222.

[d] Neither the BEA (the primary source for U. S. services trade statistics) nor the UN Service Trade Database report discrete bilateral trade data for U. S. imports from Mexico.

[e] Additionally, 82 percent reported using pharmacies and 9.8 percent reported seeking traditional healers. Byrd and Law, "Cross-border Utilization of Health Care Services," 2009, 97.

[f] Warner and Jahnke, "U.S.-Mexico Mode 2," March 3, 2010, 3.

[g] Peng, "Ultimate Outsourcing," November 19, 2008.

[h] Rivera, Ortiz, and Cardenas, "Cross-Border Purchase of Medications and Health Care," February 2009, 172; Institute for Population Health Policy, "Use of Health Care in the US-Mexico

> Border," February 2009; Byrd and Law, "Cross-border Utilization of Health Care Services," 2009, 99.
> i Su et al., "Cross-border Utilization of Health Care," December 15, 2010.
> j Warner and Jahnke, "U.S.-Mexico Mode 2," March 3, 2010, 5; *IMTJ*, "USA/Mexico," May 20, 2010.

Healthcare Systems Face Shortages of Professionals

Currently, the global workforce is estimated to need an additional 4.2 million health workers, a shortage which affects developed and developing countries alike.[299] As global demand for healthcare services has increased, many countries have addressed shortfalls in their healthcare workforces by recruiting foreign workers. Both Canada and the United States currently have a shortage of nurses, which is forecast to grow substantially over the next 20 years.[300] In developed countries, education systems frequently lack the capacity to train enough providers to meet demand; in 2009, nearly 55,000 qualified applicants were turned away from baccalaureate and graduate nursing programs in the United States due to faculty shortages and budget constraints.[301] As a result, these countries import healthcare, in the form of foreign professionals to staff their healthcare systems. In 2005–06, 22 percent of Canadian doctors and 7.7 percent of nurses were trained in a foreign country, and 8 percent of registered nurses in the United States were foreign educated in 2006.[302]

Rapid development of healthcare infrastructure in regions such as the Middle East has led developing economies to recruit foreign healthcare professionals as well. For example, Saudi Arabia's domestic workforce is not large enough to staff existing hospitals, resulting in recent recruitment of foreign medical professionals, including 1,000 doctors from Pakistan. Continued development of the Saudi healthcare infrastructure will exacerbate this shortage, as the country plans to add 750 health clinics and 15 hospitals over the next 5 years.[303] However, the practice of importing healthcare professionals has been criticized for weakening healthcare systems in the workers' countries of origin. For example, 23 percent of doctors trained in sub-Saharan Africa emigrated to work in Organization for Economic Cooperation and Development economies, attracted by higher wages and a better quality of life.[304] Partly as a result, Africa is estimated to need at least another 818,000 doctors, nurses, or midwives to meet the World Health Organization's minimum threshold of care.[305]

Governments, particularly in developed countries, have recognized that recruitment of foreign professionals is a temporary solution to the healthcare shortage, and is increasingly unsustainable as global healthcare demand continues to grow. Instead, governments have launched policies and programs intended to increase the domestic supply of educated, trained workers. For example, Canada has focused on increasing both capacity and enrollment in Canada's nursing schools. As a result, enrollment in nursing schools increased 60 percent from 1997 to 2005.[306] Recent U. S. legislation initiated similar measures: the American Recovery and Reinvestment Act of 2009 and the Affordable Care Act, passed in fall 2010, included provisions to fund training of healthcare professionals. The Affordable Care Act also included measures to address the pay disparities between primary care physicians, whose relatively low pay threatens supply, and other specialists.[307]

Governments Look to the Private Sector to Increase the Quality and Supply of Healthcare Facilities

Around the world, governments have entered into partnerships with private sector healthcare firms in order to meet growing demand for higher-quality health services. Governments have worked with private healthcare firms in the past, but in most countries private sector participation was limited to owning and maintaining infrastructure, such as hospitals, which the government used to provide services.[308] Now, governments are increasingly allowing private firms to provide healthcare services.[309] These relationships with the private sector take two forms: in countries with ample infrastructure, such as markets where public and private healthcare systems run in tandem, governments are including local private firms in the public system; in countries where there is not enough infrastructure to meet local demand, governments are trying to attract foreign investment in the healthcare sector.

Increasingly, governments have begun allowing private domestic firms to provide services or enter reimbursement networks. For example, between 2001 and 2005, reforms in the UK increased competition by allowing greater participation of private firms in healthcare provision in the NHS, and reforms currently under debate would further increase their participation.[310] Similarly, in Malaysia, government reforms allowed private dialysis firms to enter the government reimbursement network and qualify for public subsidies. These changes expanded the number of providers available to dialysis patients and subsequently increased treatment rates more than eightfold between 1990 and 2005.[311]

In contrast, in countries where construction of healthcare infrastructure may lag behind rapidly growing incomes, governments partner with the private sector by creating opportunities for foreign firms and investors. For example, in 2010, representatives from Ethiopia traveled to India in an effort to entice India's private hospital chains to set up branches in Addis Ababa.[312] China has also reached out to foreign healthcare investors in order to increase its healthcare infrastructure and meet growing demand for private healthcare facilities.[313] In December 2010, China announced it would liberalize restrictions on foreign investment in healthcare, gradually removing foreign equity limitations and eventually allowing wholly foreign-owned hospitals on a trial basis, as well as allowing foreign facilities to participate in the state medical reimbursement system.[314]

Trade Trends

Cross-Border Trade

U.S. exports have always been competitive in the global market, as U. S. hospitals are known for advanced treatments and complex care.[315] Such facilities often market to foreign patients, who visit the United States for treatments not available in their home country or to seek care from globally recognized specialists or facilities.[316] U. S. cross- border exports of healthcare services (box 6.2) continued to substantially exceed cross- border imports during 2004 through 2009 (figure 6.3), principally because foreign individuals sought treatment from U. S. healthcare facilities. In 2009, U. S. exports totaled $2.6 billion, while the United States imported $879 million of healthcare services. Overall, the U. S. healthcare trade surplus increased from $1.24 billion in 2004 to $1.74 billion in 2009.

However, U. S. exports of healthcare services slowed to 6.3 percent in 2009, compared to average annual growth rates of 10.4 percent during 2004–08. This slowdown is likely a result of the economic downturn. The depressed global economy caused foreign currencies to fall against the dollar, making U. S. exports more expensive and reducing the number of foreign patients seeking costly treatment at U. S. facilities.

The leading U. S. export destinations in 2007 demonstrate the importance of geographic proximity for trade in healthcare services: over 25 percent of U. S. exports went to Mexico and Canada (figure 6.4).[317] During 2007, Mexico was the top single country destination for U. S. exports, which totaled $434 million, following average annual growth of almost 80 percent between 2004 and 2007.[318] This growth was likely driven by affluent Mexican patients who sought higher-quality care or complicated treatment in the United States.[319] Cross-border exports to Canada totaled $160 million in 2007, making Canada the third-largest export market (following the United Kingdom). Although Canada has universal healthcare, Canadians frequently visit the United States to avoid long waits or to receive treatments unavailable locally.[320] Markets in Europe were also important destinations for U. S. exports of healthcare services, accounting for over 44 percent of such exports in 2007. During 2004 through 2007, U. S. exports to Europe more than doubled, growing from $434.7 million to over $1 billion in 2007 as Europeans took advantage of a weak dollar to seek healthcare—in particular, high-quality elective procedures—in the United States.[321]

Box 6.2. Understanding Available Data on Trade in Healthcare Services

Healthcare services are traded via all four modes of services trade,[a] but very little usable data exist on global trade in these services.[b] Trade in healthcare services may be included with trade in other services. For example, healthcare services provided using information and communication technologies may be reported as trade in computer services. Further, the variety among sources of healthcare financing, coupled with disparities in pricing for services and the absence of an international standard for data collection, frequently result in statistics that are not comparable across countries.[c]

This chapter's discussion of cross-border trade primarily uses data from the Bureau of Economic Analysis (BEA), of the U. S. Department of Commerce (USDOC), supplemented by United Nations (UN) data for analysis of specific export markets. The BEA data on cross-border trade in medical services estimate spending on healthcare services purchased abroad (consumption abroad or mode 2) through 2009.[d]

U.S. export figures estimate spending on care provided by U. S. hospitals to foreign patients, and include both emergency services required during travel and services for individuals who travel to the United States for the express purpose of receiving medical treatment. Such statistics are calculated using estimates of foreign patient volumes and cost of care in a hospital setting, including both inpatient and outpatient services.[e]

Data on U. S. imports estimate medical expenditures by U. S. residents traveling abroad. Import statistics are based on the number of U. S. travelers, the estimated share of U. S. travelers who require incidental care due to accident or illness while outside the United States, and an estimate of the average cost per treatment. In addition, import estimates also capture spending by U. S. residents who travel to Mexico or Canada specifically seeking medical services, such as dental treatments or cosmetic surgery.[f]

Cross-border trade data reported in the UN Service Trade database likewise estimate spending by those traveling for medical reasons through 2007; however, unlike the BEA data, the UN offers information on bilateral trade flows between the United States and selected countries.

Data on affiliate transactions in medical services also come from the BEA. Such statistics capture sales to foreign consumers by foreign healthcare affiliates of U. S. firms and purchases by U. S. consumers from U. S. healthcare affiliates of foreign firms.

[a] For example, foreign specialists provide remote consultations using information and communication technologies (mode 1); individuals seek treatment outside their home countries (mode 2); healthcare facilities establish branches in foreign markets (mode 3); and individual medical professionals migrate across borders (mode 4). For a more detailed explanation of the modes of services trade, see box 1.1 on p. 1-4.
[b] Mortensen, "International Trade in Health Services," 2008, 11.
[c] Helble, "The Movement of Patients across Borders," November 26, 2010.
[d] BEA also reports data on trade in healthcare services via mode 1, which occurs when the service supplier and consumer remain in their respective countries. Discrete data on such trade are not available, but are included in the subcategory "Other" within "Other business, professional, and technical services." USDOC, BEA representative, email to USITC staff, October 22, 2008.
[e] Export estimates do not include spending on ambulatory treatment or prescriptions received outside the hospital setting. USDOC, BEA representative, e-mail message to USITC staff, October 22, 2008; Bach, "U.S. International Transactions," July 1999.
[f] Bach, "Annual Revision of the U. S. International Accounts," July 2005, 67.

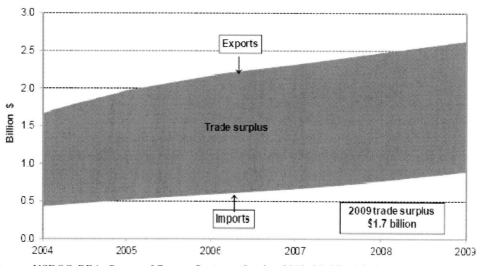

Source: USDOC, BEA, *Survey of Current Business*, October 2010, 36–37, table 1.
[a] Cross-border trade consists of expenditures on medical services by patients in foreign countries and thus are transactions between unaffiliated parties.

Figure 6.3. Healthcare services: The United States maintained a surplus in cross-border trade[a] in medical services, 2004–09.

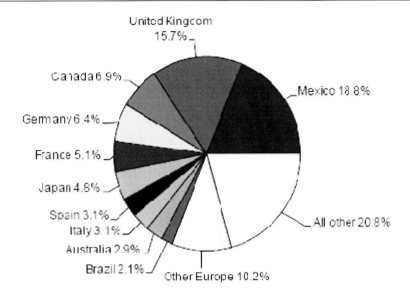

Total = $2.3 billion

Source: United Nations, UN Service Trade Database.

Figure 6.4. Healthcare services: Mexico was the United States' largest export market for healthcare services in 2007.

U.S. imports of healthcare services grew steadily in recent years, increasing 16 percent in 2009 (reaching $879 million) following growth of 15.8 percent during 2004–08.[322] Unfortunately, very few market data exist that indicate the specific countries from which the United States imports healthcare services. A handful of countries report exports of healthcare-related travel expenditure to the United States (table 6.3).[323] Of the few countries that report, Poland had the largest volume ($26.1 million), followed by France ($23.7 million) and the United Kingdom ($12.5 million); however, these countries report exporting less than 10 percent of all healthcare services imported by the United States in 2009. Although a number of Southeast Asian countries have marketed cost competitive care for Western patients, anecdotal evidence suggests that the majority of U. S. healthcare imports are purchased from North American trading partners,[324] particularly Mexico.[325] The steady growth trajectory in imports during recent years is likely a result of the growing number of uninsured Americans, who drive demand for competitively priced healthcare imports.

Affiliate Transactions

Trends in affiliate transactions reflect the importance of the U. S. market for global healthcare firms. Purchases from U. S. affiliates of foreign firms substantially exceed sales by foreign healthcare affiliates of U. S. firms (figure 6.5).[326] In 2006 (the last year for which comparable data are available), purchases from U. S. affiliates totaled $9.2 billion, far outpacing sales by foreign affiliates of U. S. firms, which totaled $1.6 billion.[327] During 2005 through 2007,[328] healthcare purchases from U. S. affiliates of foreign firms declined slightly before rebounding in 2008.

Table 6.3. Healthcare services: Countries that report exports of healthcare services to the United States, 2009

Reporter	Exports ($)
Poland	26,116,273
France	23,720,411
UK	12,528,954
Czech Republic	6,584,889
Sweden	4,073,308
Slovenia	147,904
Hungary	144,805
Estonia	43,073

Source: UN, UN Service Trade Database.

Note: Since most countries do not report trade in healthcare services broken down by country of recipient, we estimate that these figures probably represent less than 10 percent of total healthcare exports to the United States.

By virtue of being the largest healthcare services market in the world, the U. S. market offers a desirable and potentially profitable opportunity for foreign healthcare firms. As a result, foreign firms have sought opportunities to invest in the U. S. market, either by acquiring U. S. healthcare firms or establishing new U. S. affiliates. For example, in 2006, Fresenius Medical Care, a German manufacturer of dialysis supplies, became the largest outpatient supplier of dialysis services in the United States after acquiring U. S. -based Renal Care Group, Inc.[329] Acquisitions such as these drive up the numbers for affiliate transactions because, following the acquisition, spending by U. S. patients on dialysis supplied by Renal Care Group, Inc., is now a purchase from a U. S. affiliate of a foreign firm.

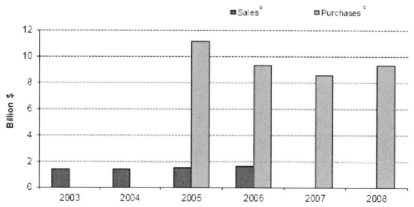

Source: USDOC, BEA, *Survey of Current Business*, various issues.

[a] BEA reports "services supplied" by foreign affiliates. In the healthcare services industry, "services supplied" correspond to "sales."

[b] Data were suppressed in 2007 and 2008 to avoid disclosure of individual company data.

[c] Data were suppressed in 2003 and 2004 to avoid disclosure of individual company data.

Figure 6.5. Healthcare services: Purchases from U. S. affiliates of foreign firms declined due to the downturn in the economy, but still exceeded sales by foreign affiliates of U. S. firms,[a] 2003–08.

In contrast, foreign affiliates of U. S. firms report lower sales in foreign markets. Such sales totaled $1.6 billion in 2006, representing average annual growth of about 4 percent since 2003.[330] In general, it is more difficult for U. S. firms to operate in foreign markets than for foreign firms to operate in the U. S. market, largely due to the presence of universal health coverage or public healthcare in other countries. This is best illustrated by U. S. and foreign investment data: in 2008, foreign investment in healthcare services in the United States reached $8.3 billion, compared to $1.1 billion of direct investment abroad in healthcare by U. S. firms.[331] However, shifts in government policies toward privatization of healthcare (as in the UK) and aging populations have created opportunities for U. S. firms such as U. S.-based Sunrise Senior Living, which operates retirement communities in the United Kingdom and Canada.[332] The majority of sales by affiliates of U. S. firms appear to be to European consumers; in 2003, such sales accounted for $1.1 billion of a total $1.4 billion.

Multilateral Negotiations, Liberalization, and Remaining Barriers

A number of barriers remain to trade in healthcare services. They are difficult to address through multilateral agreements such as the General Agreement on Trade in Services (GATS)[333]—partly due to the extent of government participation in healthcare services,[334] but also because many barriers either fall outside the scope of the GATS or are related to economy-wide policies such as immigration. For example, the largest barriers to trade in healthcare services—reimbursement policies and procedures of health insurance, both public and private—fall outside the scope of the GATS. Health insurers' reimbursement networks impede trade conducted via foreign presence (mode 3) if such networks exclude foreign providers or establishments; additionally, insurance coverage is frequently restricted to a given region or country, which impedes trade via consumption abroad (mode 2) by giving patients disincentives to seek medical treatment outside their home markets.[335] Economy-wide policies that impede trade in healthcare services are most frequently related to immigration. For example, tighter immigration policies implemented in the United Kingdom over the past decade impeded trade via movement of professionals (mode 4) and exacerbated the UK shortage of physicians as foreign physicians left the country and fewer entered.[336] Immigration policies can also impede consumption abroad; surveys in the U. S.-Mexico border region have found that among respondents, more restrictive border regulations over the past 5–10 years have deterred U. S. residents from seeking care in Mexico.[337]

On the other hand, market forces and economic interest have driven liberalization and integration in the healthcare industry. For example, new policies that permit cross-border portability of healthcare insurance were largely motivated by rising demand in developed economies for affordable healthcare. To illustrate, Singapore, which faces high healthcare costs, now allows its Medisave funds[338] to be used in approved foreign healthcare facilities in neighboring Malaysia, providing Singaporean workers with a lower-cost alternative for healthcare services.[339] Similarly, as mentioned earlier, rising demand for lower cost Mexican healthcare services motivated the development of cross-border health insurance policies that offer savings of 40 to 50 percent to U. S. citizens living in California who are willing to seek care in Mexico.[340] Additionally, regional integration is occurring in certain areas, such as in Southeast Asia, where the 10 members of the Association of Southeast Asian Nations have committed to create a more integrated regional healthcare services market. The EU is also in the process of developing an integrated healthcare services market. In the most recent action, the EU parliament voted in favor of an EU directive on patient's rights in cross-border healthcare.

Outlook

The global healthcare industry is expected to maintain the current trajectory of steady growth in the near future, as global demand for healthcare continues to rise.[341] Rapid growth in healthcare spending is forecast for the Asia-Pacific, the Middle East, and Africa, as per capita healthcare spending climbs toward global averages.[342] In China, for example, McKinsey has projected a minimum of 11 percent average annual growth in private healthcare expenditure among urban middle-class consumers over the next 20 years, based on their current high rates of saving specifically for healthcare expenses.[343]

However, markets in Western Europe and the United States are expected to continue to feel the lingering effects of the economic downturn as well as government budget cuts going forward. Some European countries have already begun to implement measures aimed at both reducing the state's share of healthcare costs and limiting price inflation for services. These reforms are expected to continue as governments face the growing burden of increasing demand and shrinking funds available for healthcare programs.[344]

Around the world, chronic disease is expected to continue to drive demand for healthcare. An epidemic of obesity-related diseases is expected in the near future; by 2030, the incidence of diabetes in the Middle East and North Africa is forecast to nearly double to 51.7 million people and chronic diseases are expected to account for 70 percent of global mortality.[345] Facing growing demand, countries are expected to continue to reform their healthcare systems to increase access to care and improve quality.[346] However, as a similar reform in Brazil in the 1990s demonstrated, the success of these reforms will depend on an adequate healthcare workforce. For example, the U. S. Affordable Health Care for America Act, which expanded coverage for the uninsured and introduced Accountable Care Organizations, is expected to exacerbate the strain on healthcare professionals;[347] the United States is predicted to have a shortfall of 63,000 physicians by 2015, and a shortage of at least 300,000 nurses by 2020.[348]

7. LEGAL SERVICES

SUMMARY

While the global legal services industry experienced a slowdown in 2009, the United States sustained growth in its cross-border trade surplus in legal services. In 2008, the latest year for which data are available, U. S. -related affiliate transactions in this section also displayed this trend. Sales by foreign legal service affiliates of U. S. firms in 2008 continued to exceed purchases from U. S. affiliates of foreign law firms; affiliate transactions in both directions continued to grow, albeit more slowly than during 2003–07. U. S. law firms managed costs during the slowdown by laying off employees and reducing other business costs, such as marketing. Offering better value or flexible payment terms may give firms an edge in the future.

In recent years European and U. S. law firms have lost global market share to firms from countries in the Asia-Pacific region. In 2009, because the total volume of legal work in the United States declined, U. S. imports of legal services decreased faster than exports of legal services. However, from 2005 through 2008 U. S. imports of legal services grew faster than exports, reflecting the growing competitiveness of foreign legal services providers. During the global downturn, markets in Asia-Pacific fared better than in the United States or Europe, the traditional market drivers. Although U. S. foreign affiliate sales remained concentrated in Europe, affiliates in the Middle East and Latin America are multiplying. In 2009, direct investment abroad by U. S. law firms increased faster than in most other professional service industries. Law firms setting up overseas often face restrictions on forms of establishment and local collaboration, and most lawyers practicing abroad can serve only as foreign legal consultants.

INTRODUCTION

Legal services[349] are a key input to international commerce: they facilitate trade and investment by increasing predictability and decreasing risk in business transactions.[350] The global increase in demand for legal services over the past few decades is largely attributed to increased international trade and capital flows.[351] In recent years, established firms in Europe and North America have confronted new challenges resulting from the global economic downturn. At the same time, other regions have expanded their legal services markets; in particular, the Asia-Pacific region has significantly increased its share of the global market since 2005.[352] This chapter discusses the effects of the downturn, the growth of emerging markets, and other factors affecting international trade in legal services as provided by law firms.[353]

Competitive Conditions in the Global Legal Services Market

The global legal services market grew at a 4.5 percent annual average rate between 2001 and 2005, and at 4.2 percent between 2005 and 2009.[354] In 2009, however, this substantial growth faltered due to the economic downturn. Global legal services revenue totaled $546.8 billion, reflecting only 0.5 percent growth in 2009 compared with 5.4 percent average annual growth during 2005–08.[355] Legal services markets in the Asia-Pacific fared better than those in the United States or Europe, due to the uneven severity of the downturn across regions.[356] While the U. S. market grew by 0.6 percent and the European market declined by 1.3 percent in 2009, the Asia-Pacific market grew by 3.9 percent.[357]

Although the Americas and Europe remained the world's largest legal services markets, their shares of the world market have declined.[358] In 2005, the Americas and Europe accounted for 61.3 percent and 33.6 percent of the global legal services market, respectively, while Asia-Pacific accounted for only 5.1 percent.[359] In 2009, the shares accounted for by the

Americas and Europe had declined to 59.2 percent and 30.4 percent, while the share of the Asia-Pacific market had risen to 10.4 percent (figure 7.1).[360]

While each region was dominated by one or two key countries, this phenomenon is especially striking in the Americas. In 2009, the United States market accounted for 80.4 percent of the Americas' legal services market and 47.6 percent of the global legal services market.[361] China accounted for the largest share of the of the Asia-Pacific legal services market in 2009, with 41.0 percent,[362] and Germany and the United Kingdom were the two largest legal services markets within Europe, with market shares of 21.4 percent and 15.5 percent, respectively.[363]

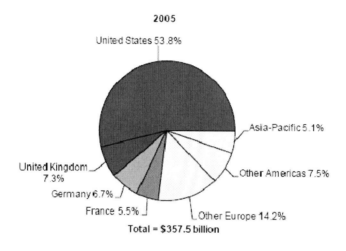

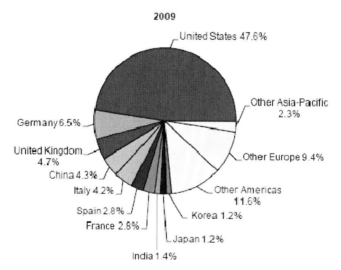

Sources: Datamonitor, "Industry Profile: Global Legal Services," July 2010, 11; Datamonitor, "Industry Profile: Global Legal Services," December 2006, 11.
[a] Market share calculated by value.

Figure 7.1. Legal services: The Asia-Pacific region increased its global market share,[a] 2005 and 2009.

Table 7.1. Legal services: Top 10 global law firms, by gross revenue, 2010

Rank	Firm	Country	Gross revenue (million $)
1	Baker and McKenzie	U.S.	2,104
2	Skadden, Arps, Slate, Meagher and Flom	U.S.	2,100
3	Clifford Chance	UK	1,875
4	Linklaters	UK	1,853
5	Latham and Watkins	U.S.	1,821
6	Freshfields Bruckhaus	UK	1,787
7	Allen and Overy	UK	1,645
8	Jones Day	U.S.	1,520
9	Kirkland and Ellis	U.S.	1,428
10	Sidley Austin	U.S.	1,357

Source: *The American Lawyer*, "The Global 100 2010," October 2010.
Note: Revenue figures refer to firms' most recently completed fiscal year.

U.S. and UK firms remain among the highest-grossing firms in the world, accounting for 91 of the 100 top-grossing firms and all of the world's top 10 law firms (table 7.1).[364] Nonetheless, profits declined for firms in both markets during the economic downturn. Among the 100 top-grossing firms, U. S. -based firms experienced a decline of 2 percent in profits per partner from 2007 to 2009, while UK-based firms experienced a decline of 7 percent.[365] Since U. S. -based firms derive more of their revenue from litigation than their counterparts in the United Kingdom, the lower rate of decline in the United States is attributed to a heavier share of countercyclical litigation work,[366] as well as the lower cost to firms of laying off employees in the United States.[367]

Larger law firms tend to focus on commercial work and are more likely to export their legal services. For example, in both the United States and China, larger firms tend to assist corporate or government clients on diverse commercial legal issues, which are typically more complex and require greater resources, while smaller firms tend to offer services in either noncommercial areas of law or specialized areas of commercial law.[368] The nature of the business conducted by large law firms makes them more likely to export (table 7.2).[369] In addition, large firms and exporters have higher labor productivity than smaller firms and nonexporters (box 7.1).[370]

Demand and Supply Factors

Demand for Legal Services Reflects Economic Conditions

Demand for legal services correlates with the level of business activity in an economy, and consequently fell in many developed markets as a result of the economic downturn. For example, in the United States, the decline in investment and corporate activity beginning in 2007 led to less commercial work for lawyers.[371] Large law firms were hit hardest:[372] the 100 highest-grossing law firms fared worse than smaller firms[373] in terms of demand, revenues, and productivity.[374] This was due to large firms' heavier reliance on commercial activities and the presence of large financial firms, which were especially vulnerable during the economic downturn.[375] Overall, the growth rate for U. S. legal services revenue slowed to 0.6 percent in

2009, compared to an average annual rate of 5.3 percent during 2005–08.[376] The situation was worse in the United Kingdom, where legal services revenue declined by 4.3 percent in 2009 after growing at an average annual rate of 3.4 percent during 2005–08.[377]

Box 7.1. Legal Services Productivity in the United States

In the United States, large legal services firms tend to be more productive than small firms.[a] Establishments of large firms (over 500 employees) had twice the labor productivity[b] of establishments of small firms (less than 500 employees) in 2007 (table 7.2, column 3).[c]

Additionally, legal services exporters tend to be more productive than nonexporters. Exporting establishments of firms of all sizes had 1.6 times the labor productivity of establishments which only served the domestic market in 2007 (table 7.2, column 4). The difference in productivity between exporters and nonexporters was driven by small firms. While there was only a slight difference in labor productivity between exporting and nonexporting establishments of large firms, exporting small and medium-sized enterprises (SMEs) had 1.5 times the labor productivity of nonexporting SMEs.[d] The largest difference in productivity between exporters and non-exporters was among firms with less than 20 employees.

[a] See USITC, *Small and Medium-Sized Enterprises*, November 2010, 2-1 to 2-2.
[b] The difference in labor productivity is referred to as the labor productivity premium, measured as ratio of labor productivity of large firms to that of small firms.
[c] Data are from the U. S. Census Bureau's Economic Census, conducted every five years. The most recent Economic Census was in 2007. When describing data in table 7.2, "Establishments" refer to a single physical location where business is conducted or where services are performed. While the data were tabulated according to the firm size categories presented in table 7.2, the data refer to establishments (rather than the firms themselves).
[d] See USITC, *Small and Medium-Sized Enterprises*, November 2010, 2-5 to 2-7, for a more detailed comparison of labor productivity for exporting versus nonexporting SMEs.

Among other developed countries, the German market did relatively well, experiencing only a modest slowdown in revenue growth. In 2009, the legal services market grew 3.2 percent, compared with an average annual rate of 4.8 percent during 2005–08.[378] Additionally, Germany's legal service firms are typically smaller and less specialized in areas like finance compared to U. S. or UK firms.[379]

Among developing legal services markets, the Chinese market experienced significant growth in 2009, though the pace was slower than earlier in the decade.[380] Industry revenue increased 7.1 percent in 2009, compared to an average annual rate of 13.7 percent from 2005 to 2008.[381] China's demand for legal services was driven by a rising volume of commercial activities, including mergers and acquisitions, initial public offerings (IPOs), and international trade.[382] For example, U. S. and UK law firms advised Chinese clients on international investments in the natural resource and automobile industries,[383] and were involved in the Agricultural Bank of China's 2010 IPO.[384] These types of commercial activities accounted for 65 percent of China's legal service industry revenue by the decade's end.[385] To meet growing demand, the number of Chinese law firms increased from approximately 13,100 in 2006 to 15,200 in 2010.[386]

Table 7.2. Legal services: Number of U. S. exporting establishments and labor productivity, by size of firm, 2007

	Number of establishments	Exporting establishments (%)	Labor productivity[a] ($/FTE)	Exporter labor productivity premium[b]
Firms with 0–19 employees				
All establishments	173,186		153,954	
Establishments with revenue from exported services	3,173	1.8	243,720	1.6
Firms with 20–99 employees				
All establishments	9,468		175,180	
Establishments with revenue from exported services	433	4.6	247,703	1.5
Firms with 100–499 employees				
All establishments	3,324		218,369	
Establishments with revenue from exported services	322	9.7	253,962	1.2
Firms with less than 500 employees				
All establishments	185,978		170,417	
Establishments with revenue from exported services	3,928	2.1	250,351	1.5
Firms with more than 500 employees				
All establishments	2,865		348,992	
Establishments with revenue from exported services	450	15.7	372,461	1.1
All firms				
All establishments	188,843		201,508	
Establishments with revenue from exported services	4,378	2.3	317,436	1.6

Sources: Data tabulated by USDOC, U. S. Census Bureau, Service Sector Statistics Division, and USITC staff calculations.

Note: Data are from the 2007 Economic Census and are tabulated by 2002 NAICS code 5411 (legal services).

[a] Labor productivity is calculated as revenue per full-time equivalent employee (FTE).

[b] The export labor productivity premium is the ratio of labor productivity of exporters to that of nonexporters.

Developing Markets Are Increasingly Important for U. S. and UK Firms

Reforms involving investment, trade, and other economic activities in developing countries have provided commercial opportunities for U. S. and UK law firms.[387] Whereas U. S. law firms' foreign mergers and partnerships have historically been with law firms in Europe and Asia, these arrangements are increasingly being pursued with firms in Latin America and the Middle East.[388] Having a presence in multiple foreign markets helped firms maintain workload during the economic downturn, which affected regions differently.[389]

Economic development has generated rising demand for legal services in the Middle East,[390] which became the fastest-growing destination for U. S. cross-border legal services exports.[391] In Saudi Arabia, for instance, private sector involvement (e.g., in infrastructure projects) has increased demand for legal services.[392] Major U. S. and UK firms such as Clifford Chance, Baker and McKenzie, and White and Case have established offices in Saudi Arabia.[393] Similarly, at least 14 U. S. and UK law firms have branches in Abu Dhabi (most of these offices were opened after 2007).[394] The branch offices assist with local clients' business activity, including the Emirati government's outbound investments. The Abu Dhabi office of Hogan Lovells (a law firm headquartered in both the United States and the United Kingdom) advises the Abu Dhabi National Energy Company,[395] and clients of the U. S. firm Dewey and LeBoeuf include the Abu Dhabi Islamic Bank and the Abu Dhabi Sewerage Services Company.[396]

Similarly, Brazil's economic growth has driven the expansion of the legal services market. Brazil was among the top 10 fastest-growing U. S. legal services export destinations between 2005 and 2008.[397] At least 17 U. S. and UK legal firms have established branches in São Paolo, 9 of which have opened since 2009.[398] These firms advise clients in several sectors, including infrastructure, banking, mergers and acquisitions, capital markets transactions,[399] and outbound investments.[400]

Clients Have Become Increasingly Price Sensitive

As costs for outside counsel[401] rose over the last several decades, the in-house legal departments of corporations increased in size and scope.[402] Corporations reduced expenditures and increased efficiency by handling more matters internally and relying on external counsel only for specialized services. For example, in the past decade DuPont decreased the number of law firms it retained to 39, from over 300 in the early 1990s.[403]

During the economic downturn, corporations continued to increase staffing in their internal law departments.[404] In a survey of U. S. corporate law departments, the share of respondents with over 30 in-house attorneys rose from 3.4 percent in 2005 to 34.1 percent in 2010.[405] Further, the share of corporate law departments that planned to decrease their use of outside counsel in the next year rose from 19.8 percent in 2005 to 40.4 percent in 2009.[406] Major European corporations also reduced their use of external law firms: Royal Dutch Shell cut its list of outside legal firms from 60 to 8, and Nokia cut by half its list of 500 law firms.[407] This trend is projected to continue, as U. S. corporations' spending on outside legal counsel, which dropped by approximately 11 percent in 2009,[408] is likely to drop by more than 25 percent in 2011.[409]

U.S. Firms Cut Labor Costs

U.S. legal services labor productivity (measured as output per unit of labor) declined during the past decade, while law firms' expenses increased. From 1999 through 2009, labor productivity declined at an average annual rate of 0.3 percent, with the sharpest drop occurring in 2009 (figure 7.2).[410] The decline in productivity can be attributed to slower growth in output than in employment; while employment grew at an annual average rate of only 0.7 percent during those 10 years, output grew at an even lower annual average rate of 0.4 percent.[411] Employment growth has coincided with rising wages, which increased at an annual average rate of 1.0 percent during 2001–09 and accounted for an estimated 40 percent of costs in 2010.[412] In total, law firm expenses rose by an estimated 10 percent per year from 2001 through 2008.[413]

In response to rising expenses and declining demand, law firms adopted cost-cutting measures, particularly freezing or reducing salaries of existing associates, delaying (deferring) hiring, and laying off employees.[414] For example, in 2009, the firm Latham and Watkins laid off 444 lawyers (the highest number of layoffs among the 250 largest U. S. law firms), and Fried, Frank, Harris, Shriver and Jacobson laid off 26.4 percent of their attorneys (the largest share of laid-off lawyers among the 250 largest U. S. law firms).[415] Overall, the number of attorneys employed by the 250 largest U. S. law firms fell by 4 percent from 131,928 attorneys in 2008 to 126,669 in 2009,[416] in contrast to 4 percent average annual growth of attorneys since 1978.[417]

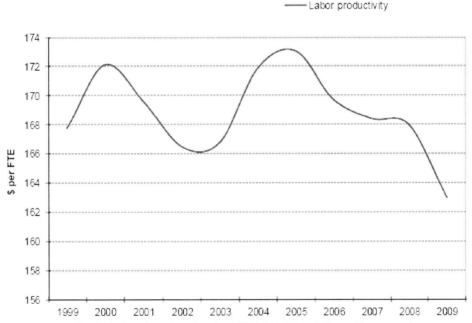

Source: USITC staff calculations based on data from USDOC, BEA, *Industry Economic Accounts*.
[a] Labor productivity is calculated as real value added by industry divided by full-time equivalent employees (FTEs) by industry.

Figure 7.2. Legal services: U. S. labor productivity[a] mostly declined during 1999–2009.

Table 7.3. Legal services: Change in total employees by location, 2005–09 (%)

Annual average rowth rate, 2005–08		Growth rate, 2008–09	Average annual growth rate, 2005–08		Growth rate, 2008–09
United States			**World**		
National sectors:			Regional:		
Professional services	3.6	(3.7)	Asia-Pacific	4.6	4.2
Legal services	(0.2)	(3.4)	Europe	3.3	1.6
			Global	2.6	(0.6)
Legal services, selected state:			Countries:		
California	(0.9)	(3.4)	Germany	3.5	1.1
Florida	(0.9)	(3.4)	France	3.9	0.6
Illinois	0.6	(3.5)	Japan	3.0	4.0
New York	0.1	(5.1)	United Kingdom	3.9	0.6
Texas	(0.5)	(3.3)	United States	1.5	(4.1)

Sources: USDOL, BLS, Current Employment Statistics; Datamonitor Legal Services Industry Profiles; USITC staff calculations.

Note: BLS estimates refer to all employees classified under NAICS code 5411 (legal services). Datamonitor estimates refer to total number of legal professionals within the following subsectors of the legal services market: commercial, criminal, legal aid, insolvency, labor/industrial, family, and taxation law.

This decline was concentrated among associates[418] and an average of 25 new associates were deferred per firm.[419] A high proportion of the decline was due to reductions in the number of attorneys in foreign offices of large global firms; for example, the U. S. firm Jones Day cut the number of attorneys in its Hong Kong and Beijing offices.[420] However, Jones Day also opened an office in Dubai, which suggests that firms continued opening offices in potentially profitable markets while reducing their total workforce. There was a 4.1 percent decline in overall employment among the legal professionals in 2009 (table 7.3).[421] Smaller firms were somewhat shielded from the economic downturn because they offered lower prices across a variety of practice areas, but still cut staff, marketing, and other business expenses.[422]

As a result of cutting labor and other costs, firms reduced expenses by 5.6 percent in 2009 and experienced less of a decline in profits per equity partner than in 2008.[423] However, there was little correlation between layoffs and increased revenue per lawyer.[424] Firms will likely have to adopt strategies, such as expanding their geographic reach and undergoing structural changes, in order to maintain competitiveness in the long run.[425]

Trade Trends

Cross-Border Trade

Although both U. S. exports and U. S. imports of legal services (box 7.2) declined in 2009, exports declined more slowly; consequently, the U. S. legal services trade surplus grew to $5.5 billion in 2009 (figure 7.3).

Box 7.2. BEA Data on Cross-border Trade and Affiliate Transactions in Legal Services

This chapter's data on cross-border trade are prepared by the Bureau of Economic Analysis (BEA) of the U. S. Department of Commerce (USDOC). Such data on legal services capture services provided when legal professionals travel abroad to provide services to clients, when clients travel abroad to engage the services of foreign attorneys, or when legal documents or advice are exchanged across national borders via the postal service, fax transmissions, the Internet, or other means.[a] Data are collected through surveys broken down by the type of service provided; companies report their sales of legal services, defined as transactions involving "legal advice or other legal services."[b] Cross-border sales of legal services therefore encompass all legal services rendered by U. S. companies through cross-border channels, irrespective of whether companies are law firms. For example, legal services rendered by a corporation's in-house counsel would be captured by cross-border trade data (though in-house attorneys would more commonly be dispensing advice internally).[c]

BEA data on affiliate transactions capture sales by foreign legal services affiliates of U. S. law firms and purchases from U. S. affiliates of foreign law firms.[d] These data are also collected through surveys; however, they are categorized based on the industry classification of the affiliate, rather than the type of service provided.[e] Thus sales of legal services by foreign affiliates of U. S. firms include only sales by affiliates which are classified under NAICS code 5411 (legal services). Consequently, the data may theoretically exclude sales by affiliates of firms in other industries that also provide legal services or include sales by legal services affiliates with secondary activities in another industry. However, neither possibility is an issue for legal services in practice.[f]

[a] BEA representative, e-mail messages to USITC staff, February 26, 2009.

[b] USDOC, BEA, form BE-125 (1-2010), "Quarterly Survey of Transactions in Selected Services," 2010, 5, 6, 8, 12; USDOC, BEA, form BE-120 (12-2006), "Benchmark Survey of Transactions in Selected Services and Intangible Assets with Foreign Persons," 3, 5; BEA representative, e-mail messages to USITC staff, January 3, 2011, February 25, 2010, and February 26, 2009; BEA representative, telephone interview by USITC staff, May 13, 2010. Statistics for cross-border trade in legal services are collected quarterly through Survey BE-125, and every five years through Survey BE-120. Both surveys collect data on affiliated and unaffiliated cross-border trade. Data for affiliated cross-border trade in legal services became available for the first time beginning in 2006; such trade accounts for a very small share of total cross-border trade in legal services. Surveys BE-125 and BE-120 can be found at http://www.bea.gov/surveys/pdf/be125.pdf and http://www.bea.gov/surveys/pdf/be12006.pdf.

[c] BEA representative, e-mail messages to USITC staff, January 3, 2011, and April 4, 2011. Similarly, any secondary (non-legal services) activity by a law firm would be classified as the type of service provided. However, both activities (secondary activities by legal services providers, and legal services provided by firms in other industries) tend to be low.

[d] BEA reports "services supplied" by affiliates; for legal services, services supplied correspond to sales.

[e] BEA representative, telephone interview by USITC staff, May 13, 2010; USDOC, BEA, form BE-10D (rev. 1/2010), "2009 Benchmark Survey of U. S. Direct Investment Abroad;" BEA representative, e-mail message to USITC staff, February 26, 2009. Statistics for transactions by majority-owned legal services affiliates are collected through BEA's surveys of U. S. Direct Investment Abroad and Foreign Direct Investment in the United States, which can be found at http://www.bea.gov/surveys/diasurv.htm and http://www.bea.gov/surveys/fdiusurv.htm.

[f] BEA representative, e-mail messages to USITC staff, January 3, 2011, and April 4, 2011.

Overall, U. S. cross-border exports of legal services decreased by 1 percent to $7.3 billion in 2009, in contrast to an average annual growth rate of 14.8 percent from 2005 through 2008.[426] U. S. imports of such services decreased by 14.5 percent to approximately $1.7

billion in 2009, compared with a 22.1 percent average annual growth rate from 2005 through 2008.

U.S. exports of legal services are concentrated among a small number of destinations. In 2009, the top five export markets for legal services accounted for 51.5 percent of total U. S. exports of such services, a decrease from 59.0 percent in 2005.[427] The United Kingdom and Japan were the two leading markets for U. S. legal services exports in 2009, accounting for 16.1 percent and 15.2 percent of such exports, respectively (figure 7.4). The other top export markets in 2009, as in 2005, included Canada, Germany, and France.

In 2009, U. S. legal exports continued to grow in Latin America (11.9 percent) and the Asia-Pacific (4.1 percent), partially offsetting decreases in Canada and Europe, where exports declined (by 2.3 percent and 5.2 percent, respectively).[428] The largest increases in U. S. cross-border legal service exports occurred in countries in the Asia-Pacific, Latin America, and the Middle East. For example, from 2005 through 2008 exports to India, Indonesia, and Malaysia grew by 52.3, 58.7, and 54.2 percent, respectively; exports to Brazil grew by 33.8 percent; and exports to Saudi Arabia grew by 44.2 percent.[429] Economic reforms, growth, and foreign direct investment have increased demand for legal services in these markets.[430]

As with exports, five countries account for over half of U. S. legal services imports. In 2009, the United Kingdom (19.5 percent), Japan (10.5 percent), Germany (8.8 percent), Canada (7.9 percent), and Israel (4.5 percent) were the top suppliers of U. S. cross-border imports (see figure 7.4). Although imports from Europe were particularly impacted by the economic downturn, Europe's share of legal services imports had already begun a steady decline in 2005.[431] Imports from Canada followed a similar trend.[432] Although imports from the Asia-Pacific also declined in 2009, the region's share of total U. S. imports of legal services increased between 2005 and 2009.[433]

Regions outside of Europe developed their legal services markets and became competitive suppliers of legal services during the last decade, and U. S. imports of legal services from Latin America, the Middle East, and Africa continued to grow in 2009.[434] These trends also reflect deeper economic ties between the United States and these regions, as U. S. direct investment in Latin America, Africa, and the Middle East grew faster from 2005 to 2009 than investment in Europe, Asia-Pacific, or Canada.[435]

The two countries with the largest increases in their share of U. S. legal services imports are Israel and Brazil.[436] Expanded exports of legal services from Brazil to the United States coincided with growing U. S. direct investment in Brazil, which rose 27.3 percent in 2009.[437] Brazil's increased share of U. S. legal services imports partly reflects the joint work of Brazilian and U. S. law firms that advise on investments.[438] For example, two Brazilian law firms (Pinheiro Neto Advogados and Barbosa Müssnich and Aragão) are working with a U. S. law firm (Cahill Gordon and Reindel) on JP Morgan's $6 billion Brazilian investment.[439] Similarly, rapidly growing imports from Israel[440] partly result from Israeli law firms advising U. S. clients on investments and business in Israel. For example, Israeli firm Herzog Fox and Neeman advises large U. S. firms such as Citibank, Hewlett-Packard, Pfizer, and UPS on their Israeli interests.[441]

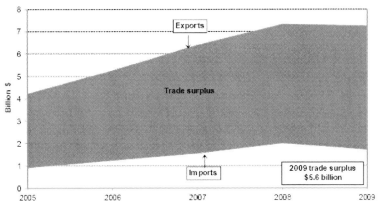

Source: USDOC, BEA, *Survey of Current Business*, October 2010, 36–37, table 1.

Figure 7.3. Legal services: U. S. cross-border trade in private-sector services resulted in a U. S. trade surplus each year during 2005–09.

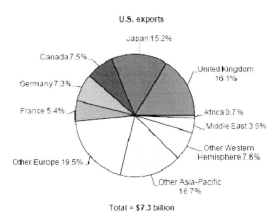

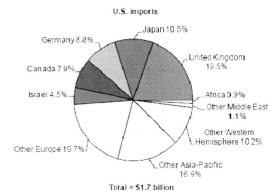

Source: USDOC, BEA, *Survey of Current Business*, October 2010, 54–55, table 7.5.
Note: Geographic regions are shaded in yellow.

Figure 7.4. Legal services: Five countries accounted for over half of U. S. exports and imports in 2009.

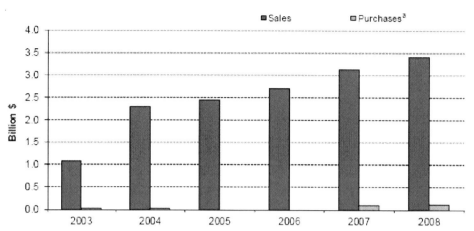

Source: USDOC, BEA, *Survey of Current Business*, various issues.

[a] BEA reports "services supplied" by foreign affiliates. In the legal services industry, "services supplied" correspond to "sales". Data were suppressed in 2005 and 2006 to avoid disclosure of individual company data.

Figure 7.5. Legal services: Both sales by foreign affiliates of U. S. law firms and purchases from U. S. affiliates of foreign law firms steadily grew, though sales continued to exceed purchases, 2003–08.

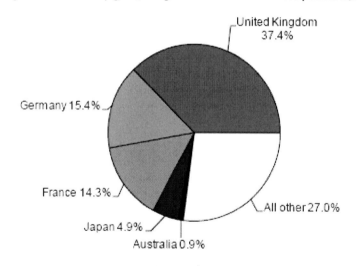

Total = $3.4 billion

Source: USDOC, BEA, *Survey of Current Business*, October 2010, 58, table 9.2.

[a] BEA reports "services supplied" by foreign affiliates. In the legal services industry, "services supplied" correspond to "sales".

Figure 7.6. Legal services: Europe accounted for the majority of foreign affiliate sales[a] in 2008.

Affiliate Transactions

Sales[442] by foreign affiliates of U. S. law firms (foreign affiliate sales) exceeded purchases from U. S. affiliates of foreign law firms in recent years (figure 7.5). In 2008, foreign affiliate sales increased 8.6 percent to $3.4 billion. This increase was well below the average annual growth rate of 30.4 percent from 2003 through 2007. In 2008, Europe accounted for 82.5 percent of foreign affiliates sales, led by the United Kingdom (37.4 percent), France (14.3 percent), and Germany (15.4 percent) (figure 7.6).[443] Japan, with 4.9 percent, ranked as the largest non-European market for foreign affiliate sales.[444] These shares remained largely unchanged since 2003.

Increasing foreign affiliate sales coincided with growth of direct investment abroad in legal services. Investment abroad by U. S. law firms increased by 28.8 percent in 2009 and rose at an average annual rate of 37.1 percent from 2005 through 2008.[445] Further, direct investment abroad in legal services increased faster than both total investment in professional services and total investment in all industries, which increased by 3.7 and 9.0 percent, respectively, in 2009, and at annual average rates of 9.3 and 12.8 percent from 2005 through 2008. Although Europe accounts for the greatest share of foreign affiliate sales, U. S. law firms are also establishing offices in non-European foreign markets, such as Latin America and the Middle East.[446]

Domestic purchases of legal services from U. S. affiliates of foreign law firms grew faster than foreign affiliate sales in 2003–07, though they started from a smaller base. In 2008, the latest year for which affiliate data are available, purchases from U. S. affiliates grew by 10.4 percent to $117 million, slower than the average annual increase of 45.0 percent from 2003 through 2007.[447]

Multilateral Negotiations, Liberalization, and Remaining Barriers

U.S. firms face significant restrictions when exporting legal services to emerging markets.[448] For example, foreign lawyers are prohibited from providing legal services or establishing a presence in India.[449] To advise on issues related to India, firms like Jones Day of the United States and Allen and Overy of the United Kingdom have entered into alliances with local firms[450] or work on Indian legal issues from nearby branch offices in Hong Kong or Singapore.[451] In 2009, the Bombay High Court directed the Indian government to clarify what foreign law firms are permitted to do,[452] and in September 2010 the government reaffirmed that India would remain closed to foreign lawyers.[453]

Brazilian regulations prohibit foreign firms from practicing local law and require local law firms to be owned and governed by Brazilian lawyers.[454] Consequently, firms like Mayer Brown, a U. S. law firm with an office in São Paolo, limit their practices to advising Brazilian clients on U. S. and British law.[455] Saudi Arabia requires foreign law firms to partner with Saudi law firms in order to establish a local presence.[456] In China, foreign lawyers and law firms face restrictions on the types of law they can practice and their ability to hire lawyers, among other stipulations.[457]

However, certain countries have taken steps to liberalize their legal service markets. For example, Korea passed the Foreign Legal Consultant Act in 2009. This act permits lawyers and law firms from countries that have a free trade agreement with Korea to establish offices as foreign legal consultants and, with three years' experience, to provide advice on public international law and the law of the foreign lawyer's jurisdiction.[458] Similarly, towards the end of 2008, Singapore granted licenses to six U. S. and British law firms which enabled them to practice Singapore law with some restrictions.[459] Previously, foreign lawyers were restricted from either practicing Singaporean law or employing lawyers qualified to practice it.

Outlook

Restructuring may be necessary for leading law firms to maintain their competitiveness.[460] Law firms may increasingly deliver their services through flexible non-hourly fee arrangements,[461] such as on a fixed-fee basis, which provides more price predictability to both the firm and the client.[462] In the United States, it is estimated that only 1 to 2 percent of medium-sized and large firms' business is currently handled on an alternative fee basis, but that rate is projected to rise to 10–15 percent in 10 years.[463]

Technological advances[464] may provide opportunities for smaller firms. Large firms tend to be better equipped to handle complex cases, but technology increasingly allows smaller firms to efficiently gather, review, and process vast amounts of data and documents. Additionally, technological changes will be advantageous for corporate in- house counsel; for example, larger social networks now allow in-house lawyers to find and develop relationships with outside counsel more efficiently.[465]

Firms will likely continue to expand their presence in growing markets such as Brazil, China, Korea, and India.[466] Global capacity will be very important for U. S. firms in the future[467] as they seek to establish and operate in fast-growing markets, follow cross- border merger and acquisition activity, and provide services to multinational clients.[468]

8. SERVICES ROUNDTABLE

The Commission hosted its fourth annual services roundtable on December 8, 2010. These roundtables are held to facilitate discussions about important issues affecting services trade. This year's roundtable included participants from government, industry, and academia, representing a range of perspectives. Discussion topics included the effect of globalization on U. S. services jobs and wages, the net welfare effects of establishing services affiliates abroad, and the effects of technological advances on the ways in which services are produced and delivered. Participants highlighted the challenges faced in understanding services trade trends in the absence of comprehensive data, and debated the significance of globalization's impact on employment trends in U. S. services industries. This section summarizes the roundtable discussion and provides a list of participants.

Data

As in past roundtables, a recurring theme in the discussion was the need for more and better services data. It is often more difficult to measure services transactions than goods transactions due to the intangible and non-storable nature of services, so existing data on services tend to include few geographic and industry details compared to data on manufactures. Participants highlighted shortcomings of data both on domestic services activities and on international trade in services, and pointed out that researchers largely have to find ways to supplement official sources in developing data sets on trade in services.

At present, U. S. trade data are collected by multiple government agencies. One participant described the current fragmented system of trade statistics as divided between the

Customs Bureau (which collects information on goods imports), the Census Bureau (which covers goods exports), and the Bureau of Economic Analysis (BEA) (which conducts surveys covering goods and services). Within BEA's survey-based data, there is a disparity in the amount of money spent surveying manufacturing firms versus what is spent surveying services firms—one participant estimated the difference to be 10 times more for manufacturing establishments. This disparity in spending is all the more striking given that manufacturing accounts for about one-tenth of U. S. employment, while services account for as much as 80 percent. One participant suggested that the Census Bureau may be better positioned than the BEA to collect survey-based services data, given the agency's access to a more representative sample of services firms and its experience collecting export data.

The underlying challenges of services data include a lack of budget for data collection. One participant noted that statistical budgets are often sacrificed when governments face fiscal constraints, and predicted the U. S. government is unlikely to spend more on services data collection in the near future. To provide historical perspective, a participant pointed out that the U. S. government used to have stronger incentives to collect trade data due to its reliance on goods tariffs as a significant source of income. In the absence of improved government data collection, industry groups may be able to supply more information on services trade, but are constrained by the confidentiality of their internal operations.

Other challenges include differences in services categorization schemes. Opportunities to make direct year-on-year comparisons of services data become limited when categories are adjusted. One participant noted that the services categories used in negotiations over the General Agreement on Trade in Services were different from the categories used in data collection. The consequences of limited services data include increased difficulty in negotiating services agreements. A participant pointed out that developing-country representatives tend to be cautious in negotiating services agreements, in part because they have limited information on the importance of services to their trading sector. Uruguay Round negotiators discussing services commitments were paraphrased as saying, "How can we discuss this? We don't have the trade data."

Effects of Globalization on Jobs and Wages

The roundtable discussed the phenomenon of U. S. information technology (IT) firms employing many workers abroad, especially in India. Opinions diverged regarding the effects of globalization on employment in the U. S. IT industry. One participant suggested that the offshoring and outsourcing business model has been fundamentally successful in boosting the net margins of U. S. IT companies, yet has also resulted in firms cutting their workforces in the United States and put downward pressure on the wages of U. S. IT workers. However, another participant pointed out that employment and wage growth have been about the same for both tradable and nontradable services in recent years, so it is difficult to conclude that tradability has measurable economic effects—i.e., that the ability to trade IT services internationally is the driver of employment and wage trends in the IT services sector.[469]

The discussion focused on India, the leading source of U. S. imports of computer and data processing services. One participant argued that India's comparative advantage in IT services is "artificial" and likely will not persist, as India is not an especially skill- abundant place relative to other countries. There are highly skilled Indian workers, but they represent a small share of India's very large population, and arbitrage opportunities are vanishing ("at this point it's a wash [in terms of cost] whether you open a call center in Bangalore or Detroit."). This was affirmed by another participant who pointed out that the current supply of engineers coming from the Indian Institutes of Technology is limited, and that firms seeking to hire such engineers compete with firms like Infosys (an Indian firm). For this reason, Indian engineers now command wages comparable to their U. S. counterparts.

The roundtable discussed the fact that offshoring can be viewed either in terms of employment or in terms of profits. Researchers and policymakers are currently focusing on ways to increase employment, yet companies that invest abroad tend to make offshoring decisions on the basis of profit opportunities. One participant suggested that we need to think more broadly about the costs and benefits of offshoring than the effects on a single firm: for example, U. S. firms have maintained their overall leadership in IT sectors in part through establishing Indian operations. Additionally, importers and exporters generally pay higher wages and are bigger, more productive, and more capital intensive than their non-importing or -exporting counterparts. In considering the broader effects of investment abroad, participants noted that the "headquarters effect" of foreign investment on domestic employment—jobs created at multinational firms' headquarters as a result of expanding abroad—is hard to identify, and may not be a significant phenomenon. However, the second-order domestic employment gains—jobs created from increased purchases of inputs by multinational companies—may be more significant.

The roundtable concluded with a discussion of challenges facing U. S. services industries going forward. One participant emphasized that there is now global competition for labor at all skill levels, as nontradable sectors are small and diminishing in number (with many activities becoming newly tradable). This elevates the importance of education and the need for the United States to invest in areas where it has comparative advantages. A participant pointed out that one challenge faced by the United States has been the strong incentive for students with mathematics skills to work in the investment banking sector, rather than sectors like computer science or engineering. The roundtable discussed the many export opportunities for U. S. services firms in engineering, architecture, and other sectors in which the United States is highly competitive. However, fewer people understand the opportunities for exporting services like these, compared to goods like aerospace manufactures. Additionally, small U. S. services firms may be more likely to focus on domestic clients due to unfamiliarity with the languages and cultures of potential export markets.

List of external participants at the Commission's services roundtable held on December 8, 2010

Name	Title / Affiliation
Bernie Ascher	Adjunct Professor of Global Business and Public Policy
	University of Maryland University College
Christine Bliss	Assistant United States Trade Representative for Services and Investment USTR
John Goyer	Vice President, International Trade Negotiations and Investment Coalition of Services Industries
Ron Hira	Associate Professor of Public Policy

	Rochester Institute of Technology
Geoff Huntington	Executive Vice President of Research
	Phi Power Communications Inc.
J. Bradford Jensen	Associate Professor of International Business and Economics
	McDonough School of Business at Georgetown University
David Long	Director of the Office of Services Industries
	U.S. Department of Commerce
Sherry M. Stephenson	Institutional Relations
	Organization of American States
Marc S. Tucker	President and CEO
	National Center on Education and the Economy
J. Robert Vastine	President
	Coalition of Services Industries

BIBLIOGRAPHY

[1] Borchert, Ingo and Aaditya, Mattoo. "*The Crisis-Resilience of Services Trade.*" World Bank Policy Research Working Paper 4917, April 2009.

[2] Cattaneo, Olivier; Michael Engman; Sebastián Sáez and Robert M. Stern, eds. *International Trade in Services*. Washington, DC: World Bank, 2010.

[3] Federal Maritime Commission (FMC). *48th Annual Report for Fiscal Year 2009*. Washington, DC: FMC, 2009. http://www.fmc.gov/assets/ 1/Page/Annual Report FY 2009.pdf.

[4] JP Morgan. "*Global Trade: Lifeblood in the Global Financial Crisis.*" n.d. http://www.jpmorgan.com/tss/ General/Global_Trade_Lifeblood _in_the_Global_ Financial_Crisis/ 1254435214927 (accessed November 5, 2010).

[5] U.S. Department of Commerce (USDOC). Bureau of Economic Analysis (BEA). "*Full-Time Equivalent Employees by Industry.*" Interactive tables: Gross-Domestic-Product-by-Industry Accounts, August 5, 2010. http://www.bea.gov/industry/gpotables/ gpo_action. cfm?anon=508764andtable id=25734andformat type=0.

[6] ———. "*Real Value Added by Industry.*" Interactive tables: Gross-Domestic-Product-by-Industry Accounts, May 25, 2010. http://www.bea.gov/industry/ gpotables/ gpoaction.cfm?anon= 508764 andtable id=25700andformat type=0.

[7] ———. *Survey of Current Business* 86, no. 10, (October 2006).

[8] ———. *Survey of Current Business* 88, no. 10, (October 2008).

[9] ———. *Survey of Current Business* 89, no. 10, (October 2009).

[10] ———. *Survey of Current Business* 90, no. 10, (October 2010).

[11] ———. "Table 3a. Private Services Transactions." U. S. International Transactions Accounts Data, December 16, 2010. http://www.bea.gov/ international/bp_web/ list.cfm?anon=71andregistered=0.

[12] ———. "*Table 6.6D: Wage and Salary Accruals Per Full-Time Equivalent Employee by Industry.*" Interactive tables: National Income and Product Accounts Table, August 5, 2010. http://www.bea.gov/national/nipaweb/TableView.asp?SelectedTable=

190andFreq=YearandFirstYear=2006andLastYear= 2007 (accessed September 9, 2010).

[13] World Trade Organization (WTO). "*Chapter 1: Basic Purpose and Concepts.*" General Agreement on Trade in Services Training Module, n.d. http://www.wto.org/english/ tratop e/serv e/ cbt_course_e/c 1s2p 1_e.htm (accessed April 7, 2009).

[14] ———. *International Trade Statistics 2010*. Geneva: WTO Secretariat, 2010. http://www.wto.org/english/res e/statis e/its2009 e/its09 toc e.htm.

[15] ———. "*Trade Likely to Grow by 13.5% in 2010, WTO Says.*" Press release, September 20, 2010. http://www.wto.org/english/news e/pres 10 e/pr6 16 e.htm.

[16] Bosworth, Barry P. and Jack, Triplett. "*Is the 21st Century Productivity Expansion Still in Services? And What Should Be Done About It?*" Prepared for American Economic Association, Chicago, IL, January 5–7, 2007.

[17] Brainard, Lael; Susan M. Collins, eds. *Brookings Trade Forum: 2005, Offshoring White-Collar Work—The Issues and Implications* (Brookings Institution Press: 2006).

[18] Cattaneo, Olivier; Michael Engman; Sebastián Sáez and Robert M. Stern, eds. *International Trade in Services*. Washington, DC: World Bank, 2010.

[19] Conway, Paul and Giuseppe, Nicoletti. "*Product Market Regulation in the Non-Manufacturing Sectors of OECD Countries: Measurement and Highlights.*" OECD Economics Department Working Papers No. 530, December 7, 2006.

[20] *Economist*. "Smart Work: Faster Productivity Will Be an Important Part of Rich Economies' Revival," October 7, 2010. http://economist.com/ node/17173903/print.

[21] Garner, C. Alan. "Offshoring in the Service Sector: Economic Impact and Policy Issues." Federal Reserve Bank of Kansas. *Economic Review*, Third Quarter, 2004.

[22] Hoekman, Bernard; Aaditya Mattoo and André Sapir. "The Political Economy of Services Trade Liberalization: A Case for International Regulatory Cooperation?" *Oxford Review of Economic Policy,* 23, no. 3 (2007): 367–9 1.

[23] Høj, Jens; Toshiyasu Kato and Dirk Pilat. "Deregulation and Privatisation in the Service Sector." *OECD Economic Studies* No. 25, 1995/II.

[24] Jensen, J. Bradford and Lori G. Kletzer. "*Tradable Services: Understanding the Scope and Impact of Services Outsourcing.*" Institute for International Economics. Working Paper Series, September 2005.

[25] Levine, Linda. "Offshoring (a.k.a. Offshore Outsourcing) and Job Insecurity among U. S. Workers." *CRS Report for Congress*, May 2, 2005.

[26] Liu, Runjuan and Daniel Trefler. "*Much Ado about Nothing: American Jobs and the Rise of Service Outsourcing to China and India.*" NBER Working Paper Series, June 2008.

[27] McKinsey Global Institute. "*Beyond Austerity: A Path to Economic Growth and Renewal in Europe*," October 2010.

[28] Molnar, Margit; Nigel Pain and Daria Taglioni. "Globalisation and Employment in the OECD." *OECD Economic Studies* No. 44, December 2008.

[29] Nicoletti, Giuseppe and Stefano Scarpetta. "*Regulation, Productivity and Growth: OECD Evidence.*" World Bank Policy Research Working Paper no. 2944, January 2003.

[30] Spohr, George. "IBM Layoffs Hit Hundreds in Latest Round." *Times-Herald Record*, August 4, 2009. http://www.recordonline.com/apps/ pbcs.dll/article?AID=/20090804/ BIZ/908049969.

[31] Triplett, Jack and Barry P. Bosworth. "*Productivity in the Services Sector.*" Prepared for the American Economic Association, Boston, MA, January 7–9, 2000.

[32] U.S. Department of Commerce (USDOC). Bureau of Economic Analysis (BEA). "*Full-Time Equivalent Employees by Industry.*" Interactive tables: Gross-Domestic-Product-by-Industry Accounts, August 5, 2010. http://www.bea.gov/industry/gpotables/ gpo_action.cfm? anon=508764andtable id=25734andformat type=0.

[33] ———. "*Real Value Added by Industry.*" Interactive tables: Gross-Domestic-Product-by-Industry accounts, May 5, 2010.

[34] ———. *Survey of Current Business,* 86, no. 10 (October 2010).

[35] U.S. Department of Labor (DOL). Bureau of Labor Statistics (BLS). "Table 32: Unemployed Persons by Occupation, Industry and Duration of Employment, 2008." Current Population

[36] Survey—Household Data—Annual Averages, 2008. ftp://ftp.bls.gov/pub/special. requests/lf/aa2008/pdf/cpsaat32.pdf (accessed April 29, 2011).

[37] ———. "Table 32: Unemployed Persons by Occupation, Industry and Duration of Employment, 2009." Current Population Survey—Household Data—Annual Averages, 2009. ftp://ftp.bls.gov/pub/special.requests/lf/aa2009/pdf/cpsaat32.pdf (accessed April 29, 2011).

[38] U.S. Government Accountability Office (U.S. GAO). Report to Congressional Requesters. "Airline Deregulation: Changes in Airfares, Services Quality and Barriers to Entry (GAO/RCED-99-92)," March 1999.

[39] U.S. International Trade Commission (USITC). *Recent Trends in U. S. Services Trade: 2010 Annual Report.* USITC Publication 4163. Washington, DC: USITC, June 2010.

[40] Van Zandweghe, Willem. "Why Have the Dynamics of Labor Productivity Changed?" Federal Reserve Bank of Kansas City. *Economic Review,* Third Quarter, 2010.

[41] Von Bergen and Jane M. "In Epidemic of Layoffs, No One Is Immune." *Philadelphia Inquirer,* April 5, 2009.__http://www.istockanalyst.com/ article/viewiStockNews/ articleid/3177048.

[42] Wölfl, Anita. "*Productivity Growth in Service Industries: An Assessment of Recent Patterns and the Role of Measurement.*" OECD Science, Technology and Industry Working Papers 2003/7, June 2003.

[43] ———. "*The Interaction between Manufacturing and Services and Its Potential Role for Productivity Growth.*" Paper presented at "En route vers Lisbonne: Second Colloque Luxembourgeois sur l'Economie de la Connaissance dans une Perspective Européenne," a conference held in Luxembourg, November 9–10, 2006.

[44] Amobi, Tuna N. "Movies and Entertainment." *Standard and Poor's Industry Surveys.* New York: Standard and Poor's, September 9, 2010.

[45] Bernstein, Richard. "An Aging Europe May Find Itself on the Sidelines." *New York Times,* June 29, 2003. http://query.nytimes.com/gst/fullpage.html? res=9C07E4DD 173AF93AA15755C0A9659C8B63.

[46] BoxOfficeMojo.com. "2009 Worldwide Grosses," n.d. http://boxofficemojo.com/ yearly/chart/?view2 =worldwideandyr=2009andp =.htm (accessed November 3, 2010).

[47] Center for Entertainment Industry Data and Research (CEIDR). *The Global Success of Production Tax Incentives and the Migration of Feature Film Production from the U. S. to the World, Year 2005 Production Report.* Encino, CA: CEIDR, 2006.

[48] Dickey, Josh. "'Avatar's' True Cost–and Consequences." TheWrap.com, December 3, 2009. http://www.thewrap.com/movies/ article/avatars-true-cost-and-consequences-11206.

[49] Digital Cinema Initiatives. "About DCI," n.d. http://www.dcimovies.com/ (accessed January 29, 2011). *Economist.* "Hollow-wood," March 11, 2010.

[50] ———. "The Worldwide Cinema Boom: The Box Office Strikes Back," May 6, 2010. ———. *"To Catch a Thief,"* May 13, 2010.

[51] ———. *"Nollywood: Lights, Camera, Africa,"* December 16, 2010.

[52] European Audiovisual Observatory (EAO). *Focus 2009: World Film Market Trends.* Strasbourg, France: EAO, 2009. http://www.obs.coe.int/oea_publ/market/focus.html.

[53] ———. *Focus 2010: World Film Market Trends.* Strasbourg, France: EAO, 2010. http://www.obs.coe.int/oea publ/market/focus.html.

[54] *Film Journal International.* "Moviegoer Quick Facts: Nielsen PreView Reveals Audience Preferences," July 15, 2009. http://www.filmjournal.com/filmjournal/content _ display/news-andfeatures/features/cinemas/e3ie3cb96740c26f800a294d7506ba771da.

[55] Gallagher, Chris. "In Japan, 3D Films Get Kicked by New Samurai Flicks." Reuters, October 14, 2010. http://www.reuters.com/ article/2010/10/15/us-samurai-idUSTRE 69E03820101015 (accessed February 7, 2011).

[56] Garrahan, Matthew. "Hollywood Braced for Budget Cuts." FT.com, October 6, 2009. http://www.ft.com/cms/s/0/edd9a0e8-b29e-11de-b7d2-00144feab49a.html.

[57] ———. *"MGM Studio Emerges from Bankruptcy."* FT.com, December 21, 2010. http://cachef.ft.com/cms/s/0/a6cc5bf6-0c9c-11e0-a0a2-00144feabdc0.html#axzz1EuNk mqZg.

[58] GlobalServicesMedia.com. *"Lights, Camera, Action...,"* February 27, 2008. http://www. globalservicesmedia.com/IT-Outsourcing/Emerging-IT-Services/Lights,-Camera,-Action. /22/26/0/industry-more200802273786.

[59] Hanson, Gordon H. and Chong Xiang. *"International Trade in Motion Picture Services."* National Bureau of Economic Research, January 2008. http://irps. ucsd.edu/assets/ 022/8777.pdf.

[60] HighBeam.com. *"Industry Report: Motion Picture and Video Tape Production,"* n.d. http://business.highbeam.com/industry-reports/personal/motion-picture-video-tape-production (accessed November 23, 2010).

[61] IBIS World. "Global Movie Production and Distribution: Q8711 -GL." *IBIS World Industry Report*, April 15, 2010.

[62] *LiveTradingNews.com.* "The Worldwide Cinema Boom," May 8, 2010. http://www.live tradingnews.com/the-worldwide-cinema-boom-13168.htm.

[63] Márquez, Huberto. "Petrodollars for Local Film Industry." *IPSnews.net*, January 12, 2007. http://ipsnews.net/news.asp?idnews=361 51.

[64] Motion Picture Association of America (MPAA). *Theatrical Movie Statistics 2009.* Los Angeles/Washington, DC: MPAA, 2010. http://www.mpaa.org/Resources/091af5d6-faf7-4f58- 9a8e-405466c 1 c5e5.pdf.

[65] ———. *Trade Barriers to Exports of U. S. Filmed Entertainment.* Los Angeles/Washington, DC: MPAA, October 2010. http://www.mpaa.org/Resources/ 69721865-ac82-4dc4-88ec-01ee84c651a1.pdf.

[66] Pells, Richard. "Is American Culture 'American'?" *America.gov* (blog), February 1, 2006. http://usinfo.americancorner.org.tw/st/business-english/2006/February/ 20080608102136xjyrreP0. 3622858.html (accessed February 2, 2011).

[67] Ryan, Orla. "*Nollywood Comes of Age.*" FT.com, October 1, 2010. http://www.ft.com/cms/s/2/afbaa850- cce9- 11 df-9bf0-00 144feab49a.html#axzz1EthD t0G1 (accessed October 20, 2010).

[68] Schuker, Lauren A.E. "Will It Play in Korea?" *Wall Street Journal: Classroom Edition*, November 2010. http://www.wsjclassroom.com/cre/articles/10novmediforeign film.htm.

[69] Schwinke, Theodore. "Will Cheap Deals Tempt the Bargain Hunters?" ScreenDaily, July 2, 2009. http://www.screendaily.com/screenbase/eastern-europe/will-cheap-deals-tempt-the-bargainhunters/5003 1 30.article.

[70] Screen Digest. "*World Film Production/Distribution.*" London: June 2006.

[71] ———. "*World Film Production Drops Again.*" London: August 2010.

[72] ———. "*Global Box Office Hits New High.*" London: November 2010.

[73] ShowBizData.com. "*Worldwide Global Theatrical Market Shares for 2009*," n.d. http://www.showbizdata.com/worldshares.cfm?year=2009andt distributor=SPCandview detail=1and (accessed October 20, 2010).

[74] United Nations Education, Scientific and Cultural Organization (UNESCO). Institute for Statistics (UIS). *Analysis of the UIS Survey of Feature Film Statistics*. Montreal: UNESCO, March 3, 2010. http://www.uis.unesco.org/ev.php?ID=7651 201andID2=DO TOPIC.

[75] U.S. Department of Commerce (USDOC). Bureau of Economic Analysis (BEA). *Survey of Current Business* 90, no. 10 (October 2010).

[76] U.S. Department of Labor (DOL). Bureau of Labor Statistics (BLS). *Motion Picture and Video Industries, 2010–11*, December 17, 2009. http://www.bls.gov/oco/cg/ cgs038.htm.

[77] USITC. *China: Effects of Intellectual Property Infringement and Indigenous Innovation Policies on the U. S. Economy*. USITC Publication 4426. Washington, DC: USITC May 2011.

[78] USTR. "*Korea-U.S. Free Trade Agreement.*" http://www.ustr.gov/trade-agreements/free-tradeagreements/korus-fta (accessed April 6, 2011).

[79] Vogel, Harold L. *Entertainment Industry Economics*. Cambridge, United Kingdom: Cambridge University Press, 2004.

[80] World Trade Organization (WTO). "*Audiovisual Services*," n.d. http://www.wto.org/english/tratop_e/ serv_e/audiovisual_e/audiovisual_ e.htm (accessed January 4, 2011).

[81] ———. "*Audiovisual Services: Background Note by the Secretariat.*" S/C/W/3 10, January 12, 2010.

[82] ———. "*Communication from Switzerland, GATS 2000: Audiovisual Services.*" S/CSS/W/74, May 4, 2001.

[83] ———. "*Communication from the United States: Audiovisual and Related Services.*" S/CSS/W/2 1, December 18, 2000.

[84] ———. Council for Trade in Services (CTS). "*Communication from Brazil: Audiovisual Services.*" S/CSS/W/99, July 9, 2001.

[85] ———. Special Session. "*Communication from Hong Kong China, Japan, Mexico, the Separate Customs Territory of Taiwan, Penghu, Kinmen and Matsu and the United*

States: Joint Statement in the Negotiations on Audiovisual Services." TN/S/W/49, June 30, 2005.

[86] Alejandro, Lisa; Eric, Forden; Allison, Gosney; Erland, Herfindahl; Dennis, Luther; Erick, Oh; Joann, Peterson; Matthew, Reisman and Isaac, Wohl. "*An Overview and Examination of the Indian Services Sector.*" USITC Office of Industries Working Paper ID-26, August 2010.

[87] Amazon. "*What is AWS?*" http://aws.amazon.com/what-is-aws/ (accessed January 4, 2011).

[88] Barnes, Taylor. "Why Indian IT Companies Are Outsourcing—to US." *Christian Science Monitor*, April 12, 2010. http://www.csmonitor.com/Business/2010/0412/Why-Indian-IT-companies-areoutsourcing-to-US.

[89] Bureau van Dijk. Orbis Companies Database. http://orbis.bvdep.com (accessed December 27, 2010).

[90] Cathers, Dylan. "Computers; Commercial Services." *Standard and Poor's Industry Survey*; New York: Standard and Poor's, May 6, 2010.

[91] Columbus, Louis. "Roundup of Cloud Computing Forecasts and Market Estimates, 2011." *A Passion for Research* (blog), January 1, 2011. http://softwarestrategiesblog.com/2011/01/01/roundup-ofcloud-computing-forecasts-and-market-estimates-20 11/.

[92] Conneally, Tim. "U.S Border Security Bill Could Strain U. S. -India Tech Relations." *Betanews,* August 6, 2010.

[93] Crosman, Penny. "Inside IBM's Mega Outsourcing Projects with ABN Amro and Bank of Ireland." *Bank Systems and Technology,* January 21, 2011. http://www.banktech.com/ architectureinfrastructure/229100013.

[94] Dacey, Jessica. "*Opposition to Work Permit Quotas Grows.*" *Swissinfo. ch,* April 21, 2010. http://www.swissinfo.ch/eng/swiss_news/ Opposition_to_work_permit_quotas_grows.html?cid=8 714906.

[95] Dai, Richard. "IBIS World Industry Report 54151: IT Consulting in the US." *IBIS World Industry Report*, August 2010.

[96] Das, Shyamanuja. "The Rise and Rise of Services." *Dataquest,* January 22, 2010. http://dqindia.ciol.com/content/industrymarket/focus/2010/ 110012202.asp.

[97] Díaz-Pinés, Agustín. *Indicators of Broadband Coverage.* Paris: OECD, December 10, 2009. http://www.oecd.org/dataoecd/41/39/44381795.pdf.

[98] Dzubeck, Frank. "Five Cloud Computing Questions." *Network World,* August 5, 2008. http://www.networkworld.com/columnists/2008/ 080508-dzubeck.html.

[99] Economist Intelligence Unit (EIU). "*World: Healthcare Outlook.*" *Views Wire,* December 9, 2010. http://viewswire.eiu.com/index.asp?layout=ib3Articleandarticle_id= 1917690976andpubtypeid=1152 462500andchannel _id=andcompany _id=andcategory _id=andcountry _id=andindustry _id=andpage _title=Lat est+analysisandfs=true (accessed January 3, 2011; subscription required).

[100] Engman, Michael. "Exporting Information Technology Services: In the Footsteps of India." In *International Trade in Services: New Trends and Opportunities for Developing Countries*, edited by Olivier Cattaneo, Michael Engman, Sebastián Sáez and Robert M. Stern. Washington, DC: World Bank, 2010.

[101] European Commission. "*Communication from the Commission to the European Parliament, the Council, the Economic and Social Committee and the Committee of the Regions: A Comprehensive Approach on Personal Data Protection in the European*

Union." COM(20 10) 609 final, November 4, 2010. http://ec.europa.eu/justice/news/consulting public/0006/com 2010 609 en.pdf.

[102] ———. *The Future of Cloud Computing: Opportunities for European Cloud Computing Beyond 2010.*

[103] Brussels: European Commission, January 2010. http://cordis.europa.eu/fp7/ict/ssai/events20100126-cloud-computing en.html.

[104] Farber, Dan. "Oracle's Ellison Nails Cloud Computing." *CNET News*, September 26, 2008. http://news.cnet.com/8301-13953 3-10052188-80.html.

[105] Forrester. "*Forrester: Mixed Economic Outlook Shifts Technology Demands.*" News release, January 10, 2011. http://www.forrester.com/ER/Press/Release/0,1769,1363,00.html.

[106] Fried, Ina. "HP Revamps Line of Inkjet Printers." *CNET News,* July 1, 2003. http://news.cnet.com/HPrevamps-line-of-inkjet-printers/2 100-1041 3- 1022459.html.

[107] Gartner. "*Gartner Says Worldwide Cloud Services Market to Surpass $68 Billion in 2010.*" News release, June 22, 2010. http://www.gartner. com/it/page.jsp?id=1389313.

[108] Gilmore, Agatha, Mike Prokopeak, Kellye Whitney, Deanna Hartley, Lindsay Edmonds Wickman and Brian Summerfield. "*Salary Survey 2008.*" *Certification Magazine*, December 2008. http://www.certmag. com/read.php?in=3656.

[109] Golden, Bernard. "The Skinny Straw: Cloud Computing's Bottleneck and How to Address It." *CIO,* August 6, 2009.

[110] Gray, Mike. "*Cloud Computing: Demystifying IaaS, PaaS and SaaS.*" *ZDNet News,* October 21, 2010. http://www.zdnet.com/news/cloud-computing-demystifying-iaas-paas-and-saas/477238.

[111] Herbst, Moira. "*Study: No Shortage of U. S. Engineers.*" *Bloomberg Business Week*, October 28, 2009. http://www.businessweek.com/ bwdaily/dnflash/content/oct2009/db20091027 723059.htm.

[112] IBM. *Form 10-K Annual Report.* March 31, 1994. http://www.sec.gov/Archives/edgar/data/51143/0000950112-94-000794.txt.

[113] ———. *2009 Annual Report.* March 5, 2010. www.ibm.com/ annualreport/2009/2009_ibm_annual.pdf.

[114] IHS Global Insight. *Digital Planet 2010.* Vienna, VA: World Information Technology and Services Alliance, October 2010.

[115] Kirk, Jeremy. "Microsoft: Cloud Computing Troubled by EU Data Rules." *Techworld,* November 10, 2010. http://news.techworld.com/ applications/3247456/microsoft-cloud-computing-troubled-byeu-data-rules/?olo=rss.

[116] Kristensen, Thomas Myrup. "Revising the EU Data Protection Directive." *Digital Policy: Microsoft's European Activities* (blog), April 1, 2010. http://www.microsoft.eu/Posts/Viewer/tabid/120/article Type/ArticleView/articleId/588/Revising-the-EU-Data-Protection-Directive.aspx.

[117] McAfee andrew. "The Weird and Wonderful Economics of Digitization." *Andrew McAfee* (blog), March 29, 2010. *Harvard Business Review*. http://blogs.hbr.org/hbr/mcafee/2010/03/the-weird-andwonderful-econom.html.

[118] Microsoft. "*City of Miami: City Government Improves Service Offerings, Cuts Costs with 'Cloud' Services Solution.*" Microsoft Case Studies, February 24, 2010. http://www.microsoft.com/ casestudies/case study detail.aspx?casestudyid=400000 6568.

[119] ———. "Microsoft Office 365." http://office365.microsoft.com/en-US/online-services.aspx (accessed October 28, 2010).

[120] ———. "Microsoft Services Overview." http://www.microsoft.com/microsoftservices/en/us/overview.aspx (accessed October 28, 2010).

[121] NASSCOM. "Executive Summary." *The IT-BPO Sector in India: Strategic Review 2010*. New Delhi:

[122] NASSCOM, February 2010. http://www.nasscom.in/upload/SR10/ExecutiveSummary.pdf.

[123] ———. "*India Inc.—An Overview of the Indian IT-BPO Industry.*" Presentation for the Gujarat Electronics and Software Industries Association, April 2010. http://www.gesia.org/images/gesia2010/ vadodara10/India%20Inc-April-2010-Final-1.pdf.

[124] ———. *The IT-BPO Sector in India: Strategic Review 2009*. New Delhi: NASSCOM, February 2009.

[125] Nordas, Hildegunn Kyvik. "Trade and Regulation: Computer Services and Other Business Services." Paper prepared for the OECD Services Experts Meeting in Business Services, Paris, June 24, 2008.

[126] O'Brien, Kevin. "Cloud Computing Hits Snag in Europe." *New York Times*, September 19, 2010. http://www.nytimes.com/2010/09/20/ technology/20cloud.html.

[127] OECD. "Services Trade Restrictiveness: Computer and Related Services." Paper prepared for the OECD Experts Meeting on the Services Trade Restrictiveness Index (STRI), Paris, July 2–3, 2009.

[128] Recovery Accountability and Transparency Board. Recovery.gov database (accessed April 4, 2011). http://www.recovery.gov/Pages/default.aspx.

[129] Salesforce. "*Restoration Hardware Taps Sale sforce CRM to Provide Foundation for Highly Successful To-the-trade Team*," n.d. http://www.salesforce.com/showcase/stories/restoration.jsp (accessed January 4, 2011).

[130] ———. "What is PaaS?" http://www.salesforce.com/paas/ (accessed February 1, 2011).

[131] Schifferes, Steve. "*Multinationals Lead India's IT Revolution.*" BBC News, January 24, 2007. http://news.bbc.co.uk/2/hi/business/ 6288247.stm.

[132] Shimanek, Anna. "Do You Want Milk with Those Cookies? Complying with the Safe Harbor Privacy Principles." *Journal of Corporation Law*, 26, no. 2 (Winter 2001): 455–77.

[133] Staten, James. "*Cloud Computing for the Enterprise.*" Presentation, February 3, 2009. http://www.forrester.com/imagesV2/uplmisc/Cloud ComputingWebinarSlideDeck.pdf.

[134] Sudan, Randeep; Seth, Ayers; Philippe, Dongier; Arturo, Muente-Kunigami and Christine, Zhen-Wei Qiang. *The Global Opportunity in IT-Based Services: Assessing and Enhancing Country Competitiveness*. Washington, DC: World Bank, 2010.

[135] TCS. "*Infineon: Reliable Backing for Corporate Planning.*" TCS Case Studies, December 14, 2010. http://www.tcs.com/resources/case studies/Pages/default.aspx.

[136] ———. "*TCS Enters into a Long-term Engagement with Infineon Technologies AG.*" News release, March 10, 2009. http://www.tcs.com/news events/press releases/Pages/TCS-engagementInfineon-Technologies-AG.aspx.

[137] United Nations Statistical Commission. *Manual on Statistics of International Trade in Services 2010 (MSITS 2010): Draft Unedited Version*. New York: United Nations,

February 2010. http://unstats.un.org/unsd/tradeserv/TFSITS/MSITS/MSITS2010%20%20for%20the%20SC%20 201 0%20at%202.22.20 1 0.pdf.

[138] U.S. Department of Commerce (USDOC). U. S. Bureau of the Census. "2007 NAICS Definition: Sector 54; Professional, Scientific and Technical Services; 54151; Computer Systems Design and Related Services." *North American Industry Classification System*, 2007. http://factfinder.census.gov/servlet/MetadataBrowserServlet? type=codeRefandid =54 15 1andibtype=NAICS2007anddsspName=ECN 2007and lang=en.

[139] ———. 2007 Nonemployer Statistics Database. http://censtats.census.gov/cgibin/nonemployer/nonsect.pl (accessed December 29, 2010).

[140] USDOC. Bureau of Economic Analysis (BEA). International Services Surveys Conducted by the Bureau of Economic Analysis: Reporting Requirements for Forms BE-9, BE-29, BE-30, BE-37, BE-45, BE-120, BE-125, BE-140, BE-150, BE-180, BE-185. January 2010. http://www.bea.gov/surveys/pdf/surveysu.pdf.

[141] ———. *Quarterly Survey of Transactions in Selected Services and Intangible Assets with Foreign Persons.* Form BE-125, January 2010. http://www.bea.gov/surveys/pdf/be125.pdf.

[142] ———. *Survey of Current Business,* 90, no. 10 (October 2010).

[143] ———. "Table 7: Business, Professional and Technical Services." In U. S. *International Services,* 2006– 09. http://www.bea.gov/international/internationalservices.htm.

[144] ———. "Table 9: Services Supplied to Foreign Persons by U. S. MNCs through Their MOFAs, Industry of Affiliate by Country of Affiliate." In U. S. *International Services,*" 2006–08. http://www.bea.gov/ international/international service s.htm.

[145] ———. "Table 10: Services Supplied to U. S. Persons by Foreign MNCs through Their MOUSAs, Industry of Affiliate by Country of UBO." In U. S. *International Services,* 2006–08. http://www.bea.gov/ international/international service s.htm.

[146] ———. "*Value Added by Industry as a Percentage of Gross Domestic Product.*" Interactive tables: Gross-Domestic-Product-by-Industry Accounts. December 14, 2010. http://www.bea.gov/industry/gpotables/gpo_action.cfm?anon=872106andtable_id= 26752andformat _type=0 (accessed January 21, 2011).

[147] ———. "Where Can I Find Information about Computer Services Supplied to Foreign Markets by U. S. Companies or Individuals?" *Frequently Asked Questions*, no. 556 (November 3, 2010). http://www.bea.gov/faq/index.cfm?faqid=556andsearchQuery=and start=0andcat id=0.

[148] U.S. Department of Labor (DOL). Bureau of Labor Statistics (BLS). Employment, Hours and Earnings— National Database. http://data.bls.gov/cgi-bin/dsrv?ce (accessed January 21, 2011).

[149] West, Joel. "*Carly Reconsidered (II): She Was Right, I Was Wrong.*" *Open IT Strategies* (blog), February 15, 2010. http://blog.openitstrategies.com/2010/02/carly-reconsidered-ii-i-was-wrong.html

[150] World Trade Organization (WTO). Council for Trade in Services (CTS). "Communication from Albania, Australia, Canada, Chile, Colombia, Croatia, the European Communities, Hong Kong China, Japan, Mexico, Norway, Peru, the Separate Customs Territory of Taiwan, Penghu, Kinmen and Matsu, Turkey and the United

States: Understanding on the Scope of Coverage of CPC 84— Computer and Related Services." TN/S/W/60, S/CSC/W/5 1, January 26, 2007.

[151] WTO Secretariat. *"Computer and Related Services: Background Note by the Secretariat."* S/C/W/300, June 2009.

[152] Culbert, Kevin. *Colleges and Universities in the United States.* IBIS World, December 2010.

[153] Douglass, John Aubrey. *"Higher Education Budgets and the Global Recession: Tracking Varied National Responses and Their Consequences."* Center for Studies in Higher Education. Research and Occasional Papers Series, CSHE.4. 10, February 2010 http://cshe.berkeley.edu/publications/docs/ROPS.5Douglass.HEGlobalRecession.3.13.10.pdf.

[154] *Economist.* "The Brains Business," September 8, 2005.

[155] ———. *"Foreign University Students: Will They Still Come?"* August 5, 2010.

[156] ———. *"Globalisation and Higher Education: Learning without Frontiers,"* October 28, 2010.

[157] ———. *"Reassuringly Expensive,"* March 10, 2011.

[158] ———. *"Repointing the Spires,"* January 27, 2005.

[159] ———. *"Universities: Can Foreigners Prop Them Up?"* January 15, 2009.

[160] ———. *"Wandering Scholars,"* September 8, 2005.

[161] Fischer, Karin. "American Colleges Look to Private Sector for Global Recruiting." *Chronicle of Higher Education,* May 30, 2010.

[162] ———. "China Props Up Foreign Students' Numbers in U. S. " *Chronicle of Higher Education,* November 19, 2010.

[163] ———. "Ethical Debates Surround U. S. College's Use of International Recruiters." *USA Today,* June 1, 2010.

[164] Hannah, Mario. "Indian Students Continue to Shun Australia Visas." Global Visas, November 30, 2010. http://www.globalvisas.com/news/indian students continue to shun australia visas2777.html.

[165] Institute of International Education (IIE). *"Open Doors 2010 Fast Facts."* Data summary, released at news conference, Washington, DC, November 15, 2010.

[166] Johnson, Nicholas; Phil Oliff and Erica Williams. *"An Update on State Budget Cuts."* Center on Budget and Policy Priorities, February 9, 2011. http://www.cbpp.org/files/3-13-08sfp.pdf.

[167] Kakuchi, Suvendrini. "Japan: University Internationalization Scaled Back." *University World News,* November 28, 2010. http://www.universityworldnews.com.

[168] Koh Chin, Hey-Kyung, ed. *Open Doors.* New York, NY: Institute for International Education, 2004.

[169] Maslen, Geoff. "Australia: Alarming Fall in Chinese Student Numbers." *University World News,* November 7, 2010. http://www.university worldnews.com/.

[170] ———. "Australia: Uncertain Times Ahead for Universities." *University World News,* January 9, 2011. http://www.universityworldnews.com/.

[171] McNichol, Elizabeth; Phil, Oliff and Nicholas, Johnson. "States Continue to Feel Recession's Impact." Center on Budget and Policy Priorities, March 9, 2011. http://www.cbpp.org/cms/? fa=viewandid=711.

[172] NAFSA: Association of International Educators. *"The Economic Benefits of International Education to the United States: A Statistical Analysis."* Summary data,

[173] ———. "*The Economic Benefits of International Education to the United States for the 2004–2005 Academic Year: A Statistical Analysis.*" Summary data. http://www.nafsa.org//File/ /eis2005/usa.pdf (accessed December 2, 2010).

[174] ———. "*The Economic Benefits of International Education to the United States for the 2005–2006 Academic Year: A Statistical Analysis.*" Summary data. http://www.nafsa.org/ /File/ / eis2006/usa.pdf (accessed December 2, 2010).

[175] ———. "*The Economic Benefits of International Education to the United States for the 2006–2007 Academic Year: A Statistical Analysis.*" Summary data. http://www.nafsa.org/public_policy.sec/ international education 1/eis 2007/ (accessed December 2, 2010).

[176] ———. "*The Economic Benefits of International Education to the United States for the 2007–2008 Academic Year: A Statistical Analysis.*" Summary data. http://www.nafsa.org/ /File/ / eis08/Guam.pdf (accessed December 2, 2010).

[177] ———. "*The Economic Benefits of International Education to the United States for the 2008–2009 Academic Year: A Statistical Analysis.*" Summary data. http://www.nafsa.org/publicpolicy/default.aspx?id= 17174 (accessed December 2, 2010).

[178] ———. "*The Economic Benefits of International Education to the United States for the 2009–2010 Academic Year: A Statistical Analysis.*" Summary data. www.nafsa.org/ /File/ /eis2010/Guam.pdf (accessed December 2, 2010).

[179] OECD. Center for Educational Research and Innovation. "*Highlights from Education at a Glance 2010*," 2010. http://www.oecd-ilibrary.org/education/highlights-from-education-at-a-glance-2010 eag highlights-20 1 0-en;jsessionid=7ap5uoc5uhoe.delta.

[180] ———. Program on Institutional Management in Higher Education. "The Post-Crisis Context: Investing in Tertiary Education for Sustainable Growth." *IMHE Info*, August 2010, 3. http://www.oecd.org/dataoecd /56/34/45878140.pdf

[181] Redden, Elizabeth. "A Shifting International Mix." *Inside Higher Ed*, August 25, 2010. http://www.insidehighered.com/news/2010/08/ 25/chinese.

[182] ———. "Downturn Down Under." *Inside Higher Ed*, November 30, 2010. http://www.insidehighered.com/news/2010/11/30/australia.

[183] ———. "*Ethical Debates Surround U. S. College's Use of International Recruiters.*" USA Today, June 1, 2010.

[184] Stripling, Jack. "……………*More Tuition Struggles Projected.*" *Inside Higher Ed*, December 17, 2010. http://www.insidehighered.com/news/2010/12/17/moody_s_forecasts_falling_tuition_revenues_a t colleges.

[185] United Nations Education, Scientific and Cultural Organization (UNESCO). Institute for Statistics (UIS). *Global Education Digest 2009: Comparing Education Statistics across the World.* Montreal, Quebec, Canada: UNESCO Institute for Statistics, 2009. http://www.uis.unesco.org/template/pdf/ged/2009/GED 2009 EN.pdf.

[186] ———. *Global Education Digest 2010: Comparing Education Statistics across the World.* Montreal, Quebec, Canada: UNESCO Institute for Statistics, 2010. http://www.uis.unesco.org/template/pdf/ged/2010/GED 2010 EN.pdf.

[187] U.S. Department of Commerce (USDOC). Bureau of Economic Analysis (BEA). *Survey of Current Business* 90, no. 10 (October 2010).

[188] VanDuzer, J. Anthony. "Navigating between the Poles: Unpacking the Debate on the Implications for Development of GATS Obligations Relating to Health and Education

Services." In *Reforming the World Trading System: Legitimacy, Efficiency and Democratic Governance*, edited by Ernst- Ulrich Petersmann. Oxford: Oxford University Press, 2005.

[189] West, Charlotte. "Ripple Effects: The Bologna Process, Ten Years On." *International Educator*, November–December 2010.

[190] World Trade Organization (WTO). "*Services Signaling Conference: Report by the Chairman of the TNC.*" Job(08)/93, July 30, 2008. http://www.wto.org/english/news_e/news08_e/serv_ signallingjuly08 e.htm.

[191] Aiken, Linda H.; Robyn B. Cheung and Danielle M. Olds. "*Education Policy Initiatives to Address the Nurse Shortage in the United States.*" Health Affairs–Web Exclusive 28, no. 4 (June 2009): w646–56.

[192] Al-Dhibyani, Falih. "*Demand for Foreign Health Workers to Increase.*" Saudi Gazette, February 7, 2011.

[193] Al-Maskari, Fatma. "*Lifestyle Diseases: An Economic Burden on the Health Services.*" UNChronicle 47, no. 2 (2010). http://www.un.org/wcm/content/site/chronicle/home/archive/issues2010/achieving_global_health/economicburdenonhealthservices?ctnscroll_articleContainerList= 1_0andc tnlistpagination articleContainerList=true.

[194] American Association of Colleges of Nursing (AACN). "*Nursing Shortage Fact Sheet*," September 20, 2010. http://www.aacn.nche. edu/media/pdf/NrsgShortageFS.pdf.

[195] Anstett, Patricia. "*Canadians Visit U. S. to Get Health Care.*" Detroit Free Press, August 20, 2009.

[196] Association of American Medical Colleges (AAMC). "*AAMC Releases New Physician Shortage Estimates Post-Reform.*" News alert, September 30, 2010.

[197] Avila, Oscar. "Mexico/USA Spending: Mexico Is the New Dental Destination for Americans." *Chicago Tribune*, March 24, 2009.

[198] Bach, Christopher L. "Annual Revision of the U. S. International Accounts 1991–2004." *Survey of Current Business* (Bureau of Economic Analysis, U. S. Department of Commerce), July 2005: 54–67.

[199] ———. "U.S. International Transactions, Revised Estimates for 1982–98." *Survey of Current Business* (Bureau of Economic Analysis, U. S. Department of Commerce), July 1999: 60–74.

[200] Bastida, Elena; H. Shelton Brown and José A. Pagán. "Health Insurance Coverage and Health Care Utilization along the U. S. -Mexico Border: Evidence from the Border Epidemiologic Study on Aging." In *The Health of Aging Hispanics: The Mexican-Origin Population*, edited by Jacqueline L. Angel and Keith E. Whitfield, 222–34. New York, NY: Springer, 2007.

[201] Bitrán, Ricardo; Liliana Escobar and Patricia Gassibe. "After Chile's Health Reform: Increase in Coverage and Access, Decline in Hospitalization and Death Rates." *Health Affairs* 29, no. 12 (December 2010): 2161–70.

[202] Bloom, David E. and David Canning. "*Population Health and Economic Growth.*" Commission on Growth and Development. Working Paper No. 24, 2008.

[203] Board of Governors of the Federal Reserve System. St. Louis Federal Reserve. "*U.S./U.K Foreign Exchange Rate*," April 1, 2011.

[204] Boseley, Sarah. "*Health Worker Shortage is a Truly Global Crisis.*" Guardian UK, January 18, 2011. Buchanan, Michael. "Doctor Shortage Sees New Recruitment Drive

in India." *BBCNews*, June 1, 2010. Bureau van Dijk. Orbis Companies Database. https://orbis.bvdep.com (accessed January 31, 2011).

[205] ———. *Zephyr Mergers and Acquisitions Database.* https://zephyr.bvdep.com (accessed February 10, 2011).

[206] Byrd, Theresa L. and Jon G. Law. "Cross-border Utilization of Health Care Services by United States Residents Living near the Mexican Border." *Pan American Journal of Public Health,* 26, no. 2 (2009): 95–100.

[207] Canadian Nurses Association. "*Tested Solutions for Eliminating Canada's Registered Nurse Shortage,*" May 2009. http://www.cna-nurses.ca/CNA/issues/hhr/default e.aspx.

[208] Cattaneo, Olivier. "Health without Borders: International Trade for Better Health Systems and Services." In *International Trade in Services: New Trends and Opportunities for Developing Countries,* edited by Olivier Cattaneo, Michael Engman, Sebastián Sáez and Robert M. Stern, 99–140. Washington, DC: World Bank, 2010.

[209] Center for Disease Control and Prevention. "*Chronic Disease Prevention and Health Promotion,*" July 7, 2010. http://www.cdc.gov/ chronicdisease/overview/index.htm.

[210] Cortez, Nathan. "Recalibrating the Legal Risks of Cross-Border Health Care." *Yale Journal of Health Policy, Law and Ethics,* 10, no.1 (2010). http://papers.ssrn.com/sol3/papers.cfm?abstract id= 1424788.

[211] Crone, Robert K. "Flat Medicine? Exploring Trends in the Globalization of Health Care." *Academic Medicine* 83, no. 2 (2008): 117–21.

[212] Dall, Timothy M.; Yiduo Zhang; Yaozhu J. Chen; William W. Quick; Wenya G. Yang and Jeanene Fogli. "The Economic Burden of Diabetes." *Health Affairs,* 29, no. 2 (February 2010): 297–303.

[213] Daswani, Kavita. "My You Look Rested: Cosmetic Surgery for Foreigners." *WWD Scoop,* September 29, 2008 (posted on the Beverly Hills Institute of Aesthetic and Reconstructive Surgery Web site). http://www.bevhills.com/media/print/my-you-look-rested/.

[214] Deardorff, Alan V. "*The Economics of Government Market Intervention and Its International Dimension.*" University of Michigan. School of Public Policy. Research Seminar in International Economics Discussion paper no. 455, February 10, 2000.

[215] Dumont, Jean-Christophe, Pascal Zurn, Jody Church and Christine LeThi. "*International Mobility of Health Professionals and Health Workforce Management in Canada.*" OECD Health Working Papers No. 40, 2008.

[216] *Economic Times.* "Ethiopia Woos Indian Hospitals to Set Up Branches," June 18, 2010.

[217] Economist Intelligence Unit (EIU). "Asia and Australasia: Healthcare Outlook." *Healthcare Briefing,* June 14, 2010.

[218] ———. "United Kingdom: Healthcare and Pharmaceuticals Report." *Healthcare Briefing,* November 9, 2010.

[219] ———. "World: Healthcare Outlook." *Industry Briefing,* September 28, 2010.

[220] ———. "World: Healthcare Outlook." *Industry Briefing,* December 9, 2010.

[221] European Central Bank. "*Euro Exchange Rates USD,*" April 11, 2011. http://www.ecb.int/stats/exchange/eurofxref/html/eurofxref-graph-usd.en.html.

[222] European Commission. Eurostat. "*Impact of the Economic Crisis on Unemployment,*" February 9, 2011. http://epp.eurostat.ec.europa.eu/ statistics explained/index.php/ Impact of the economic crisis o n unemployment.

[223] Fakkar, Galal. "Health Ministry to Hire 3,000 Foreign Doctors." *Arab News*, October 12, 2010. Feder, Barnaby. "Hip Surgery with a Future." *New York Times*, April 14, 2007.
[224] Fields, Robin. "God Help You. You're on Dialysis." *The Atlantic*, December 2010.
[225] *Global Health Resources*. "International Factoid: Diabetes in the Middle East and North Africa," February 24, 2011.
[226] Greene, Jay. "Canadian Patients Give Detroit Hospitals a Boost." *Crain's Detroit Business*, April 18, 2008.
[227] HCA, Inc. "About Our Company," n.d. http://hcahealthcare.com/about.
[228] HCA International. "*Key Facts and Figures*," n.d. http://www.hcainternational.com/about-hca-key-factsand-figures.asp.
[229] Health Canada. "*Health Care System Delivery*," October 7, 2005. http://www.hc-sc.gc.ca/hcssss/delivery-prestation/index-eng.php.
[230] Helble, Matthias. "The Movement of Patients across Borders: Challenges and Opportunities for Public Health." *Bulletin of the World Health Organization*, November 26, 2010.
[231] Herman, Lior. "*Assessing International Trade in Healthcare Services.*" European Centre for International Political Economy. ECIPE Working Paper No. 03/2009, 2009.
[232] Holahan, John. "The 2007–09 Recession and Health Insurance Coverage." *Health Affairs, 30*, no. 1 (January 2011): 145–52.
[233] Iglehart, John K. "Despite Tight Budgets, Boosting U. S. Health Workforce May Be Policy That Is 'Just Right.'" *Health Affairs*, 30, no. 2 (February 2011): 191–92.
[234] Institute for Population Health Policy. "*Use of Health Care in the US-Mexico Border.*" University of Texas—Pan American. Research Brief 09-02, February 2009.
[235] *International Medical Travel Journal (IMTJ)*. "China: China Opens the Door for Foreign Healthcare Providers," January 12, 2011.
[236] ———. "*Mexico, USA: Mexico Expects More Medical Tourists As U. S. Outbound Medical Tourism Stagnates,*" October 21, 2010.
[237] ———. "*USA: U. S. Hospitals Promoting Inbound and Domestic Medical Tourism,*" January 19, 2011. ———. "USA/Mexico: Aetna Introduces New Cross-Border Health Insurance," May 20, 2010. KPMG. "The Future of Global Healthcare Delivery and Management," 2010.
[238] Lee, Olivia F. and Tim R. V. Davis. "International Patients: A Lucrative Market for U. S. Hospitals." *Health Marketing Quarterly,* 22, no. 1 (2004): 41–56.
[239] Lim, Teck-Onn; Adrian Goh; Yam-Ngo Lim; Zaki Morad Mohamed Zaher and Abu Bakar Suleiman. "How Public and Private Reforms Dramatically Improved Access to Dialysis Therapy in Malaysia." *Health Affairs* 29, no. 12 (December 2010): 2214–21.
[240] Lusardi, Annamaria; Daniel J. Schneider and Peter Tufano. "*The Economic Crisis and Medical Care Usage.*" National Bureau of Economic Research. Working Paper no. 15843, March 2010.
[241] Ma, Sai and Neeraj Sood. "*A Comparison of the Health Systems in China and India.*" RAND Center for Asia Pacific Policy. Occasional Paper, 2008.
[242] Martin, Anne; David Lassman; Lekha Wittle; Aaron Catlin and the National Health Expenditure Accounts Team. "Recession Contributes to Slowest Annual Rate of Increase in Health Spending in Five Decades." *Health Affairs, 30*, no. 1 (January 2011): 11–22.

[243] *Modern Healthcare*. "10 Largest Healthcare Systems, By Revenue," June 7, 2010.

[244] Mortensen, Jon. "*International Trade in Health Services: Assessing the Trade and the Trade-offs.*" Danish Institute for International Studies. Working Paper no. 2008/11, 2008.

[245] Pearson, Thomas A. "Cardiovascular Disease: Have We Really Made Progress?" *Health Affairs,* 26, no. 1 (January/February 2007): 49–60.

[246] Peng, Tina. "Ultimate Outsourcing." *Newsweek*, November 19, 2008.

[247] PricewaterhouseCoopers. "*Build and Beyond: The Revolution of Healthcare PPPs.*" Health Research Institute, December 2010.

[248] ———. "Emerging Trends in Chinese Healthcare: The Impact of a Rising Middle Class," 2010.

[249] Prince, Rosa. "*Recession Sees First Fall in Private Health Spending in 20 Years.*" *The Telegraph*, April 4, 2009. http://www.telegraph.co.uk/health/healthnews/5100101/Recession-sees-first-fall-in-privatehealth-spending-in-20-years.html.

[250] Rivera, José O.; Melchor Ortiz and Victor Cardenas. "Cross-Border Purchase of Medications and Health Care in a Sample of Residents of El Paso, Texas and Ciudad Juarez, Mexico." *Journal of the National Medical Association,* 101, no. 2 (February 2009), 167–73.

[251] Robert Wood Johnson Foundation. "*Nursing Study Analyzes Trends and Impact of Foreign-Educated Nurses on U. S. Health Care System,*" September 2007. http://www.rwjf.org/reports/grr/052892.htm.

[252] Ross, Lester and Tao Xu. "*China Opens the Door Wider to Private and Foreign Investment in Healthcare.*" *Legal Insights* (WilmerHale), December 17, 2010.

[253] Rundle, Rhonda L. "Europeans Take Beauty Trip to U. S. " *Wall Street Journal*, July 8, 2008.

[254] Scheffler, Richard, M.; Chris Brown Mahoney, Brent, D. Fulton, Mario R. Dal Poz and Alexander S. Preker. "Estimates of Health Care Professional Shortages in Sub-Saharan Africa by 2015." *Health Affairs–Web Exclusive,* 28, no. 3–4 (August 2009): w849–w862.

[255] Schoen, Cathy; Robin, Osborn; Sabrina, K.H. How; Michelle, M. Doty and Jordan Peugh. "In Chronic Condition: Experiences of Patients with Complex Health Care Needs, In Eight Countries, 2008." *Health Affairs – Web Exclusive,* 28, no. 1–2 (November 13, 2008): w1–w16.

[256] Statistics Canada. "Study: Canada's Employment Downturn." *The Daily*, November 12, 2009. http://www.statcan.gc.ca/daily-quotidien/091112/ dq091112a-eng.htm.

[257] Steenhusyen, Julie and Kate Kelland. "*Obesity Epidemic Risks Heart Disease 'Tsunami.'*" Reuters, February 4, 2011.

[258] *Straits Times*. "Use of Medisave Overseas," February 10, 2010.

[259] Su, Dejun; Chad Richardson; Ming Wen and José Pagán. "Cross-Border Utilization of Health Care: Evidence from a Population-Based Study in South Texas." *Health Services Research*, December 15, 2010.

[260] Suhrcke, Marc; Martin McKee; Regina Sauto Arce; Svetla Tsolova and Jørgen Mortensen. "*The Contribution of Health to the Economy in the European Union.*" Health and Consumer Protection Directorate-General. European Commission. Luxembourg: Office for Official Publications of the European Communities, August 23, 2005.

[261] Swiss Re. "To Your Health: Diagnosing the State of Healthcare and the Global Private Medical Insurance Industry." *Sigma*, 2007, no. 6.

[262] United Nations (UN). UN Service Trade Database (accessed February 21, 2011). http://unstats.un.org/unsd/ServiceTrade/default.aspx.

[263] U.S. Department of Commerce (USDOC). Bureau of Economic Analysis (BEA). *Foreign Direct Investment in the U. S. : Balance of Payments and Direct Investment Position Data.* "Industry Detail – Position on a Historical-Cost Basis," 2005–09. http://www.bea.gov/ international/di1fdibal.htm.

[264] ———. *Survey of Current Business,* 90, no. 10 (October 2010): 18–60. http://www.bea.gov/scb/toc/1010cont.htm.

[265] ———. U. S. *Direct Investment Abroad: Balance of Payments and Direct Investment Position Data.* "Industry Detail — Position on a Historical-Cost Basis," 2005–09. http://www.bea.gov/international/ di1usdbal.htm.

[266] ———. U. S. *International Services.* "*Table 9: Services Supplied to Foreign Persons by U. S. MNCs Through Their MOFAs*," 2004–05 and 2006–08. http://www.bea.gov/international/international service s.htm.

[267] ———. U. S. *International Services.* "*Table 10: Services Supplied to U. S. Persons by Foreign MNCs Through Their MOUSAs*," 2002–05 and 2006–08. http://www.bea.gov/international/international service s.htm.

[268] ———. "*Value Added by Industry as a Percentage of Gross Domestic Product.*" Interactive tables: Gross-Domestic-Product-By-Industry Accounts, December 14, 2010 (accessed February 6, 2011).

[269] U.S. Federal Trade Commission. "*Maintaining Competition, FTC Allows Fresenius' $3.5 Billion Deal to Buy Rival Dialysis Provider Renal Care Group.*" News release, March 30, 2006.

[270] U.S. International Trade Commission, *Caribbean Region: Review of Economic Growth and Development.* USITC Publication 4000. Washington, DC: USITC, May 2008.

[271] Waeger, Patricia. "*Trade in Health Services: An Analytical Framework.*" Kiel Institute for the World Economy. Advanced Studies in International Economic Policy Research. Working Paper no. 441, October 2008.

[272] Warner, David C. and Lauren R. Jahnke. "*U.S.-Mexico Mode 2 Imports and Exports of Healthcare Services.*" Report to the Organisation for Economic Co-operation and Development, March 3, 2010.

[273] Weisfeldt, Myron and Susan J. Zieman. "Advances in the Prevention and Treatment of Cardiovascular Disease." *Health Affairs,* 26, no. 1 (January/February 2007): 25–37.

[274] World Bank. World dataBank Database. http://databank.worldbank. org/ddp/home.do (accessed December 13, 2010).

[275] World Diabetes Foundation. "Diabetes Facts," February 5, 2010. http://www.worlddiabetesfoundation.org/composite-35.htm.

[276] World Health Organization (WHO). "*Chronic Diseases and Health Promotion,*" n.d. http://www.who.int/chp/en/ (accessed January 31, 2011).

[277] ———. "*Health Topics: Chronic Diseases,*" n.d. http://www.who.int/ topics/chronic_diseases/en/ (accessed January 31, 2011).

[278] ———. "*Migration of Health Workers,*" July 2010. http://www.who.int/mediacentre/factsheets/fs30 1/en/index.html.

[279] ———. Global Health Observatory (GHO) Database. http://apps.who.int/ghodata/ (accessed December 30, 2010).
[280] ———. National Health Accounts. "*Glossary of Terms and Financing Flows*," n.d. http://www.who.int/nha/glossary/en/index.html (accessed January 25, 2011).
[281] ———. National Health Accounts. "United Kingdom," March 2010. http://www.who.int/nha/country/gbr.pdf (accessed February 9, 2011).
[282] ———. Regional Office for Europe. *The European Health Report: Health and Health Systems*. Copenhagen, Denmark: WHO, 2009.
[283] Allen and Overy. "People and Offices: Brazil." http://www.allenovery.com/ AOWEB/PeopleOffices/Country.aspx?countryID=18603andprefLangID=4 10 (accessed December 8, 2010).
[284] ———. Web site. "People and Offices: India Group." http://www.allenovery.com/AOWEB/PeopleOffices/Country.aspx?countryID=18853 andprefLangID=41 0 (accessed February 1, 2011).
[285] Altman Weil, Inc. "*2010 Chief Legal Officer Survey: An Altman Weil Flash Survey*," 2010. http://www.altmanweil.com/dir_docs/resource/ 473ed6e1-1c5d-4a8d-ae00-085ad1b2bd14 document.pdf.
[286] *American Lawyer*. "Behind the Numbers: Noteworthy Trends in This Year's AM Law 100 Report," May 2010, 96–101.
[287] ———. "*Field Reports*," October 1, 2009. http://www.law.com/ jsp/tal/PubArticle TAL.jsp?id=1 202433874427 [fee required].
[288] ———. "*The Future is Now: The Booming Brazilian Market*" (video), October 1, 2010. http://www.law.com/jsp/tal/PubArticleTAL.jsp?id= 1202472726561.
[289] ———. "*The Global 100 2010: The World's Highest-Grossing Law Firms*," October 1, 2010. http://www.law.com/jsp/tal/PubArticleTAL. jsp?id=1202471809600.
[290] Association of Corporate Counsel and Altman Weil, Inc. "2005 Chief Legal Officer Survey: The Opinions of Chief Legal Offices on Issues of Importance," 2005. http://www.altmanweil.com/dir_docs/resource/ 0b629558-1f19-4ee5-a525-8b7 1 70a8da73 document.pdf.
[291] Baxter, Brian. "*India Again Closes Door on Foreign Firms.*" *American Lawyer*, September 29, 2010. http://amlawdaily.typepad.com/ amlawdaily/2010/09/india-foreign-firms.html.
[292] Blakely, Rhys and Alex Spence. "Brief for India's Outsourcing Lawyers: Keep it Cheap." *The Times* (London), January 15, 2010. http://business.timesonline.co.uk/tol/business/industry_sectors/ support services/article6988773.ece.
[293] Breitman, Rachel. "*Overseas Practices Keep British Firms Afloat.*" *American Lawyer*, September 9, 2008. http://www.law.com/ jsp/article.jsp?id=1202424375522andslreturn =1and.
[294] Bronstad, Amanda. "Asia Practice Special Report." *The National Law Journal*, November 16, 2010. http://www.law.com/jsp/article.jsp?id= 1202474903864andAsia_Practice_Special_Report_Competi tion Heats Up in China.
[295] Burk, Bernard A. and David McGowan. "*Big but Brittle: Economic Perspectives on the Future of the Law Firm in the New Economy*." Rock Center for Corporate Governance at Stanford University. Working Paper No. 87, August 2010.
[296] Cattaneo, Olivier and Peter Walkenhorst. "Legal Services: Does More Trade Rhyme with Better Justice?" In *International Trade in Services: New Trends and Opportunities*

for *DevelopingCountries*, edited by Oliver Cattaneo, Michael Engman, Sebastián Sáez and Robert M. Stern, 67– 97. Washington, DC: World Bank, 2010.

[297] Combs, Drew. "No Place to Hide." *The American Lawyer*, June 1, 2010. http://www.law.com/jsp/tal/ PubArticleTAL.jsp?id= 1202458447280.

[298] Cresswell, Rosie. "JP Morgan Looks to Brazil." *Latin Lawyer*, October 2010. http://www.pinheironeto.com.br/upload/tb_pinheironeto_release/pdf/281010144127JP Morgan_L L.pdf.

[299] Culbert, Kevin. "Law Firms in the US: 54111." *IBIS World Industry Report*, September 2010.

[300] Datamonitor. "*Industry Profile: Global Legal Services*." EBSCOhost Business Source Complete Database, December 2006.

[301] ———. "*Industry Profile: Global Legal Services*." EBSCOhost Business Source Complete Database, November 2007.

[302] ———. "*Industry Profile: Global Legal Services*." EBSCOhost Business Source Complete Database, July 2010.

[303] ———. "*Industry Profile: Legal Services in Asia-Pacific*." EBSCOhost Business Source Complete Database, July 2010.

[304] ———. "*Industry Profile: Legal Services in Europe*." EBSCOhost Business Source Complete Database, July 2010.

[305] ———. "*Industry Profile: Legal Services in France*." EBSCOhost Business Source Complete Database, July 2010.

[306] ———. "*Industry Profile: Legal Services in Germany*." EBSCOhost Business Source Complete Database, July 2010.

[307] ———. "*Industry Profile: Legal Services in Japan*." EBSCOhost Business Source Complete Database, July 2010.

[308] ———. "*Industry Profile: Legal Services in the United Kingdom*." EBSCOhost Business Source Complete Database, July 2010.

[309] ———. "*Industry Profile: Legal Services in the United States*." EBSCOhost Business Source Complete Database, July 2010.

[310] Dewey and LeBoeuf. "*Abu Dhabi*." http://deweyleboeuf.com/en/ Services/WhereWeWork/Locations/AbuDhabi (accessed December 8, 2010).

[311] DiPetro, Daniel. "Priced to Sell." *American Lawyer*, May 1, 2010. http://www.law.com/jsp/tal/PubArticleTAL.jsp?id=1202448396657 [fee required].

[312] DuPont Legal. "Primary Service Providers." http://www.dupontlegalmodel.com/psp-list/ (accessed January 25, 2010).

[313] *Economist*. "Laid-off Lawyers, Cast-off Consultants," January 21, 2010. http://www.economist.com/node/15330702?story id= 15330702.

[314] Freshfields Bruckhaus Deringer. "Freshfields Advises Geely on Its $1.8 Billion Acquisition of Volvo Car Corporation." http://www.freshfields.com/news/media releases/mediarelease.asp?id=2064.

[315] Goldhaber, Michael D. "*The Global 100 2010: Sound as a Pound*." American Lawyer, October 1, 2010. http://www.law.com/ jsp/tal/PubArticleTAL.jsp?id=1202472314818.

[316] Government of China, Ministry of Commerce, Department of Trade in Services. "*Developments in the Legal Services Industry*." http://tradeinservices.mofcom.gov.cn/upload/2010/10/22/ 1287714390688 83889.pdf (accessed January 12, 2011).

[317] Haberbeck andreas. "Bridging the Gulf." *The Lawyer*, May 28, 2007. http://www.thelawyer.com/bridging-the-gulf/126155.article.

[318] Heineman, Ben W. and William F. Lee. "The Time Has Come." *American Lawyer*, October 1, 2009. http://www.law.com/jsp/tal/PubArticle TAL.jsp?id=1202433957821 [fee required].

[319] Herzog Fox and Neeman. "*Practice Areas: Banking and Finance.*" http://www.hfn.co.il/ enUS/Practice83.aspx (accessed December 20, 2010).

[320] Hildebrandt Baker Robbins and Citi Private Bank. "*2010 Client Advisory*," March 3, 2010. http://www.hbrconsulting.com/ 2010ClientAdvisory.

[321] Hogan Lovells. "*Offices: Abu Dhabi.*" http://www.hoganlovells. com/abu-dhabi/ (accessed December 7, 2010).

[322] Hook, Alison. "*Sectoral Study on the Impact of Domestic Regulation on Trade in Legal Services.*" Paper prepared for the OECD-World Bank Sixth Services Expert Meeting: Domestic Regulation and Trade in Professional Services, Paris, France, February 15–16, 2007.

[323] IBIS World. "Attorney and Legal Services in China: 7421." *IBIS World Industry Report*, January 8, 2010.

[324] International Monetary Fund (IMF). World Economic Outlook Database. http://www.imf.org/external/pubs/ft/weo/2010/02/weodata/ index.aspx *(accessed April 4, 2011).*

[325] Johnson, Chris. "Letter from London." *American Lawyer*, September 17, 2010. http://amlawdaily.typepad.com/amlawdaily/2010/09/europefees.html.

[326] Jones Day. "*Offices: New Delhi.*" http://www.jonesday.com/newdelhi/ (accessed December 29, 2010).

[327] Jones, Leigh. "Big Firms Slashed Headcount at International Offices, NLJ 250 Shows." *The National Law Journal*, November 12, 2009. http://www.law.com/jsp/nlj/ PubArticleNLJ.jsp?id=1202435422952.

[328] ———. "Headcount Declined Sharply in New York, Atlanta and Philadelphia." *The National Law Journal*, November 10, 2009. http://www.law.com/jsp/nlj/PubArticle NLJ.jsp?id=1202435345819.

[329] ———. "So Long, Farewell." *The National Law Journal*, November 9, 2009.http://www.law.com/jsp/nlj/PubArticleNLJ.jsp?id=1202435251608.

[330] Jun He. "*About Us.*" http://www.junhe.com/en/profile1.asp? classid=5andmenu=1 (accessed December 7, 2010).

[331] Kessenides, Dimitra. "*The AM Law 100 2010: Too Big to Fail?*" *American Lawyer*, May 12, 2010. http://amlawdaily.typepad.com/ amlawdaily/2010/05/toobigtofail.html.

[332] King and Wood. "Offices." http://www.kingandwood.com/offices.aspx? language=en (accessed December 7, 2010).

[333] Kolz, Amy. "*No Easy Answers.*" *American Lawyer*, May 1, 2010. http://www.law.com/ jsp/tal/ PubArticleTAL.jsp?id= 1202448339080.

[334] Lamb, Patrick J. "25% Cut in In-House Legal Spending Translated to Even Deeper Cuts for Outside

[335] Legal Work." *ABA Journal*, October 27, 2010. http://www.abajournal.com/weekly/ article/25 cut in in-house legal spending translates to even deeper cuts for outsid?utm source =maestroandutm medium=emailandutm campaign=weekly email.

[336] Legal 500. "*Brazil.*" http://www.legal500.com/c/brazil/directory (accessed January 4, 2010)
[337] ———. "*Herzog Fox and Newman.*" http://www.legal500.com/firms/12299/offices/13928 (accessed December 20, 2010).
[338] ———. "*Saudi Arabia.*" http://www.legal500.com/c/saudi-arabia (accessed January 20, 2010).
[339] ———. "*Saudi Arabia: Legal market overview.*" http://www.legal500.com/c/saudi-arabia/legal-marketoverview (accessed December 20, 2010).
[340] *Legal Intelligencer.* "The New Firm Order," June 22, 2009. http://www.law.com/jsp/pa/PubArticlePA.jsp?id= 1202431088960.
[341] LexisNexis Research System. Martindale-Hubbell Law Directory (accessed December 8, 2010).
[342] Lin, Anthony. "Inside the Revolution." *American Lawyer,* October 1, 2010. http://www.law.com/jsp/tal/PubArticleTAL.jsp?id=1202472313481andslreturn=1andhbxlogin=1 [fee required].
[343] ———. "India: A Dream (Still) Deferred." *American Lawyer,* October 1, 2009. http://www.law.com/jsp/tal/PubArticleTAL.jsp?id=1202434045985andslreturn=1andhbx login=1 [fee required].
[344] ———. "Singapore: Feeling the West's Pain." *American Lawyer,* October 1, 2009. http://www.law.com/jsp/tal/PubArticleTAL.jsp?id= 1202433874886 [fee required].
[345] Lippe, Paul. "General Counsel to Cut Legal Spending Up to 25%: Catastrophe or Opportunity." *ABA Journal,* October 22, 2010. http://www.abajournal.com/weekly/article/general_counsel_legal_ spending cuts catastrophe or opportunity?utm source=maestroandutm medium=emailandutm ca mpaign=weekly email.
[346] Lloyd, Richard. "Storm Averted." *American Lawyer,* May 1, 2010. http://www.law.com/jsp/tal/PubArticleTAL.jsp?id=1202448399218 [fee required].
[347] ———. "Abu Dhabi: The Desert's New Hot Spot." *American Lawyer,* October 1, 2009. http://www.law.com/jsp/tal/PubArticleTAL.jsp?id= 1202433909901 *[*fee required].
[348] ———. "*The 2009 Global 100: The Great Game.*" *American Lawyer,* October 1, 2009. http://www.law.com/jsp/tal/PubArticleTAL.jsp?id= 1202433874460 [fee required].
[349] Marek, Lynne. "What to Expect in the Decade Ahead." *National Law Journal,* November 9, 2009. http://www.law.com/jsp/nlj/PubArticle NLJ.jsp?id=1202435210821 [fee required].
[350] Mayer Brown. "Offices: São Paulo." http://www.mayerbrown.com/saopaulo/ (accessed December 20, 2010).
[351] Mitev, Vesselin. "Small Firms, Solos Face Tough Economic Decisions." *New York Law Journal,* February 18, 2009. http://www.law.com/jsp/nylj/PubArticleNY.jsp?id =1202428344086.
[352] *National Law Journal.* "The 2009 NLF 250: The Nation's Biggest Firms Said Bon Voyage to more than 5,000 Lawyers," November 9, 2009. http://www.law.com/jsp/nlj/PubArticleNLJ.jsp?id=1202435209872andThe NLJ.
[353] Needles, Zack. "For Midsized Firms, Opportunities Abound." *Legal Intelligencer,* June 1, 2009. http://www.law.com/jsp/pa/PubArticlePA. jsp?id=1202431089288.
[354] *New Legal Review.* "Inside the DuPont Legal Model," May 11, 2010. http://www.cpaglobal.com/ newlegalreview/4377/inside dupont legal model.

[355] Passarella, Gina. "GCs Want Firms to Change with Times." *The Legal Intelligencer*, June 8, 2009. http://www.law.com/jsp/pa/PubArticle PA.jsp?id=1202431260925.

[356] ———. "Diamonds Are a Law Firm's Best Friend." *The Legal Intelligencer*, May 11, 2009. http://www.law.com/jsp/pa/PubArticle PA.jsp?id=1202430587522.

[357] ———. "For Large Firms, Alternative Billing Makes Inroads." *The Legal Intelligencer*, May 26, 2009. http://www.law.com/jsp/pa/PubArticlePA.jsp?id=1202430953666.

[358] ———. "Losing Lockstep, Piling on Partner Pressures." *The Legal Intelligencer*, May 18, 2009. http://www.law.com/jsp/pa/Pub ArticlePA.jsp?id=1202430756834.

[359] Passarella, Gina and Zack Needles. "After the Last Shoe Drops." *The Legal Intelligencer*, June 22, 2009. http://www.law.com/jsp/pa/PubArticlePA.jsp?id=1202431620239.

[360] Press, Aric and Greg Mulligan. "Lessons of the Am Law 100." *American Lawyer*, May 1, 2010. http://www.law.com/jsp/tal/PubArticleTAL.jsp? id=1202448340864.

[361] Ribstein, Larry E. "Death of Big Law." *Wisconsin Law Review, 2010*, no. 3 (July 12, 2010): 750–815.

[362] Rupp, Brian C. and Jae En Kim. "Korean Legal Services Set to Open Up." *National Law Journal*, February 26, 2008. http://www.law.com/jsp/article.jsp?id=1204026529251.

[363] Sawhney, Robert. "Entering the Emerging Markets of Asia: Insight for North American Law Firms." http://www.patrickmckenna.com/pdfs/Entering%20Emerging%20 Markets.pdf.

[364] Squire Sanders. "São Paulo." http://www.ssd.com/sao paulo/.

[365] Swift, James. "Singapore's Swing." *The Lawyer*, August 9, 2010. http://www.thelawyer.com/singapore'sswing/1 005245.article.

[366] Todd, Ross. "The Future Is Now." *American Lawyer*, October 1, 2010. http://www.law.com/jsp/ tal/PubArticleTAL.jsp?id= 1202472307554.

[367] United Nations (UN). *Manual on Statistics of International Trade in Services 2010*. Geneva, Luxembourg, New York, Paris, Washington, DC: 2010. http://unstats.un.org/unsd/statcom/doc10/BG-MSITS20 1 0.pdf.

[368] UN Statistics Division Web. "Detailed Structure and Explanatory Notes: CPC Ver.1.1 Code 821." http://unstats.un.org/unsd/cr/registry/ regcs.asp?Cl=16andLg=1andCo=821 (accessed February 25, 2011).

[369] U.S. Department of Commerce (USDOC). Bureau of Economic Analysis (BEA). *Survey of Current Business*, 90, no. 9 (September 2010).

[370] ———. *Survey of Current Business*, 90, no. 10 (October 2010).

[371] ———. "Table 7: Business, Professional and Technical Services." In *U. S. International Services: Cross-Border Trade 1986–2008 and Services Supplied through Affiliates, 1986–2007*. 2006–09 and 2001–05 datasets. http://www.bea.gov/international/ intlserv.htm (accessed December 16, 2010).

[372] ———. "Table 9: Services Supplied to Foreign Persons by U. S. MNCs through Their MOFAs," 2006–08 and 2001–05. In *U. S. International Services: Cross-Border Trade 1986–2008 and Services Supplied through Affiliates, 1986–2007*. http://www.bea.gov/international/intlserv.htm (accessed December 16, 2010).

[373] ———. "Table 10: Services Supplied to U. S. Persons by Foreign MNCs through Their MOUSAs," 2006–08 and 2001–05. In *U.S International Services: Cross-Border Trade*

1986–2008 and Services Supplied through Affiliates, 1986–2007. http://www.bea.gov/international/intlserv.htm (accessed December 16, 2010).

[374] USDOC. U. S. Census Bureau Web site. "Industry Statistics Sampler: NAICS 5411–Legal Services." http://www.census.gov/econ/ industry/def/d5411.htm (accessed January 3, 2011).

[375] USDOC. U. S. Commercial Service. *"Doing Business in Saudi Arabia: 2010 Country Commercial Guide for U. S. Companies,"* 2010. http://www.buyusainfo.net/docs/x_7168692.pdf.

[376] U.S. Department of Labor (DOL). Bureau of Labor Statistics (BLS). Current Employment Statistics Survey (National). http://www.bls.gov/ces/ (accessed September 29, 2010).

[377] U.S. International Trade Commission (USITC). *Small and Medium-Sized Enterprises: Characteristics and Performance.* USITC Publication 4189. Washington, DC: USITC, November 2010. http://www.usitc.gov/publications/332/pub4189.pdf.

[378] United States-Korea Free Trade Agreement, Annex II: Non-Conforming Measures for Services and Investment. http://www.ustr.gov/sites/ default/files/uploads/agreements/fta/korus/asset upload file355 12750.pdf

[379] USTR. "China." *2010 National Trade Estimate Report on Foreign Trade Barriers.* Washington, DC: USTR, 2010. http://www.ustr.gov/ sites/default/files/uploads/reports/2010/NTE/2010 NTE China final.pdf.

[380] ———. "India." *2010 National Trade Estimate Report on Foreign Trade Barriers.* Washington, DC: USTR, 2010. http://www.ustr.gov/sites/default/files/uploads/reports/2010/NTE/2010 NTE India final.pdf.

[381] ———. "Korea." *2010 National Trade Estimate Report on Foreign Trade Barriers.* Washington, DC: USTR, 2010. http://www.ustr.gov/sites/default/files/uploads/reports/2010/NTE/2010 NTE Korea final.pdf.

[382] ———. "Singapore." *2010 National Trade Estimate Report on Foreign Trade Barriers.* Washington, DC: USTR, 2010. http://www.ustr.gov/sites/default/files/uploads/reports/2010/NTE/2010 NTE Singapore final.pdf.

[383] Vinson and Elkins. "VandE Assists Sinopec International Petroleum Exploration and Production Corporation in its Acquisition of Addax Petroleum Corporation." News release, n.d. http://www.velaw.com/ resources/news_detail.aspx?id=15328 (accessed January 20, 2011).

[384] Wines, Michael. "China Bank I.P.O. Raises $19 Billion." *New York Times*, July 6, 2010. http://www.nytimes.com/2010/07/07/ business/global/07ipo.html.

[385] Zillman, Claire. "Brazil: The Waiting Game." *American Lawyer*, October 1, 2009. http://www.law.com/jsp/tal/PubArticleTAL.jsp?id= 1202434045738andslreturn=1and hbxlogin=1 [fee required].

End Notes

[1] Cross-border trade occurs when suppliers in one country sell services to consumers in another country, with people, information, or money crossing national boundaries in the process. Affiliate trade occurs when firms provide services to foreign consumers through affiliates established in host (i.e. foreign) countries.

[2] Beginning in 2008, the Recent Trends report has discussed the professional and infrastructure service subsectors in alternate years. This division allows more detailed analysis of the individual services industries. Professional

services are characterized as labor-intensive industries employing highly skilled and highly educated individuals in positions that frequently require specialized licensing or training. Infrastructure services are capital intensive, providing critical inputs to industrial activity and economic growth, and are consumed by every firm irrespective of economic sector. For the purposes of this report, infrastructure services include banking, insurance, securities, transportation, telecommunications, electric power, and retail services.

[3] For the computer services industry, sales through foreign affiliates are the predominant mode of supply.

[4] The discussions of individual service industries use a wide variety of industry specific data sources; as a result, the time periods discussed in these chapters reflect the most recent data available.

[5] In addition to the industries identified above, subsequent editions of *Recent Trends* may discuss other professional services, including accounting, auditing, and bookkeeping services; advertising services; architectural, engineering, and other technical services; and construction services. Beginning in 2008, the Recent Trends report has discussed the professional and infrastructure service subsectors in alternate years. This division allows for more detailed analysis of the individual industries. Professional services are characterized as labor-intensive industries, employing highly skilled and highly educated individuals in positions that frequently require specialized licensing or training. Infrastructure services are capital-intensive: they provide critical inputs to industrial activity and economic growth, and are consumed by every firm irrespective of economic sector. For the purposes of this report, infrastructure services include banking, insurance, securities, transportation, telecommunication, electric power, and retail services.

[6] BEA data are compiled from surveys of services directed to specific service industries or types of investment. For more information, see USDOC, BEA, *Survey of Current Business*, October 2010.

[7] Data on affiliate transactions lag those on cross-border services trade by one year. Thus, while analyses of cross-border trade data compare performance in 2009 to trends from 2004 through 2008, analyses of affiliate transactions compare performance in 2008 to trends from 2005 through 2007. Note also that in 2009, BEA changed its method of reporting affiliate trade data. New affiliate data report "services supplied," a measure that better reflects services output than the prior measure, "sales of services." The change is retroactive for data from years 2005–08. For more information, see USDOC, BEA, *Survey of Current Business*, October 2009, 34–36.

[8] For purposes of this report, Commission staff calculated labor productivity by dividing gross domestic product for each industry by the number of full-time equivalent employees.

[9] USDOC, BEA, "Real Value Added by Industry," May 25, 2010; USDOC, BEA, "Table 6.5D," August 5, 2010; USDOC, BEA, "Table 6.6D," August 5, 2010. Value added is a measure of an industry's contribution to gross domestic product; it is the difference between gross industry output and intermediate inputs.

[10] Cattaneo et al., *International Trade in Services*, 2010, 3.

[11] USDOC, BEA representative, telephone interview by USITC staff, February 25, 2009. The term "commercial services," used by the World Trade Organization (WTO), is like the term "private services"; both refer to services offered by the private, rather than the public, sector. WTO trade data are sourced from the International Monetary Fund (IMF).

[12] WTO, *International Trade Statistics 2010*, 2010, 189–91, table A8.

[13] Ibid., table A9.

[14] The $149.0 billion trade surplus estimated by the BEA differs from the $143.3 billion WTO estimate, presented above in the "Global Services Trade" section. The data are drawn from different sources, as both sets of data are not available in a single source. The WTO provides global services trade data whereas BEA provides U. S. services trade data.

[15] Values are reported before deductions for expenses and taxes, as gross values are most directly comparable across countries, industries, and firms.

[16] USDOC, BEA, *Survey of Current Business*, October 2010, 34. Travel services are measured through the purchase of goods and services while traveling abroad. Such items include, for example, food, lodging, recreation, local transportation, and entertainment.

[17] Ibid., 36–37.

[18] Cross-border services trade, as reported in the current account, includes both private and public sector transactions. The latter principally reflect operations of the U. S. military and embassies abroad. However, because public-sector transactions are not considered to reflect U. S. service industries' competitiveness and may introduce anomalies resulting from events such as international peace-keeping missions, this report will focus solely on private sector transactions, except when noted.

[19] According to the BEA, "Trade-related services consist of auction services, Internet or online sales services, and services provided by independent sales agents. For exports, 'merchanting' services are also included; these exports are measured as the difference between the cost and resale prices of goods that are purchased and resold abroad with significant processing." USDOC, BEA, *Survey of Current Business*, October 2010, 37.

[20] This encompasses freight transportation and port services, but does not include air passenger transport services (i.e., passenger fares). In 2009, U. S. exports of passenger fares decreased by 16 percent from the previous year.

[21] Between 2008 and 2009, U. S. exports of financial services decreased 8.8 percent, whereas U. S. imports decreased by more than twice that amount, at 18.4 percent, contributing to a net U. S. surplus. The United States has maintained a trade surplus in financial services for at least the past 10 years which, prior to 2009, was due in part to a sharper rise in U. S. exports of financial services relative to U. S. imports.

[22] USDOC, BEA, *Survey of Current Business*, October 2010, 54–55.

[23] Ibid., 36–37.

[24] Ibid. The vast majority of these payments are recorded as unaffiliated transactions, as they are undertaken on behalf of third-party policyholders.

[25] U. S.-owned foreign affiliates are affiliates owned by a U. S. parent company and located abroad; conversely, foreign-owned U. S. affiliates are affiliates located in the United States and owned by foreign parent companies.

[26] The main source for this section is the USDOC, BEA, *Survey of Current Business*, October 2006– October 2010.

[27] Data for professional services are underreported due to the suppression of data by BEA to avoid disclosure of confidential firm information.

[28] USDOC, BEA, *Survey of Current Business*, October 2010, 56–60, tables 8–10.2.

[29] See chapter 2 for an in-depth discussion on professional services.

[30] For the purposes of this report, professional services include accounting, auditing, and bookkeeping services; advertising services; architectural, engineering, and other technical services; construction services; industrial engineering services; computer and data processing services; computer systems design and related services; legal services; scientific research and research and development services; management of companies and enterprises; education services; and healthcare and social assistance services.

[31] Beginning in 2008, the *Recent Trends* report has discussed the professional and infrastructure service subsectors in alternate years. This division allows more detailed analysis of the individual services industries. Professional services are characterized as labor-intensive industries employing highly skilled and highly educated individuals in positions that frequently require specialized licensing or training. Infrastructure services are capital intensive, providing critical inputs to industrial activity and economic growth, and are consumed by every firm irrespective of economic sector. For the purposes of this report, infrastructure services include banking, insurance, securities, transportation, telecommunication, electric power, and retail services.

[32] U. S. Department of Labor (DOL), Bureau of Labor Statistics (BLS), "Table 32: Unemployed Persons by Occupation, Industry, and Duration of Employment, 2008," 2008, and "Table 32: Unemployed Persons by Occupation, Industry, and Duration of Employment, 2009," 2009. For education and healthcare services, the average (median) duration of unemployment was 9.2 weeks in 2008, and 13.6 weeks in 2009.

[33] Triplett and Bosworth, "Productivity in the Services Sector," January 2000, 8.

[34] Von Bergen, "In Epidemic of Layoffs, No One Is Immune," April 5, 2009; Spohr, "IBM Layoffs Hit Hundreds in Latest Round," August 4, 2009.

[35] Von Bergen, "In Epidemic of Layoffs, No One Is Immune," April 5, 2009.

[36] Nicoletti and Scarpetta, "Regulation, Productivity, and Growth," January 2003, 6; *Economist*, "Smart Work," October 7, 2010.

[37] Cattaneo et al., *International Trade in Services*, 2010, 10; Conway and Nicoletti. "Product Market Regulation in the Non-Manufacturing Sectors of OECD Countries: Measurement and Highlights," December 7, 2006, 20. Among OECD countries, professional services that face the largest degree of regulation are legal services, followed by accounting, architectural, and engineering services.

[38] Nicoletti and Scarpetta, "Regulation, Productivity, and Growth," January 2003, 9. Past studies cited by Nicoletti and Scarpetta indicate a positive relationship between competition and innovation. Competition is measured by market concentration, firm profits, and import penetration. Innovation is recognized in firm behaviors such as the adoption of new technology and investment in research and development. Further, studies have found a positive relationship between trade liberalization and productivity in that such liberalization increases competition and innovation in the market.

[39] *Economist*, "Smart Work," October 7, 2010; McKinsey Global Institute, "Beyond Austerity," October 2010, 73; GAO, Airline Deregulation," March 1999, 2; Høj, Kato, and Pilat, "Deregulation and Privatisation in the Service Sector," 1995, 55. In the telecommunications industry, price decreases occurred largely with respect to long-distance services.

[40] Hoekman, Mattoo, and Sapir, "The Political Economy of Services Trade Liberalization," 2007, 384.

[41] Molnar, Pain, and Taglioni, "Globalisation and Employment in the OECD," December 2008, 4. Where firms outsource the production of intermediate goods and services to offshore entities, they may purchase such goods and services from either foreign affiliates (sometimes referred to as international insourcing) or from unaffiliated firms.

[42] Wölfl, "Productivity Growth in Service Industries," June 2003, 9.

[43] Jensen and Kletzer, "Tradable Services," September 2005, 11. Tradable services are those that can be provided "at a distance" (i.e., from foreign locations). Such services do not require face-to-face contact and may instead be delivered through electronic networks.

[44] Ibid.

[45] Garner, "Offshoring in the Service Sector," 2004, 12–17. Garner distinguishes between two types of labor markets: one composed largely of unskilled labor that is both cheap and plentiful (China and India); the other, of an abundance of physical and human capital (United States). As education levels rise in developing economies that have historically been sources of unskilled labor, these economies acquire outsourced jobs of increasingly higher skill.

[46] Jensen and Kletzer, "Tradable Services," September 2005, 2–3; Levine, "Offshoring (a.k.a. Offshore Outsourcing)," May 2, 2005, 4.

[47] See Brainard and Collins, *Brookings Trade Forum: 2005*, 2006, 107 and 121, for a number of papers discussing this issue. For example, Jensen and Kletzer find that, during the period 1999–2003, white collar workers in tradable occupations faced higher job displacement rates (9.4 percent) than white collar workers in non-tradable occupations (6.5 percent). However, other academic researchers suggest that the extent to which the former result may have been due to offshoring rather than the cyclical effects of the economy is uncertain.

[48] Wölfl, "Productivity Growth in Service Industries," June 2003, 9; Wölfl, "The Interaction between Manufacturing and Services," November 2006, 4. In her 2006 paper, Wölfl states that services that are (1) relatively price elastic and (2) exposed to international competition experience a downward pressure on price, causing them to become more productive. These more productive services make higher contributions to "aggregate labor productivity."

[49] BEA official, e-mail correspondence with USITC staff, March 30, 2011. BEA measures professional services' contribution to GDP as "value added by industry," which represents the contribution of each industry's labor and capital to its gross output and the overall GDP. USDOC, BEA, "Gross-Domestic-(GDP)- by-Industry Data," 1998–2010.

[50] USDOC, BEA, "Full-Time Equivalent Employees by Industry," August 5, 2010; USDOC, BEA, "Real Value Added by Industry," May 5, 2010.

[51] Ibid.

[52] For purposes of this report, USITC staff calculated labor productivity by dividing GDP by industry by full-time equivalent employees.

[53] USDOC, BEA, "Full-Time Equivalent Employees by Industry," August 5, 2010; USDOC, BEA, "Real Value Added by Industry," May 5, 2010.

[54] Management consulting includes administrative, human resources, management, marketing, and logistic services, but also includes allocated expenses received by parent companies from affiliates for general overhead and expenses.

[55] USDOC, BEA, *Survey of Current Business*, October 2010, 54–55, table 7.2. For the purposes of the cross-border trade discussion, data on professional services include management, consulting, and public relations services; education, RandD and testing services; computer and data processing services; legal services; architectural, engineering, and other technical services; industrial engineering; medical services; and construction services.

[56] Affiliate transactions data include architectural, engineering, and related services; management, scientific, and technical services; advertising and related services; accounting, tax preparation, bookkeeping, and payroll services; scientific research and development; healthcare and social assistance; educational services; computer systems design and related services; and construction services. For 2008, complete data for U. S. -owned foreign affiliate sales of computer system design and related services, specialized design services, healthcare and social assistance, and other professional services were not available.

[57] For the purpose of this discussion, "audiovisual services" refers to the production and distribution of motion pictures, comprising primarily feature films, television programs, and documentaries. These services are distributed to consumers through projection in theaters, commercial flights, and other public venues; rental or sale of prerecorded works; broadcast, cable, and satellite television, including DVDs (digital video discs), Blu-ray discs, video on demand, and the Internet. Sound recording industries have been excluded from this discussion since most of their official trade data are either unavailable or have been suppressed to avoid disclosure of data of individual companies.

[58] The motion picture industry consists of a three-part industrial structure. After a movie or a video has been (i) produced, it is usually transferred to a (ii) distributor, which in turn arranges to make the product accessible to the consumer through (iii) movie theaters, video rental and/or sale outlets, and television broadcasts.

[59] HighBeam.com, "Industry Report," n.d. (accessed November 23, 2010). Success in the film production industry is largely predicated on two factors: a wide distribution network and access to the substantial capital required for film production. Thus major film companies, which are primarily based in the United States, enjoy obvious economy-of-scale advantages. In addition to distribution capabilities, many of the major studios have been operating long enough to build up sizable film libraries, which provide revenue through video sales or through sale or rental to television stations. These well-established companies are likely to wield substantial financial leverage and control physical production facilities.

[60] WTO, "Audiovisual Services: Background Note," January 12, 2010, 1.

[61] *Screen Digest*, "Global Box Office Hits New High," November 2010, 337–40.

[62] Vogel, *Entertainment Industry Economics*, 2004, 50–51.

[63] *Screen Digest*, "Global Box Office Hits New High," November 2010, 338. The Russian box office dropped by about 12 percent in dollar terms, masking an actual increase in local currency values in the region of about 13 percent. The number of admissions in Russia actually rose by over 11 percent to reach 132 million, confirming that the box office fall was attributed largely to currency issues.

[64] Ibid., 337–40. The decline in Indian box office revenue is largely due to the recent multiplex-producer strike, but local observers also point to poorer movie content and unforeseen factors such as swine flu and turbulent general elections.

[65] Ibid., 339. Total screens rose to reach 5,334 in 2009. Exhibitors, in particular, have been investing heavily in digital cinema, primarily for 3-D screenings, and by the midpoint of 2010, there were over 600 3-D screens across Latin America, up from just 84 at the end of 2008.

[66] Ibid. In terms of overall cinema attendance in 2009, the top five markets were India (2.9 billion), the United States (1.3 billion), China (264 million), France (201 million), and Mexico (174 million).

[67] Ibid., 340.

[68] Ibid., 337.

[69] HighBeam.com, "Industry Report," n.d. (accessed November 23, 2010). Production companies can be classified into three major categories: the "majors," the "mini-majors," and the "independents" or "indies." The majors include large conglomerates such as Disney, Sony, and Viacom. In such companies, a single corporate structure often controls both the production and distribution of films, as well as an array of related operations through which the corporation can market movie soundtracks, toys, and other promotional tie-ins. Slightly smaller companies, often called "mini-majors" (e.g., United Artists, Columbia Pictures), may have weaker distribution power and may specialize in a specific segment of the film market, such as art films or action films. Small independent filmmakers (e.g., Republic Pictures, Monogram Pictures) often have no distribution capability at all and must depend entirely on outside distribution companies.

[70] *Screen Digest*, "World Film Production Drops Again," August 2010, 1–9.

[71] Ibid., 1.

[72] Ibid., 1–9; WTO, "Audiovisual Services: Background Note by the Secretariat," January 12, 2010, 7–9.

[73] In the year 2006.

[74] BoxOfficeMojo.com, "2009 Worldwide Grosses," n.d. (accessed November 3, 2010).

[75] European Audiovisual Observatory (EAO), *Focus 2009*, 2009.

[76] *Screen Digest*, "Global Box Office Hits New High," November 2010, 340. Egypt's film market has been growing rapidly, with overall attendance reaching about 29.1 million in 2009, an increase of about 10 million since 1999. Egypt has the highest cinema attendance level in the Middle East region and the 23rd highest level worldwide, just ahead of the Netherlands (27.2 million) and only slightly behind Thailand (29.9 million).

[77] WTO, "Audiovisual Services: Background Note," January 12, 2010, 9. Domestic films accounted for about 91 percent of India's market; Egypt, 85 percent; China, 61 percent; and Japan, 60 percent.

[78] Ibid., 8.

[79] *Screen Digest*, "World Film Production Drops Again," August 2010, 7.

[80] Amobi, "Movies and Entertainment," September 9, 2010, 3–5.

[81] ShowBizData.com, "Worldwide Global Theatrical Market Shares for 2009," n.d. (accessed October 20, 2010). The studios are Warner Brothers (part of Time Warner Inc.), Twentieth Century Fox (News Corp.), Buena Vista/Disney (Walt Disney Co.), Sony Pictures (Sony Corp.), Universal Pictures (General Electric Co.), and Paramount Pictures (Viacom Inc.).

[82] WTO, "Audiovisual Services: Background Note," January 12, 2010, 8–11; Amobi, "Movies and Entertainment," September 9, 2010, 3–5; U. S. Department of Labor (DOL), Bureau of Labor Statistics (BLS), *Motion Picture and Video Industries*, 2010–11. Although studios and other production companies are responsible for financing, producing, publicizing, and distributing a film or program, the actual making of the film is done by hundreds of local small businesses and independent contractors hired by the studios on an as-needed basis. These companies provide a wide range of services, such as equipment rental, lighting, special effects, set construction, and costume design. The industry also contracts with a large number of workers in other industries that supply support services to the crews while they are filming, such as truck drivers, caterers, electricians, and makeup artists. Many of these workers, particularly those in Los Angeles and Mumbai, are wholly dependent on the motion picture industry.

[83] Dickey, "Avatar's True Cost," December 3, 2009.

[84] Amobi, "Movies and Entertainment," September 9, 2010, 3–5.

[85] DOL, BLS, *Motion Picture and Video Industries*, 2010–11.

[86] *Economist*, "The Worldwide Cinema Boom," May 6, 2010.

[87] Hanson and Xiang, "International Trade in Motion Picture Services," January 2008, 8–11. An important issue in using data on box office revenue is how to classify the nationality of a motion picture. *Screen Digest*, the primary box office and production data source for our discussion, defines the origin country for a film by the location of the company that produces the film. However, double-counting of reported revenue and production levels often becomes a problem when two or more international studios collaborate to produce a single film.

[88] WTO, "Audiovisual Services: Background Note," January 12, 2010, 8.

[89] Ibid.; *Screen Digest*, "World Film Production/Distribution," June 2006, 205.
[90] Vogel, *Entertainment Industry Economics*, 2004, 13.
[91] Ibid.
[92] Motion Picture Association of America (MPAA), *Theatrical Market Statistics 2009*, 9; *Film Journal International*, "Moviegoer Quick Facts," July 15, 2009.
[93] Vogel, *Entertainment Industry Economics*, 2004, 12–14.
[94] Ibid., 13; *Economist*, "The Worldwide Cinema Boom," May 6, 2010.
[95] *Economist*, "The Worldwide Cinema Boom," May 6, 2010; EAO, *Focus 2010*, 2010, 43.
[96] LiveTradingNews.com, "The Worldwide Cinema Boom," May 8, 2010.
[97] Bernstein, "An Aging Europe May Find Itself on the Sidelines," June 29, 2003.
[98] *Economist*, "The Worldwide Cinema Boom," May 6, 2010; EAO, *Focus 2010*, 2010, 14.
[99] EAO, *Focus 2010*, 2010, 53.
[100] Gallagher, "In Japan, 3D films Get Kicked by New Samurai Flicks," October 14, 2010.
[101] Digital Cinema Initiatives, "About DCI," n.d. (accessed January 29, 2011). The initiative was created in March 2002 and is a joint venture of Disney, Fox, Paramount, Sony, Universal, and Warner Brothers to establish and document voluntary specifications for an open architecture for digital cinema that ensures a uniform high level of technical performance, reliability, and quality control. Because of the relationship of DCI to many of Hollywood's key studios, conformance to DCI's specifications is considered a requirement by software developers or equipment manufacturers targeting the digital cinema market.
[102] EAO, *Focus 2010*, 2010, 7. The VPF model's basic premise is that a third party pays up front for the digital equipment, and then recoups the cost of the equipment over time, through payments from distributors and exhibitors.
[103] *Economist*, "The Worldwide Cinema Boom," May 6, 2010.
[104] MPAA, *Theatrical Market Statistics 2009*, 15.
[105] Garrahan, "Hollywood Braced for Budget Cuts," October 6, 2009.
[106] WTO, "Audiovisual Services: Background Note," January 12, 2010, 10; DOL, BLS, *Motion Picture and Video Industries*, 2010–11.
[107] *Economist*, "Hollow-wood," March 11, 2010.
[108] Ibid.; WTO, "Audiovisual Services: Background Note," January 12, 2010, 10.
[109] *Economist*, "Hollow-wood," March 11, 2010; WTO, "Audiovisual Services: Background Note," January 12, 2010, 10.
[110] *Economist*, "Hollow-wood," March 11, 2010.
[111] Center for Entertainment Industry Data and Research (CEIDR), *The Global Success of Production Tax Incentives*, 2006, 2–3; Schwinke, "Will Cheap Deals Tempt the Bargain Hunters?" July 2, 2009. For instance, Bulgaria, Hungary, Poland, Romania, and Serbia have been particularly active in offering production incentives to foreign filmmakers.
[112] WTO, "Audiovisual Services: Background Note," January 12, 2010, 10; DOL, BLS, *Motion Picture and Video Industries*, 2010–11.
[113] The first year in which the U.S.-Singapore Free Trade Agreement (FTA) went into effect.
[114] GlobalServicesMedia.com, "Lights, Camera, Action....," February 27, 2008. Lucasfilm's overseas projects have included the creation of special effects for the movie *Rush Hour 3* and the Star Wars-based television series, *Clone Wars*.
[115] Ibid.
[116] WTO, "Audiovisual Services: Background Note," January 12, 2010, 1.
[117] Industry official, interview by USITC staff, Washington, DC, November 9, 2010.
[118] Ibid.
[119] MPAA, *Trade Barriers to Exports of U.S. Filmed Entertainment*, October 2010 and industry official, interview by USITC staff, Washington, DC, November 9, 2010. The MPAA as well as the International Intellectual Property Alliance (IIPA) has advocated the establishment of stronger online legal protections for copyright owners, which include: adequate notice and takedown provisions; clearly defined Internet service provider (ISP) liability guidelines; the protection of temporary copies; and stronger enforcement of the World Intellectual Property Organization (WIPO) Copyright Treaty (WCT) and the WIPO Performance and Phonograms Treaty (WPPT). See also, the USITC's report, *China: Effects of Intellectual Property Infringement and Indigenous Innovation Policies on the U.S. Economy*.
[120] *Economist*, "To Catch a Thief," May 13, 2010. The technique developed by NEC, a Japanese technology company, and Mitsubishi Electric, has been adopted by the International Organization for Standardization (ISO) for MPEG-7, the latest standard for transmitting audiovisual content.
[121] Ibid.
[122] Amobi, "Movies and Entertainment," September 9, 2010, 3–5.
[123] USDOC, BEA, *Survey of Current Business*, October 2010, 46–49.
[124] Pells, "Is American Culture 'American'?" February 1, 2006.
[125] Ibid.

[126] USDOC, BEA, *Survey of Current Business*, October 2010, 47–49.
[127] Márquez, "Petrodollars for Local Film Industry," January 12, 2007. In 2006, the government opened the "Villa del Cine" just 30 kilometers east of Caracas. The complex offers soundproof studies with fully equipped lighting, audio and video equipment, and facilities for casting, wardrobe, and post production.
[128] USDOC, BEA, *Survey of Current Business*, October 2010, 46–49.
[129] WTO, "Audiovisual Services," 2010–11.
[130] For a more detailed explanation of the modes of services trade, see box 1.1 on p. 1-4.
[131] WTO, "Audiovisual Services," 2010–11.
[132] USTR, "Korea-U.S. Free Trade Agreement," n.d. (accessed April 6, 2011).
[133] WTO, "Audiovisual Services," 2010–11.
[134] Garrahan, "MGM Studio Emerges from Bankruptcy," December 21, 2010.
[135] Amobi, "Movies and Entertainment," September 9, 2010, 1–9; IBIS World, "Global Movie Production and Distribution," April 15, 2010, 40.
[136] Amobi, "Movies and Entertainment," September 9, 2010, 5, 9; IBISWorld, "Global Movie Production and Distribution," April 15, 2010, 49–50.
[137] State Administration of Radio, Film, and Television.
[138] *Screen Digest*, "Global Box Office Hits New High," November 2010, 340.
[139] *Screen Digest*, "World Film Production Drops Again," August 2010, 9.
[140] Nordas, "Trade and Regulation," June 24, 2008, 7.
[141] The computer services industry comprises numerous business segments. Much of the analysis in this chapter focuses on "computer systems design and related services" as defined in the North American Industry Classification System (NAICS). It has been selected because it spans a variety of services requiring specialized skills and training, in keeping with the focus of this report on professional services. It is defined as "establishments primarily engaged in providing expertise in the field of information technologies through one or more of the following activities: (1) writing, modifying, testing, and supporting software to meet the needs of a particular customer; (2) planning and designing computer systems that integrate computer hardware, software, and communication technologies; (3) on-site management and operation of clients' computer systems and/or data processing facilities; and (4) other professional and technical computer-related advice and services." USDOC, U. S. Bureau of the Census, "2007 NAICS Definition," 2007.
[142] USDOC, BEA, "Value Added by Industry," December 14, 2010. The shares of output correspond to value added as a percentage of gross domestic product.
[143] U. S. Department of Labor (DOL), Bureau of Labor Statistics (BLS), Employment, Hours, and Earnings—National Database. Statistics cited are for January 1994 and January 2009.
[144] USDOC, BEA, "Table 7," 2006–09.
[145] This definition corresponds to that found in United Nations Statistical Commission, *Manual on Statistics of International Trade in Services 2010* (MSITS 2010), February 2010. The previous edition of the MSITS (2002) left unresolved whether non-customized software delivered over the Internet should be classified as a computer service within international trade statistics. MSITS 2010 clarified that it should.
[146] IHS Global Insight, *Digital Planet 2010*, October 2010, 26. This source defines computer services as "outsourced services—whether domestic or offshore—such as information technology consulting, computer systems integration, outsourced custom software development, outsourced world wide web page design, network systems, network systems integration, office automation, facilities management, equipment maintenance, web hosting, computer disaster recovery, and data processing services." The data represent spending by country and region rather than revenues. Mexico is grouped within North America in the dataset.
[147] Two other Indian firms, Wipro and Infosys, were just outside the top 10.
[148] Gilmore et al., "Salary Survey 2008," December 2008, 4.
[149] Cathers, "Computers," May 6, 2010, 10.
[150] IDC, cited in Cathers, "Computers," May 6, 2010, 17. IT consulting is defined in this source as "a service provider providing an analysis or assessment of the clients' IT operations or strategy."
[151] Data processing is the use of computers to perform operations on data, such as merging, sorting, and tabulation. Data processing also includes data entry, retrieval, analysis, and reporting.
[152] Crosman, "Inside IBM's Mega Outsourcing Projects," January 21, 2011.
[153] USDOC, U. S. Bureau of the Census, 2007 Nonemployer Statistics Database. The database states that nonemployer firms are typically "self-employed individuals operating very small unincorporated businesses, which may or may not be the owner's principal source of income."
[154] Nordas, "Trade and Regulation," June 24, 2008, 8.
[155] NASSCOM, *The IT-BPO Sector in India*, February 2009, 185.
[156] Nordas, "Trade and Regulation," June 24, 2008, 25.
[157] Some observers believe the United States has a shortage of computer specialists, but others disagree. Herbst, "Study: No Shortage," October 28, 2009.
[158] Nordas, "Trade and Regulation," June 24, 2008, 23–24. For a more detailed explanation of the modes of services trade, see box 1.1 on p. 1-4.

[159] Rubalcaba and Kox, "The Growth of European Business Services," August 10, 2007, cited in OECD, "Services Trade Restrictiveness," July 2009, 7.
[160] TCS, "TCS Enters into a Long-term Engagement," March 10, 2009; TCS, "Infineon," December 14, 2010, 2.
[161] To illustrate, in fiscal year 2010, financial services firms accounted for 41 percent of India's export revenues from IT and business process outsourcing. NASSCOM, "India Inc." April 2010, 19. The statistic quoted here is for banking, other financial services, and insurance. India's fiscal year begins on April 1 and ends on March 31. The 2010 fiscal year ended on March 31, 2010.
[162] NASSCOM, "Executive Summary," February 2010, 6; Dai, "IBISWorld Industry Report 54151," August 2010, 7.
[163] Dai, "IBIS World Industry Report 54151," August 2010, 7; Recovery Accountability and Transparency Board, Recovery.gov database.
[164] EIU, "World: Healthcare Outlook," December 9, 2010.
[165] NASSCOM, "Executive Summary," February 2010, 6.
[166] IBM, *2009 Annual Report,* March 5, 2010, 26.
[167] Company representative, interview by USITC staff, December 14, 2009. IBM's total revenues grew from $68.9 billion in 1990 to $95.8 billion in 2009. IBM, *2009 Annual Report,* March 5, 2010, 19, and *Form 10-K Annual Report,* March 31, 1994, 70.
[168] Microsoft, "Microsoft Services Overview."
[169] Microsoft, "Microsoft Office 365."
[170] West, "Carly Reconsidered (II)," February 15, 2010; Fried, "HP Revamps," July 1, 2003.
[171] Das, "The Rise and Rise of Services," January 22, 2010.
[172] Staten, "Cloud Computing for the Enterprise," February 3, 2009, 11.
[173] Dzubeck, "Five Cloud Computing Questions," August 5, 2008.
[174] A platform is a set of resources that a developer uses to create software. It may include an operating system, databases, Web servers, and other software and hardware. Salesforce, "What is PaaS?"
[175] Larry Ellison, the CEO of Oracle Corporation, called cloud computing "everything that we already do." Farber, "Oracle's Ellison Nails Cloud Computing," September 26, 2008.
[176] Gartner, "Gartner Says," June 22, 2010.
[177] Ibid.
[178] Dzubeck, "Five Cloud Computing Questions," August 5, 2008.
[179] European Commission, *The Future of Cloud Computing,* 2010, 52.
[180] Nordas, "Trade and Regulation," June 24, 2008, 9.
[181] Díaz-Pinés, *Indicators of Broadband Coverage,* December 10, 2009, 38. Broadband is defined by the OECD as "a communication service that enables access to the Internet at data transmission rates above a specific threshold." The OECD and the International Telecommunications Union (ITU), two widely consulted sources of data, use a download speed of 256 kilobits per second as the threshold for their broadband statistics.
[182] Nordas, "Trade and Regulation," June 24, 2008, 9; WTO Secretariat, "Computer and Related Services," June 2009, 17.
[183] IMF, Balance of Payments Statistics Database.
[184] ITU, ICT Statistics Database.
[185] IMF, Balance of Payments Statistics Database.
[186] Golden, "The Skinny Straw," August 6, 2009.
[187] Sudan et al., *The Global Opportunity in IT-Based Services,* 2010, 16 and 21.
[188] ITU, *Measuring the Information Society,* 2009, cited in Engman, "Exporting Information Technology Services," 2010, 231.
[189] Unless otherwise indicated, the analysis in this section is based on data found in USDOC, BEA, *Survey of Current Business,* October 2010, 36–37, 54–55, tables 1 and 7.2.
[190] For years before 2006, BEA's data for trade in computer and data processing services reflect transactions between unaffiliated parties only. BEA's data for 2006–09 also include affiliated (intrafirm) trade, which comprises transactions between U. S. parents and their foreign affiliates and between U. S. affiliates and their foreign parents.
[191] BEA representative, e-mail to USITC staff, January 31, 2011.
[192] USDOC, BEA, "Table 7," 2006–09.
[193] BEA representative, e-mail to USITC staff, January 31, 2011.
[194] Schifferes, "Multinationals Lead India's IT Revolution," January 24, 2007.
[195] Alejandro et al., "An Overview and Examination," August 2010, 14.
[196] Unless otherwise indicated, the analysis in this section is based on data found in USDOC, BEA, "Table 9," 2006–08, and "Table 10," 2006–08.
[197] BEA reports "services supplied" by foreign affiliates. In the affiliate statistics for the computer systems design and related services industry, services supplied correspond to sales. Thus, sales and services supplied are used interchangeably in this section.
[198] USDOC, BEA, "Where Can I Find Information?" November 3, 2010.

[199] 2006 is the latest year for which total data are available. BEA suppressed them for later years to avoid disclosure of individual company data.

[200] BEA provided only limited data by country for affiliate sales. "Top six" here refers to the top six among the eight individual countries for which BEA provided this information for 2006. The six were, in descending order, Japan, the United Kingdom, Canada, the Netherlands, Australia, and Germany.

[201] See, for example, Nordas, "Trade and Regulation," June 24, 2008, 23–24.

[202] BEA provided country-specific data for only five countries in 2008: the United Kingdom, France, Canada, Japan, and the Netherlands. Together these countries accounted for only about a fifth of sales by foreign parents' U. S. affiliates in computer systems design and related services.

[203] Barnes, "Why Indian IT Companies Are Outsourcing," April 12, 2010.

[204] WTO Secretariat, "Computer and Related Services," June 2009, 7.

[205] Dacey, "Opposition to Work Permit Quotas Grows," April 21, 2010. The United States is another country that limits the entry of temporary workers. It raised fees for some temporary worker visas in 2010. A leading computer services industry association in India suggested that the measure could negatively affect Indian investment in the United States. Conneally, "U.S. Border Security Bill," August 6, 2010.

[206] Kirk, "Microsoft: Cloud Computing," November 10, 2010.

[207] Kristensen, "Revising the EU Data Protection Directive," April 1, 2010. Formally known as "Directive 95/46/EC of the European Parliament and of the Council of 24.10.1995 on the protection of individuals with regard to the processing of personal data and on the free movement of such data," the directive adopts principles from the OECD's Guidelines on the Protection of Privacy and Transborder Flows of Personal Data, issued in 1980. Shimanek, "Do You Want Milk with Those Cookies?" 2001.

[208] O'Brien, "Cloud Computing Hits Snag in Europe," September 19, 2010.

[209] WTO, CTS, "Communication from Albania," January 26, 2007, 1.

[210] European Commission, "Communication from the Commission," November 4, 2010, 18.

[211] European Union-United States Trade Principles for Information and Communication Technology Services, April 4, 2011.

[212] Free Trade Agreement between the United States of America and the Republic of Korea, Article 15.8. As of June 2011, the agreement had not been approved by Congress.

[213] Forrester, "Forrester: Mixed Economic Outlook," January 10, 2011.

[214] IHS Global Insight, *Digital Planet 2010*, October 2010, 15.

[215] Gartner, "Gartner Says," June 22, 2010. Other analysts' forecasts vary according to the specific cloud services and geographic markets they examine, but they generally point toward robust growth for cloud-based services. For a summary of a number of forecasts, see Columbus, "Roundup of Cloud Computing Forecasts," January 1, 2011.

[216] NAFSA: "The Economic Benefits of International Education," 2010; additional data for each academic year beginning in 2003–04.

[217] *Economist*, "Will They Still Come?" August 5, 2010.

[218] Fischer, "American Colleges Look to Private Sector," May 30, 2010.

[219] *Economist*, "Wandering Scholars," September 8, 2005; *Economist*, "The Brains Business," September 8, 2005.

[220] Culbert, *Colleges and Universities in the United States*, December 2010, 22, 25.

[221] Fischer, "American Colleges Look to Private Sector," May 30, 2010.

[222] Redden, "A Shifting International Mix," August 25, 2010.

[223] OECD, "Highlights from Education at a Glance 2010," 2010, 33.

[224] Council of Australian Governments, "International Students Strategy for Australia," November 1, 2010. For example, revised rules require applicants to deposit into an Australian financial institution sufficient tuition and living expenses for the entire program of study instead of, as formerly, for one year only. Foreign students must also demonstrate greater English-language proficiency than previously required. Moreover, the government sharply reduced the number of occupations in prime demand in the economy and for which completed coursework tended to offer the most rapid path to permanent residency under the skilled migration program. This action could affect several hundred thousand foreign students enrolled in now unapproved courses and over 100,000 applicants for permanent residency.

[225] Australian Visa Bureau, "China Says Australian Visa Barriers Are Steering Chinese Students Away," November 3, 2010; Maslen, "Australia: Alarming Fall in Chinese Student Numbers," November 7, 2010.

[226] Maslen, "Australia: Uncertain Times Ahead for Universities," January 9, 2011; Hannah, "Indian Students Continue to Shun Australia Visas," November 30, 2010; Redden, "Downturn Down Under," November 30, 2010. In addition to amendments to student visa and skilled migrant programs, the decline in student visa issuance can also be attributed to a strong Australian dollar, the adverse impacts of the global recession on foreign students' financial resources, delays in processing student visas under revised requirements, and a decline in applications for student visas from India following violent attacks on several Indian students in 2009.

[227] Australian Government, Department of Immigration and Citizenship, "Terms of Reference: Strategic Review of the Student Visa Program," "Overview of Student Visa Changes to Assist International Education Sector,"

December 2010; Maslen, "Australia: Uncertain Times Ahead for Universities," January 9, 2011; Australian Government, "Submissions Invited for Student Visa Review," February 3, 2011.

[228] The visas would be awarded contingent upon applicants enrolling mostly in courses predetermined to be required for degrees. Applicants would be required to demonstrate a higher level of English-language competency before entering the country. Moreover, the proposals would inter alia place new limits on allowable employment during study, as well as on the entry and employment of dependents, and would require graduates to leave the country on graduating unless progressing to the next level of education.

[229] American Association of State Colleges and Universities, "State Outlook," November 2010, 1, 5.

[230] McNichol, Oliff, and Johnson, "States Continue to Feel Recession's Impact," January 21, 2011. State-based financial support for universities will likely decline even further, with 44 state governments projecting budgetary shortfalls totaling approximately $125 billion in 2012 and 20 states anticipating further shortfalls in 2013.

[231] Johnson, Oliff, and Williams, "An Update on State Budget Cuts," November 5, 2010. In most states, the fiscal year ends on June 30.

[232] American Association of State Colleges and Universities, "State Outlook," November 2010, 6, 7.

[233] Stripling, "More Tuition Struggles Projected," December 17, 2010.

[234] The decline in funding would begin in 2011 and continue for four years; funding for instruction in science, technology, engineering, and mathematics was not reduced.

[235] *Economist*, "Reassuringly Expensive," March 10, 2011.

[236] Douglass, "Higher Education Budgets and the Global Recession," February 2010; Kakuchi, "Japan: University Internationalization Scaled Back," November 28, 2010.

[237] Redden, "Ethical Debates Surround U. S. Colleges' Use of International Recruiters," June 1, 2010; *Economist*, "Will They Still Come?" August 5, 2010; *Economist*, "Can Foreigners Prop Them Up?" January 13, 2005. In some countries, foreign students are charged substantially higher tuition than their domestic counterparts.

[238] Fischer, "American Colleges Look to Private Sector for Global Recruiting," May 30, 2010; Redden, "Ethical Debates Surround U. S. College's Use of International Recruiters," June 1, 2010.

[239] *Economist*, "Build It and They Will Come," January 15, 2009.

[240] *Economist*, "Will They Still Come?" August 5, 2010; *Economist*, "Can Foreigners Prop Them Up?" January 13, 2005; *Economist*, "Repointing the Spires," January 27, 2005.

[241] *Economist*, "Learning without Frontiers," October 28, 2010.

[242] Fischer, "China Props Up Foreign Students' Numbers in U. S. ," November 19, 2010, A22. The increasing concentration of these countries' students at U. S. institutions is described by some education industry representatives as inconsistent with universities' stated goals of promoting cultural and national diversity among foreign student populations on U. S. campuses.

[243] VanDuzer, "Navigating between the Poles," 2005, 183.

[244] WTO, "Services Signaling Conference," July 30, 2008, 3.

[245] West, "Ripple Effects: The Bologna Process," November–December 2010, 25–29.

[246] *Economist*, "Will They Still Come?" August 5, 2010.

[247] McNichol, Oliff, and Johnson, "States Continue to Feel Recession's Impact," January 21, 2011.

[248] Redden, "Ethical Debates Surround U. S. Colleges' Use of International Recruiters," June 1, 2010; Fischer, "American Colleges Look to Private Sector," May 30, 2010.

[249] *Economist*, "Will They Still Come?" August 5, 2010.

[250] The healthcare industry comprises providers (doctors, nurses, and other health professionals) who offer individualized and specialized services in medical facilities, including hospitals; medical offices, clinics, and other ambulatory facilities; and nursing and residential care facilities. Swiss Re, "To Your Health," 2007, 8.

[251] The inverse relationship is also true; higher national incomes promote health through access to better nutrition, sanitation, and quality care. Bloom and Canning, "Population Health and Economic Growth," 2008, 1.

[252] The health of their constituents is of interest to governments because an individual's earning potential and labor productivity is affected by personal health. If a citizen suffers catastrophic illness, the cost of treatment may exceed the citizen's accumulated savings. Further, ongoing illness may limit the ability of such persons to work, reducing the labor force and possibly increasing the state's burden. Additionally, healthier populations have longer life expectancies and save accordingly, resulting in higher levels of national savings and wealth. Mortensen, "International Trade in Health Services," 2008, 5; Suhrcke et al., "The Contribution of Health," August 23, 2005, 22, 38, and 67; Swiss Re, "To Your Health," 2007, 10.

[253] Global healthcare expenditure consists of public (government) spending and private spending. Private expenditure comprises spending by private prepaid plans, households' out-of-pocket expenditure, and other private resources for health, such as nonprofit organizations which provide households with goods and services free or for negligible prices. WHO, National Health Accounts, "Glossary of Terms and Financing Flows," n.d. (accessed January 25, 2011).

[254] Data from 2008 are the most recent available. Data on healthcare expenditure is reported by the WTO as ratios. Expenditure volumes are estimated by USITC staff using these ratios and nominal GDP data reported by the

World Bank to get estimated nominal healthcare expenditure. World Health Organization (WHO), Global Health Observatory (GHO) Database and World Bank, World dataBank Database.

[255] The United States accounted for over 60 percent of global private spending in 2008. WHO, GHO Database.

[256] U. S. private spending on healthcare accounted for a relatively steady share of GDP (around 8.5 percent) during 2003–08, but growth in actual spending on health slowed, due to the slow growth of the U. S. GDP during the recent recession. USITC staff calculations using data from the WHO's GHO Database and the World Bank's World dataBank database.

[257] The incidence and implications of chronic diseases are discussed in detail in the Demand and Supply Factors section.

[258] WHO Regional Office for Europe, *The European Health Report 2009*, 2009, 7 1–72.

[259] The European region is consistent with the WHO's definition. Healthcare spending by European governments remained steady at roughly 6.8 percent of GDP throughout the period. USITC staff calculations using data from the WHO's, GHO Database and the World Bank's World dataBank database.

[260] The Middle East region corresponds to the region defined as East Mediterranean by the WHO. From 2003 through 2008, private expenditure more than doubled in the Middle East, reaching $41.1 billion, while in Africa it rose from $18.8 billion to $35.1 billion. USITC staff calculations using data from the WHO's GHO Database and the World Bank's World dataBank database.

[261] PricewaterhouseCoopers, "Emerging Trends in Chinese Healthcare," 2010, 10.

[262] Healthcare systems are networks of individual providers and facilities that operate as a group to offer healthcare services to a specific population, such as members of an insurance plan or residents of a specific geographic location.

[263] HCA, "About Our Company," n.d.; HCA International, "Key Facts and Figures," n.d.

[264] No international regulatory body exists to govern healthcare industries across countries; instead, the industry is regulated by national or regional agencies.

[265] There is wide variation in a number of healthcare factors across countries, including methods of delivery and sources of financing. Ma and Sood, "A Comparison of Health Systems in China and India," 2008, 1.

[266] Governments generally intervene in markets to achieve noneconomic objectives, to redistribute income, or to address market distortions. Deardorff, "The Economics of Government Market Intervention," February 10, 2000, 3.

[267] Third-party payers refer to organizations that intervene in the relationship between the individual patient and a healthcare provider. These may be insurance carriers, nonprofit organizations, health maintenance organizations (HMOs), or governments.

[268] Swiss Re, "To Your Health," 2007, 8–9.

[269] Employers and employees generally have different criteria in choosing insurance plans. Employers tend to focus on cost, while employees consider the types of services or treatments they need. Ibid.

[270] Government provision of healthcare is limited to public hospitals, such as Veterans Affairs facilities; the majority of care in the U. S. market is provided by private entities.

[271] The Medicare program provides healthcare for elderly populations, while Medicaid serves the low- income population.

[272] PricewaterhouseCoopers, "Emerging Trends in Chinese Healthcare," 2010, 10.

[273] Prince, "Recession Sees First Fall in Private Health Spending in 20 Years," April 4, 2009; WHO, National Health Accounts, "United Kingdom," March 2010.

[274] Private expenditure on healthcare in China accounted for 53.3 percent of total healthcare spending in 2008; this was almost identical to the share of private spending in the U. S. market (53.5 percent). See table 6.1. WHO, GHO Database.

[275] Statistics Canada, "Study," November 12, 2009; European Commission, Eurostat, "Impact of the Economic Crisis," February 9, 2011.

[276] In France, 12 percent of respondents reported a reduction in seeking medical care since the financial crisis, compared to 10.3 percent in Germany, 7.6 percent in the United Kingdom, and 5.6 percent in Canada. Lusardi, Schneider, and Tufano, "The Economic Crisis and Medical Care Usage," March 2010, 7.

[277] Holahan, "The 2007–09 Recession and Health Insurance Coverage," January 2011, 148.

[278] Lusardi, Schneider, and Tufano, "The Economic Crisis and Medical Care Usage," March 2010, 7. A different survey found 36 percent of Americans reported seeing a healthcare professional less frequently in 2009 due to the recession. Martin et al., "Recession Contributes to Slowest Annual Rate," January 2011, 18.

[279] The American Recovery and Reinvestment Act passed by Congress extended the Consolidated Omnibus Budget Reconciliation Act (COBRA) premium subsidies for 2009. These premium subsidies temporarily allow recently unemployed individuals to keep their health insurance coverage for a cost below market price.

[280] Martin et al., "Recession Contributes to Slowest Annual Rate," January 2011, 11.

[281] In some cases, national health plans cover care in a foreign market—usually for care not available in the home market. For example, some Middle Eastern governments will reimburse care sought abroad because local infrastructure lacks capacity; similarly, in special cases and with preapproval, the Canadian government will

reimburse care received in the United States for treatments not available in Canada. Mortensen, "International Trade in Health Services," 2008, 18; Cattaneo, "Health Without Borders," 2010, 105.

[282] *International Medical Travel Journal (IMTJ)*, "Mexico, USA," October 21, 2010. Two Mexican hospitals in the Angeles Health International hospital system report providing an estimated $11.5 million worth of care to U. S. citizens and residents annually. The hospitals reported serving an average of 1,600 American patients, offering services at an average cost of $7,200; the majority of services were weight-loss surgeries. Warner and Jahnke, "U.S.-Mexico Mode 2," March 3, 2010, 8.

[283] *IMTJ*, "Mexico, USA," October 21, 2010. Also see USITC, *Caribbean Region*, May 2008, 2-24–2- 25 for a discussion of Caribbean destinations.

[284] Avila, "Mexico/USA Spending," March 24, 2009; Warner and Jahnke, "U.S.-Mexico Mode 2," March 3, 2010, 8.

[285] The British pound had a favorable exchange rate against the U. S. dollar for several years, beginning around 2004, but the euro gained strength in late 2007. Most reports suggest Europeans took advantage of this exchange rate during the first half of 2008, before the dollar strengthened against the euro and the pound towards the last quarter of the year. European Central Bank, "Euro Exchange Rates USD," April 11, 2011; Board of Governors of the Federal Reserve System, "U.S./U.K Foreign Exchange Rate," April 1, 2011; Rundle, "Europeans Take Beauty Trip to U. S.," July 8, 2008; Daswani, "My You Look Rested," September 29, 2008.

[286] U.S. plastic surgeons specifically targeted European patients by taking out advertisements in trans- Atlantic in-flight magazines. Rundle, "Europeans Take Beauty Trip to U. S.," July 8, 2008.

[287] Chronic diseases are defined as long-term, uncurable conditions with generally slow progression. WHO, "Health Topics: Chronic Diseases," n.d. (accessed January 31, 2011); Al-Maskari, "Lifestyle Diseases," 2010.

[288] Dall et al., "The Economic Burden of Diabetes," February 2010, 299–301.

[289] Schoen et al., "In Chronic Condition," November 13, 2008, w1.

[290] Better acute cardiac care and secondary prevention after cardiovascular disease onset have contributed to declines in mortality. For example, CT scans have increased early detection of the disease, which can then be managed using statins (a pharmaceutical) or intracoronary stents. Weisfeldt and Zieman, "Advances in the Prevention and Treatment of Cardiovascular Disease," January/February 2007, 28–33.

[291] Pearson, "Cardiovascular Disease," January/February 2007, 50.

[292] Center for Disease Control and Prevention, "Chronic Disease Prevention and Health Promotion," July 7, 2010.

[293] The four largest risk factors leading to chronic diseases are physical inactivity, poor nutrition, tobacco use, and excessive alcohol consumption.

[294] Obesity leads to cardiovascular disease, diabetes, some cancers, and arthritis, among other conditions. Steenhuysen and Kelland, "Obesity Epidemic Risks Heart Disease," February 4, 2011.

[295] Currently, India has the world's highest incidence of diabetes, with 50.8 million diabetics, followed by China, with 43.2 million. World Diabetes Foundation, "Diabetes Facts," February 5, 2010.

[296] WHO, "Chronic Diseases and Health Promotion," n.d. (accessed January 31, 2011).

[297] The reform required the social health insurance system to provide coverage for 56 conditions, many of which are chronic conditions. Chile's social health insurance system comprises a large public program and a number of private insurers. Bitrán, Escobar, and Gassibe, "After Chile's Health Reform," December 2010, 2162.

[298] Ibid., 2168.

[299] Boseley, "Health Worker Shortage," January 18, 2011.

[300] The Canadian Nurses Association estimated a shortage of 11,000 full time Registered Nurses (RNs) in 2007, and in the Untied States, the national RN vacancy rate was reported to be 8.1 percent in 2008. American Association of Colleges of Nursing (AACN), "Nursing Shortage Fact Sheet," September 20, 2010; Canadian Nurses Association, "Tested Solutions," May 2009.

[301] AACN, "Nursing Shortage Fact Sheet," September 2010.

[302] Dumont et al., "International Mobility of Health Professionals," 2008, 9; Robert Wood Johnson Foundation, "Nursing Study Analyzes Trends," September 2007.

[303] Fakkar, "Health Ministry to Hire 3,000 Foreign Doctors," October 12, 2010; Al-Dibyani, "Demand for Foreign Health Workers to Increase," February 7, 2011.

[304] Boseley, "Health Worker Shortage," January 18, 2011; WHO, "Migration of Health Workers," July 2010.

[305] Scheffler et al., "Estimates of Health Care Professional Shortages," August, 2009, w849.

[306] Dumont et al., "International Mobility of Health Professionals," 2008, 22–24.

[307] Iglehart, "Despite Tight Budgets," January 2011, 191.

[308] PricewaterhouseCoopers, "Build and Beyond," December 2010, 7.

[309] EIU, "United Kingdom: Healthcare and Pharmaceuticals Report," November 9, 2010.

[310] These reforms would allow general practitioners to contract for services from hospitals and clinics, including those in the private sector.

[311] Lim et al., "How Public and Private Reforms Dramatically Improved Access," December 2010, 2216.

[312] *Economic Times*, "Ethiopia Woos Indian Hospitals to Set Up Branches," June 18, 2010.

[313] *IMTJ*, "China," January 12, 2011.

[314] Ross and Xu, "China Opens the Door Wider to Private and Foreign Investment in Health Care," December 17, 2010.

[315] For example, U. S. hospitals are known for coronary bypass surgery, cosmetic procedures, and oncology treatments. Lee and Davis, "International Patients," 2004, 43.

[316] Many U. S. hospitals market their healthcare exports because exports are profitable for U. S. providers. Most foreign patients use out-of-pocket private funds to pay for services and, on average, return 80 to 100 cents on the dollar; publicly or privately insured domestic patients generally return 40 to 60 cents on the dollar. Lee and Davis, "International Patients," 2004, 42; *IMTJ*, "USA," January 19, 2011.

[317] 2007 is the most recent year available for which geographic detail is provided for U. S. cross-border trade in healthcare services. BEA does not break down healthcare imports and exports by country. Data reported in the UN Service Trade Database appear to correspond to BEA estimates of cross-border trade, and as such, are used to analyze major U. S. markets. Mortensen, "International Trade in Health Services," 2008, 18; USITC staff calculations based on data from UN Service Trade Database.

[318] USITC staff calculations based on data from UN Service Trade Database.

[319] Rivera, Ortiz, and Cardenas, "Cross-border Purchase of Medications and Health Care," February 2009, 167.

[320] This care is often financed out of pocket, but in some cases, provincial governments have entered into arrangements with U. S. providers to offer services not available locally or, if pre-approved, will reimburse Canadian residents for care received in the United States with funds drawn from the national health insurance. For example, Detroit Hospital Center and Henry Ford Medical Center (Michigan) have entered formal partnerships with Ontario, Canada's Ministry of Health and Long Term Care to supply imaging services, bariatric procedures, and other tests not readily available in the province. Anstett, "Canadians Visit U. S. to Get Healthcare," August 20, 2009; Greene, "Canadian Patients Give Detroit Hospitals a Boost," April 18, 2008.

[321] The British pound and the Euro progressively strengthened against the U. S. dollar through mid-2008. European Central Bank, "Euro Exchange Rates USD," April 11, 2011; Board of Governors of the Federal Reserve System, "U.S./U.K Foreign Exchange Rate," April 1, 2011.

[322] BEA estimates for 2004 through 2009 show steady growth in total U. S. import volumes. These data primarily estimate incidental care sought by U. S. travelers; however, they do include spending by individuals who traveled to Mexico and Canada specifically seeking medical treatment.

[323] Reported exports of healthcare services to the United States roughly correspond to U. S. imports of such services from these countries.

[324] BEA does not report medical services trade data on a country basis, nor does the United States report healthcare-related travel expenses by country in the UN Services Trade database. A limited number of countries report exports of healthcare services to the United States; however, these data are neither comprehensive nor complete, and so will be used for illustrative purposes only.

[325] U. S. residents who purchase healthcare services in Mexico include the large population of uninsured Americans who reside along the border (for more information see box 6.1), Mexican immigrants who return home for treatment, retirees who reside in Mexico at least part of the year, and individuals who travel to Mexico for specific treatments or procedures. Warner and Jahnke, "U.S.-Mexico Mode 2," March 3, 2010, 1.

[326] BEA reports "services supplied" by affiliates; for healthcare and social assistance services, services supplied correspond to sales. Thus, "sales" and "services supplied" are used interchangeably in this section.

[327] USDOC, BEA, U. S. *International Services*, "Table 9," and "Table 10" (accessed December 21, 2010).

[328] Data on purchases from U. S. affiliates of foreign firms during 2003 and 2004 were not reported.

[329] The acquisition was valued at $3.5 billion. Bureau van Dijk, Zephyr Mergers and Acquisitions Database; Federal Trade Commission, "Maintaining Competition," March 30, 2006; Fields, "God Help You," December 2010.

[330] Data for 2006 are the most recent data available, as data for 2007 and 2008 are suppressed by BEA to avoid disclosing individual firms' data.

[331] USDOC, BEA, "U.S. Direct Investment Abroad," n.d. and "Foreign Direct Investment in the United States," n.d.

[332] Bureau van Dijk, Zephyr Mergers and Acquisitions Database.

[333] Currently, only 39 percent of WTO members have made commitments in the health sector—among the lowest percentage across all sectors. Cattaneo, "International Trade in Services," 2010, 137.

[334] Public healthcare is outside the scope of the GATS under article XIV, which stipulates exceptions for services related to human life or health.

[335] Waeger, "Trade in Health Services," October 2008, 16.

[336] Buchanan, "Doctor Shortage Sees New Recruitment Drive in India," June 1, 2010.

[337] Rivera, Ortiz, and Cardenas, "Cross-border Purchase of Medications and Health Care," February 2009, 172.

[338] Medisave is the mandatory individual health savings fund to which Singaporean workers automatically contribute.

[339] *Straits Times*, "Use of Medisave Overseas," February 10, 2010; industry representative, interview by USITC staff, March 9, 2010.

[340] Cortez, "Recalibrating the Legal Risks of Cross-Border Health Care," 2010, 69.

[341] EIU, "World: Healthcare Outlook," December 9, 2010.

[342] Ibid.; EIU, "Asia and Australasia: Healthcare Outlook," June 14, 2010.
[343] PricewaterhouseCoopers, "Emerging Trends in Chinese Healthcare," 2010, 9.
[344] EIU, "World: Healthcare Outlook," December 9, 2010.
[345] Ibid.; *Global Health Resources*, "International Factoid," February 24, 2011; WHO, "Health Topics: Chronic Diseases," n.d. (accessed January 31, 2011).
[346] KPMG, "The Future of Global Healthcare Delivery and Management," 2010, 12.
[347] Accountable Care Organizations are a concept wherein hospitals, primary care physicians, and specialists would jointly be accountable for the quality and cost of healthcare provided to a group of Medicare patients. KPMG, "The Future of Global Healthcare Delivery and Management," 2010, 12; Association of American Medical Colleges (AAMC), "AAMC Releases New Physician Shortage Estimates Post-Reform," September 30, 2010.
[348] Aiken, Cheung, and Olds, "Education Policy Initiatives," June, 2009, w646; AAMC, "AAMC Releases New Physician Shortage Estimates Post-Reform," September 30, 2010.
[349] United Nations (UN), *Manual on Statistics of International Trade in Services (MSITS)2010*, 2010, 67; U. S. Department of Commerce (USDOC), U. S. Census Bureau Web site, "Industry Statistics Sampler: NAICS 5411—Legal Services" (accessed January 3, 2011). MSITS defines legal services as "legal advisory and representation services in any legal, judicial and statutory procedures; drafting services of legal documentation and instruments; certification consultancy; and escrow and settlement services."
[350] Cattaneo and Walkenhorst, "Legal Services," 2010, 69.
[351] Hook, "Sectoral Study on the Impact of Domestic Regulation," February 15–16, 2007, 6.
[352] Datamonitor, "Industry Profile: Global Legal Services," July 2010, 11; Datamonitor, "Industry Profile: Global Legal Services," December 2006, 11.
[353] Industry representative, telephone interview by USITC staff, April 27, 2011. For example, revenue data from Datamonitor (the primary source of global and comparative country-level data for legal services), likely refers to revenue from law firms and excludes other types of firms that have lawyers.
[354] Datamonitor, "Industry Profile: Global Legal Services," July 2010, 9; Datamonitor, "Industry Profile: Global Legal Services," December 2006, 9. Continuous series using data between 2001 and 2009 are not calculated, since data for the two sets of years (2001–05 and 2005–09) are published in separate reports and differ when they overlap. The annual average rate between 2005 and 2009 includes the significant slowdown in growth between 2008–09, discussed below.
[355] Datamonitor, "Industry Profile: Global Legal Services," July 2010, 9.
[356] Lloyd, "The 2009 Global 100," October 1, 2009.
[357] Datamonitor, "Industry Profile: Legal Services in the United States," July 2010, 9; Datamonitor, "Industry Profile: Legal Services in Europe," July 2010, 9; Datamonitor, "Industry Profile: Legal Services in Asia-Pacific," July 2010, 9.
[358] Datamonitor, "Industry Profile: Global Legal Services," July 2010, 6, 11. The valuation of the global legal services market reflects only the largest legal services markets in Europe, Asia-Pacific, North America, and South America. Thus while countries in North America in this analysis include Canada, Mexico, and the United States, countries in South America include only Argentina, Brazil, Chile, Colombia, and Venezuela. Countries in Europe include Belgium, the Czech Republic, Denmark, France, Germany, Hungary, Italy, the Netherlands, Norway, Poland, Romania, Russia, Spain, Sweden, Ukraine, and the United Kingdom. Countries in the Asia-Pacific total include Australia, China, India, Japan, Singapore, Korea, and Taiwan.
[359] Datamonitor, "Industry Profile: Global Legal Services," December 2006, 11; Datamonitor, "Industry Profile: Global Legal Services," November 2007, 11; Datamonitor, "Industry Profile: Global Legal Services," July 2010, 11. A country or region's share of the global is calculated market based on revenue. The share for the Asia-Pacific region first increased between 2005 and 2006 (when the region's global share jumped from 5.1 percent to 11.2 percent). In the same year, Europe's share declined from 33.6 percent to 26.9 percent, while the Americas' share increased slightly from 61.3 percent to 61.9 percent.
[360] Datamonitor, "Industry Profile: Global Legal Services," July 2010, 11; Datamonitor, "Industry Profile: Legal Services in the United States," July 2010, 11.
[361] USITC staff calculations using data from Datamonitor, "Industry Profile: Global Legal Services," July 2010, 11 and "Industry Profile: Legal Services in the United States," July 2010, 11.
[362] Datamonitor, "Industry Profile: Legal Services in Asia-Pacific," July 2010, 11. The remaining Asia-Pacific market shares in 2009 were as follows: India (13.5 percent), Japan (11.7 percent), and Korea (11.4 percent).
[363] Datamonitor, "Industry Profile: Legal Services in Europe," July 2010, 11. The remaining European markets shares in 2009 were as follows: Spain (9.1 percent), France (9.1 percent), and the rest of Europe (31 percent).
[364] *American Lawyer*, "The Global 100 2010," October 2010. The remaining firms included five Australian firms and one firm each from Canada, France, Spain, and the Netherlands.
[365] Goldhaber, "The Global 100 2010," October 2010.
[366] Culbert, "Law Firms in the US," September 2010, 15; Hildebrandt Baker Robbins and Citi Private Bank, "2010 Client Advisory," March 3, 2010, 7. During economic downturns, demand for and revenues from bankruptcy, insolvency, and litigation typically increase; during periods of economic growth, demand for legal services related to commercial activities, such as mergers and acquisitions, increases and drives revenue. For example,

results of a survey of 193 firms, including firms from the 200 highest-grossing U. S. firms and 52 additional participants, indicated that only bankruptcy and litigation practice areas grew during most of 2009, while other practice areas, such as general corporate and capital markets, grew only during the last quarter of the year.

[367] Goldhaber, "The Global 100 2010," October 2010.

[368] IBISWorld, "Attorney and Legal Services in China," January 2010, 7, 14; Culbert, "Law Firms in the US," September 2010, 14, 15. According to IBISWorld, in both the United States and China, the commercial segment makes up the largest share of industry revenue and is defined as follows. In the United States, commercial legal services involve "merger and acquisition activity, capital raisings involving debt and equity markets, activities relating to initial public offerings (IPOs) and legal services associated with private equity transactions including leveraged buyouts" and also include bankruptcy, insolvency, and litigation. In China, commercial legal services involve commercial disputes, litigation, and arbitration. In the United States, noncommercial segments of the industry include personal injury, intellectual property, trademark and patent law, property, and other law. In China, non-commercial segments include civil, criminal, nonlitigious, and other legal services.

[369] Data exclude nonemployer firms. In 2007, 91.7 percent of all U. S. legal establishments were firms with fewer than 20 employees, with only 1.8 percent of them exporting. On the other hand, establishments with more than 500 employees accounted for only 1.5 percent of all establishments, but for 15.7 percent of firms that exported legal services. This pattern of concentrated exports (by large law firms) is similar to the relationship between firm size and the level of exports for providers of many types of goods and services in the United States.

[370] A similar pattern is seen in China, where larger Beijing-headquartered law firms have also entered the global market. For example, King and Wood and Jun He have expanded their presence internationally in recent years. Both have offices in New York and Silicon Valley, and King and Wood has an office in Tokyo as well. Their foreign branches support international clients with business and investments in China, as well as Chinese clients with business abroad. King and Wood Web site, "Offices," (accessed December 7, 2010); Jun He Web site, "About Us," (accessed December 7, 2010). King and Wood has maintained their Silicon Valley office since 2001. They opened their Tokyo and New York locations more recently—in 2005 and 2008, respectively.

[371] Culbert, "Law Firms in the US," September 2010, 5, 8.

[372] Ibid., 6; Hildebrandt Baker Robbins and Citi Private Bank, "2010 Client Advisory," March 3, 2010, 2–5. Based on a survey of 193 U. S. law firms, demand dropped 4.1 percent in 2009 and revenue dropped by 3.4 percent.

[373] The 100 highest-grossing firms are referred to as "Am Law 100" firms. The smaller firms include firms ranked 101–200 by gross revenue (the "Am Law 200") and smaller midsize firms.

[374] Hildebrandt Baker Robbins and Citi Private Bank, "2010 Client Advisory," March 3, 2010, 7. In particular, demand declined by 4 percent for the Am Law 100 compared to about 1 percent for the Am Law 200 and by about 3 percent for smaller, midsize firms; productivity dropped by about 4 percent for the Am Law 100, by 2.5 percent for the Am Law 200, and by 2 percent for midsized firms; and revenue declined by 2 percent for the Am Law 100 compared to an increase of 2 percent of the Am Law 200 and a decline of about 0.5 percent for midsize firms. Numbers published in a different source show similar trends for these groups of firms, though the percentage changes differ. See DiPetro, "Priced to Sell," May 1, 2010; *American Lawyer*, "Behind the Numbers," May 2010, 96; Press and Mulligan, "Lessons of the Am Law 100," May 1, 2010. See Combs, "No Place to Hide," June 1, 2010, for a fuller comparison between the Am Law 100 and the Am Law 200. Using different metrics, the comparison showed varying relationships between the two groups of firms.

[375] DiPetro, "Priced to Sell," May 1, 2010. Additionally, smaller firms typically charge lower or more flexible rates than their larger counterparts, which helped to maintain demand for their services.

[376] Datamonitor, "Industry Profile: Legal Services in the United States," July 2010, 9. U. S. revenue grew by 4.8 percent in 2008 (similar to 4.6 percent in 2007). Legal services market value represents law firms' total revenues.

[377] Datamonitor, "Industry Profile: Legal Services in the United Kingdom," July 2010, 9; Lloyd, "The 2009 Global 100," October 1, 2009; Datamonitor, "Industry Profile: Legal Services in France," July 2010, 9; Datamonitor, "Industry Profile: Legal Services in Japan," July 2010, 9. Between 2008 and 2009, profits per partner at large British firms such as Clifford Chance and Latham fell by over 40 and 20 percent, respectively, which is very different from their peak performance during 2004–08. As in the United Kingdom, legal services revenue in France and Japan grew 0.1 and 0.2 percent in 2009, respectively, versus annual average rates of 4.3 and 5.6 percent, respectively, during 2005–08.

[378] IMF, World Economic Outlook Database; Datamonitor, "Industry Profile: Legal Services in Germany," July 2010, 9. This sustained growth does not seem to be clearly associated with the performance of the German economy relative to other developed countries. While GDP in 2008 declined in the United Kingdom, stayed the same in the United States, and grew by only 0.1 percent in France, it continued to grow in Germany (by 1.0 percent). However, in 2009, GDP fell between 2.5 and 4.9 percent in all four countries. A similar pattern emerged with respect to employment of legal professionals. The United States experienced the sharpest drop in employment, with a decline of 4.1 percent in 2009, followed by the United Kingdom and France, where growth slowed to 0.6 percent, whereas Germany's legal services employment grew 1.1 percent in 2009.

[379] Lloyd, "Storm Averted," May 1, 2010; Culbert, "Law Firms in the US," September 2010, 7.

[380] IBISWorld, "Attorney and Legal Services in China," January 2010, 36.
[381] Ibid., 11–33. See Ministry of Commerce, 2–5, for additional estimates of industry growth, reported as 17.0 percent in 2008; revenues of foreign law firms' representative offices in China, which may be included in the domestic aggregate on which 17 percent growth figure is based, grew by 23.4 percent in 2008.
[382] IBISWorld, "Attorney and Legal Services in China," January 2010, 36.
[383] Vinson and Elkins Web site, "VandE Assists Sinopec International Petroleum Exploration and Production Corporation" (accessed January 20, 2011); Bronstad, "Asia Practice Special Report," November 16, 2010; Freshfields Bruckhaus Deringer Web site, "Freshfields Advises Geely," March 29, 2010. Examples of such investments include the acquisition by China Petroleum and Chemical Corporation (Sinopec) of Canadian Addax Petroleum Corporation in 2009 (Sinopec was represented by U. S. law firm Vinson and Elkins) and the 2010 purchase of Volvo from Ford Motor Co. by Zhejiang Geely Holding Group Co. (represented by UK firm Freshfields Bruckhaus Deringer).
[384] Bronstad, "Asia Practice Special Report," November 16, 2010; Wines, "China Bank I.P.O. Raises $19 Billion," July 6, 2010. In 2010, Agriculture Bank of China raised $22.1 billion; U. S. firm Davis Polk and Wardwell and UK firm Herbert Smith were involved with the IPO. In 2006, the Industrial and Commercial Bank of China raised $21.9 billion in IPOs.
[385] IBIS World, "Attorney and Legal Services in China," January 2010, 7. It is not clear in which year commercial legal services were 65 percent of the industry revenue, though the statistics likely refer to 2009 or 2010. USITC staff derived the 65 percent figure by adding commercial legal services (commercial disputes, litigation, and arbitration) and nonlitigious legal services (consultation, mediation, services for mergers and acquisitions, conveyancing, bankruptcies, and IPOs).
[386] Ibid., 4; Datamonitor, "Industry Profile: Legal Services in Asia-Pacific," July 2010, 10. The number of legal professionals in Asia-Pacific grew in 2009 by 4.2 percent, just under the rate for 2005–2008 (4.6 percent). This growth was largely due to China's legal services market where, according to statistics by the Chinese Ministry of Justice (see Ministry of Commerce), employment in China's legal services industry grew 9.0 percent in 2008 to 216,701.
[387] Cattaneo and Walkenhorst, "Legal Services," 2010, 70.
[388] Culbert, "Law Firms in the US," September 2010, 26.
[389] Kessenides, "The AM Law 100 2010," May 12, 2010.
[390] Breitman, "Overseas Practices Keep British Firms Afloat," September 9, 2008.
[391] USDOC, BEA, U. S. *International Services*, 2005–09, table 7. U. S. legal services exports to the Middle East grew at an average annual rate of 30.3 percent in 2005–09, almost double the rate (17.6) of exports to Asia-Pacific, the second fastest growing region.
[392] Haberbeck, "Bridging the Gulf," May 28, 2007.
[393] Legal 500 Web site, "Saudi Arabia" (accessed January 20, 2010).
[394] Lloyd, "Abu Dhabi," October 1, 2009; LexisNexis, Martindale-Hubbell Law Directory (accessed December 8, 2010).
[395] Hogan Lovells Web site, "Offices: Abu Dhabi," (accessed December 7, 2010); TAQA Web site, http://www.taqa.ae/en/index.html (accessed December 7, 2010).
[396] Dewey and LeBoeuf Web site, "Abu Dhabi" (accessed December 8, 2010).
[397] USDOC, BEA, U. S. *International Services*, 2005–09, table 7. See the trade trends section of this chapter for a fuller explanation.
[398] Zillman, "Brazil," October 1, 2009; LexisNexis, Martindale-Hubbell Law Directory (accessed December 8, 2010); Todd, "The Future is Now," October 1, 2010; Legal 500 Web site, "Brazil" (accessed January 4, 2010).
[399] Allen and Overy Web site, "People and Offices: Brazil" (accessed December 8, 2010); Squire Sanders Web site, "São Paulo" (accessed December 8, 2010).
[400] See *American Lawyer*, "Field Reports," October 2009, for information on developing legal services markets in India, Russia, and Singapore. Also see Zillman, "Brazil," October 1, 2009.
[401] Outside counsel refers to legal services law firms provide to corporations, while in-house counsel refers to corporations' own legal departments.
[402] Burk and McGowan, "Big But Brittle," 2010, 14–61.
[403] DuPont Legal Web site, "Primary Service Providers" (accessed January 25, 2010). According to this site, DuPont has "39 Primary Law Firms (PLFs), 9 Primary Service Providers (PSPs) and Diverse Legal Suppliers." See *New Legal Review*, "Inside the DuPont Legal Model," May 11, 2010.
[404] Passarella, "GCs Want Firms to Change with Times," June 8, 2009; Burk and McGowan, "Big but Brittle," 2010, 61. Companies (as well as law firms) have also used legal process outsourcing (LPO) in overseas markets for legal research and document review/drafting. However, the Indian LPO industry has not grown as swiftly as foreseen a couple of years ago, and LPOs tend to focus more on back-office functions than substantive legal work. See Lin, "Inside the Revolution," October 1, 2010, and Blakely and Spence, "Brief for India's Outsourcing Lawyers," January 15, 2010, on law firms' use of LPOs.
[405] Association of Corporate Counsel and Altman Weil, Inc., "2005 Chief Legal Officer Survey," 2005, 12; Altman Weil, Inc., "2010 Chief Legal Officer Survey," 2010, 17.

[406] Association of Corporate Counsel and Altman Weil, Inc., "2005 Chief Legal Officer Survey," 2005, 4; Altman Weil, Inc., "2010 Chief Legal Officer Survey," 2010, 5. This number decreased to 29.1 percent in 2010.
[407] Johnson, "Letter from London," September 17, 2010.
[408] Hildebrandt Baker Robbins and Citi Private Bank, "2010 Client Advisory," March 3, 2010, 2.
[409] Lippe, "General Counsel to Cut Legal Spending up to 25%," October 22, 2010; Lamb, "25% Cut in In-House Legal Spending," October 27, 2010.
[410] Data are from the BEA, and labor productivity is calculated as real value added divided by full-time equivalent employees. Legal services labor productivity did grow during 1999–2000 and again during 2003–05.
[411] Output started to decline after 2005, while employment was still growing (employment started to decline only in 2008). The sharpest drops in both employment (3.6 percent) and output (6.4 percent) occurred in 2009. By the end of the period, in 2009, employment levels matched those between 2002–03, while output reverted to the 2000 level, making labor productivity the lowest it had ever been in the ten year period from 1999 through 2009.
[412] Culbert, "Law Firms in the US," September 2010, 22, 35.
[413] Hildebrandt Baker Robbins and Citi Private Bank, "2010 Client Advisory," March 3, 2010, 5. The expenses refer to a sample of 193 firms, including firms from the 200 highest-grossing U. S. firms and 52 additional participants, from 2001 through 2008.
[414] Burk and McGowan, "Big but Brittle," 2010, 20–23.
[415] Jones, "2009 Worst Year for Lawyer Headcount in 3 Decades," November 9, 2009.
[416] *National Law Journal*, "The 2009 NLF 250," November 9, 2009; Jones, "So Long, Farewell," November 9, 2009; Jones, "Headcount Declined Sharply in New York, Atlanta, and Philadelphia," November 10, 2009. Labor declines were highest in New York City (13.3 percent, which also includes firms that closed during the survey year), followed by Philadelphia (9.6 percent) and Atlanta (9.4 percent). The least hard-hit large U. S. cities were Chicago (4.1 percent) and San Francisco (3.9 percent).
[417] The 2009 decline was also steeper than the previous two (in 1992 and 1993), when the number of attorneys fell by less than 1 percent.
[418] The number of associates declined 8.7 percent while the number of partners increased 0.9 percent. Jones, "So Long, Farewell," November 9, 2009.
[419] Jones, "2009 Worst Year for Lawyer Headcount in 3 Decades," November 9, 2009.
[420] Jones, "Big Firms Slashed Headcount at International Offices," November 12, 2009.
[421] Datamonitor, "Industry Profile: Legal Services in the United States," July 2010, 10. Table 7.3 also presents employment in legal services for the United States as reported by the U. S. Department of Labor (DOL), Bureau of Labor Statistics (BLS) Current Employer Statistics, which show a 3.4 percent decline in the same year. While the BLS estimates of total employees in legal services are classified by NAICS code (5411) and exclude the self-employed (see http://www.bls.gov/ces/cesfaq.htm), Datamonitor refers to the total number of legal professionals according to its definition of the legal services market. The decline was relatively even across states in the BLS sample. Four of the five states with the highest employment in legal services—California, Florida, Illinois, and Texas—all experienced declines ranging between 3.3 and 3.5 percent; New York experienced the highest decline at 5.1 percent. Note that the numbers given for total employees in the BLS estimate but are representative of large and small firms and include all employees in legal services. These numbers show a decline of 0.2 percent between 2005–08, while the National Law Journal (NLJ) 250 (the largest 250 U. S. firms by employment) enjoyed positive growth rates of attorneys during those years. See table 7.2 on the number of firms in the U. S. legal services industry by size. Also see Culbert, "Law Firms in the US," September 2010, 21, where it is reported that approximately 60 percent of legal services establishments are non-employer firms and 95 percent of employer firms have fewer than 20 employees.
[422] Culbert, "Law Firms in the US," September 2010, 7.
[423] Hildebrandt Baker Robbins and Citi Private Bank, "2010 Client Advisory," March 3, 2010, 5–8. Expense and profit estimates refer to a survey of 193 firms, including firms from the 200 highest-grossing U. S. firms and 52 additional participants. Profits per equity partner declined 0.3 percent in 2009 versus 3.0 percent in 2008, compared with 11.5 percent growth during the 2001–07 period. Also see DiPetro, "Priced to Sell," May 1, 2010; *Economist*, "Laid-off Lawyers, Cast-off Consultants," January 21, 2010.
[424] Kolz, "No Easy Answers," May 1, 2010.
[425] Marek, "What to Expect in the Decade Ahead," November 9, 2009.
[426] USDOC, BEA, U. S. *International Services*, 2005–09, table 7. Note that 2005 export data for legal services refer to unaffiliated services (i.e., services not provided by foreign affiliates of U. S. firms); affiliated services are reported in "other" affiliated services. From 2006 on, export data for legal services include both affiliated and unaffiliated trade.
[427] USDOC, BEA, U. S. *International Services*, 2009, table 7; USDOC, BEA, U. S. *International Services*, 2005, table 7. Regionally, Europe's share shrank from 51.9 percent in 2005 to 48.3 percent in 2009, while the Middle East increased from 2.3 percent in 2005 to 3.9 percent in 2009, and the Asia-Pacific increased from 28.6 percent in 2005 to 31.9 percent in 2009.

[428] USDOC, BEA, U. S. *International Services*, 2008–09, table 7. Exports declined by 18 percent in Africa and grew by 0.7 percent in the Middle East.
[429] The 10 fastest-growing export markets from 2005 through 2008 include the ones mentioned above, plus Australia, China, Korea, New Zealand, and Singapore. Though U. S. legal services exports to a number of these countries declined or grew more slowly in 2009 than in 2005–08, they account for the majority of the countries whose annual average (U.S. legal services) exports grew fastest from 2005 through 2008. Within the Asia-Pacific, China and Korea took the largest share of U. S. legal export after Japan, at 10.2 percent and 13.6 percent, respectively. Among all countries importing U. S. legal services, China's share increased from 2.1 percent in 2005 to 3.2 percent in 2009 and Korea's from 2.4 percent in 2005 to 4.4 percent in 2009. Within Latin America, Brazil and Mexico are the largest export markets (17.8 and 16.8 percent, respectively). Israel makes up 44.2 percent of the Middle Eastern export market, and South Africa makes up 60 percent of the African market.
[430] Cattaneo and Walkenhorst, "Legal Services," 2010, 70.
[431] Imports from Europe declined by 20.2 percent in 2009 after growing at an annual average rate of 25.7 percent during 2005–08; the share of imports from Europe among total imports fell from 57.5 percent in 2005 to 47.9 percent in 2009.
[432] Imports from Canada declined 25.4 percent in 2009, following annual average growth of 28.7 percent during 2005–08; the share of imports from Canada among total imports fell from 9.5 percent in 2005 to 7.9 percent in 2009.
[433] Imports from the Asia-Pacific declined 19.3 percent in 2009 after growing at an annual average rate of 41.1 percent during 2005–08; the share of imports from the Asia-Pacific among total imports increased from 22.9 percent in 2005 to 27.4 percent in 2009.
[434] Imports from Latin America and the Western Hemisphere increased by 29.9 percent in 2009 following annual average growth of 26.0 percent between 2005–08; the share of imports from Latin America in total imports of U.S legal services increased from 7.5 percent in 2005 to 10.2 percent in 2009. Imports from the Middle East increased by 46.2 percent in 2009 after growing at an annual average rate of 63.0 percent during 2005–08; the share of imports from the Middle East increased from 1.7 percent in 2005 to 5.6 percent in 2009. Imports from Africa increased 23.1 percent in 2009 following annual average growth of 22.9 percent between 2005 and 2008; the share of imports from Africa increased from 0.8 percent in 2005, to 0.9 percent in 2009.
[435] USDOC, BEA, *Survey of Current Business*, September 2010, table 14.
[436] USDOC, BEA, U. S. *International Services*, 2009, table 7.
[437] USDOC, BEA, *Survey of Current Business*, September 2010, table 14. This number is for investment in all industries.
[438] Todd, "The Future is Now," October 1, 2010.
[439] Cresswell, "JP Morgan Looks to Brazil," October 28, 2010.
[440] U. S. legal service imports from Israel grew 72.7 percent in 2009 to $76 million, slightly slower than the average annual growth rate between 2005 and 2008 of 94.3 percent. The share of U. S. legal services imports from Israel increased to 4.5 percent in 2009 compared with 0.7 percent in 2005. U. S. legal service imports from Brazil grew 112.5 percent in 2009 to $68 million, and grew at an annual average rate of 31.7 percent between 2005 and 2008. The share of U. S. legal services imports from Brazil has increased from 1.6 percent in 2005 to 4.0 percent in 2009.
[441] Legal 500 Web site, "Herzog Fox and Newman" (accessed December 20, 2010); Herzog Fox and Neeman Web site, "Practice Areas, Banking and Finance" (accessed December 20, 2010).
[442] BEA reports "services supplied" by foreign affiliates. In the legal services industry, services supplied correspond to sales. Thus, sales and services supplied are used interchangeably in this section.
[443] USDOC, BEA, U. S. *International Services*, 2005–09, table 7.
[444] Ibid.
[445] USDOC, BEA, *Survey of Current Business*, September 2010, table 15.
[446] Culbert, "Law Firms in the US," September 2010, 26.
[447] USDOC, BEA, U. S. *International Services*, 2003–08, table 10. Note that data for 2005 and 2006 data were suppressed to avoid disclosing individual firms' data. Hence, country-specific data on purchases from U. S. affiliates of foreign law firms are not available in enough detail to determine which countries account for the greatest shares of such transactions.
[448] For Asian markets, see Sawhney, "Entering the Emerging Markets of Asia."
[449] Office of the U. S. Trade Representative (USTR), "India," 2010, 7.
[450] Jones Day Web site, "Offices: New Delhi" (accessed December 29, 2010); Allen and Overy Web site, "People and Offices: India Group" (accessed February 1, 2011).
[451] Also see Lin, "India," October 1, 2009.
[452] USTR, "India," 2010, 7.
[453] Baxter, "India Again Closes Door on Foreign Firms," September 29, 2010.
[454] American Lawyer, "The Future is Now" (video), October 1, 2010.

[455] Mayer Brown is partnered with a local Brazilian law firm, Tauil and Chequer Advogados. Mayer Brown Web site, "Offices: São Paulo" (accessed December 20, 2010).
[456] USDOC, U. S. Commercial Service, "Doing Business in Saudi Arabia," 2010, 75; Legal 500 Web site, "Saudi Arabia, Legal market overview" (accessed December 20, 2010).
[457] For further restrictions, see USTR, "China," 2010, 24–25.
[458] USTR, "Korea," 2010, 5. Also see Rupp and Kim, "Korean Legal Services Set to Open Up," February 26, 2008; United States-Korea Free Trade Agreement, Annex II: Non-Conforming Measures for Services and Investment, 44–45. The free trade agreement between Korea and the United States, signed in 2007 but not yet ratified, includes liberalizing provisions related to legal services. For example, U. S. law firms are allowed to establish foreign legal consultant offices, and U.S-licensed attorneys are permitted to provide legal services regarding international law and laws of their home jurisdiction. Other provisions permit foreign legal consultant offices to enter into "cooperative agreements" with Korean law firms and for U. S. law firms to form joint ventures with Korean law firms.
[459] USTR, "Singapore," 2010, 2; Swift, "Singapore's Swing," August 9, 2010; Lin, "Singapore: Feeling the West's Pain," October 1, 2009.
[460] Ribstein, "Death of Big Law," 2010. See *The Legal Intelligencer*, "The New Firm Order," June 22, 2009, for a series of articles examining the effect of the economic recession on the legal industry. Examples include Passarella, "Losing Lockstep," May 18, 2009, and Passarella, "Diamonds Are a Law Firm's Best Friend," May 11, 2009, on associate hiring and compensation models. Culbert, "Law Firms in the US," September 2010, 8–9; Heineman and Lee, "The Time Has Come," October 1, 2009.
[461] Johnson, "Letter from London," September 17, 2010. Also see Passarella, "For Large Firms," May 26, 2009; Passarella and Needles, "After the Last Shoe Drops," June 22, 2009.
[462] Heineman and Lee, "The Time Has Come," October 1, 2009.
[463] Passarella, "For Large Firms," May 26, 2009.
[464] Needles, "For Midsized Firms, Opportunities Abound," June 1, 2009.
[465] Burk and McGowan, "Big but Brittle," 2010, 56–57, 63.
[466] DiPetro, "Priced to Sell," May 1, 2010. Also see Lloyd, "The 2009 Global 100," October 1, 2009.
[467] Marek, "What to Expect in the Decade Ahead," November 9, 2009.
[468] Culbert, "Law Firms in the US," September 2010, 26.
[469] Tradability refers to whether a good or service can be consumed at a location distant from the site of its production. For more detail on research conducted in this area, see box 2.1 on p. 2-4.

In: Trends in U. S. Services Trade
Editors: Charles Schneider and Thomas G. Hatchet

ISBN 978-1-62100-933-7
© 2012 Nova Science Publishers, Inc.

Chapter 2

U. S. MULTINATIONAL SERVICES COMPANIES: EFFECTS OF FOREIGN AFFILIATE ACTIVITY ON U. S. EMPLOYMENT

United States International Trade Commission

ABSTRACT[1]

This working paper examines the effect that U. S. services firms' establishment abroad has on domestic employment. Whereas many papers have explored the employment effects of foreign direct investment in manufacturing, few have explored the effects of services investment. We find that services multinationals' activities abroad increase U. S. employment by promoting intrafirm exports from parent firms to their foreign affiliates. These exports support jobs at the parents' headquarters and throughout their U. S. supply chains. Our findings are principally based on economic research and econometric analysis performed by Commission staff, services trade and investment data published by the Bureau of Economic Analysis, and employment data collected by the Bureau of Labor Statistics. In the aggregate, we find that services activities abroad support nearly 700,000 U. S. jobs. Case studies of U. S. multinationals in the banking, computer, logistics, and retail industries provide the global dimensions of U. S. MNC operations and identify domestic employment effects associated with foreign affiliate activity in each industry.

INTRODUCTION

Do the foreign activities of U. S. multinational companies (MNCs) create jobs in the United States or erode them? This question has been a focus of research and popular debate in recent years, but relatively little of this attention has been devoted to service industries.

This working paper examines how the foreign activities of multinational service firms affect employment in the United States. In chapter 1, we review some basic data on U. S. multinational service companies, then examine the relationship between these firms' foreign affiliate activities and U. S. employment. We find that domestic employment is positively correlated with such activities, and that these relationships are statistically significant. This suggests that domestic employment and foreign activity in services are complements.

Next, we present data that show how multinational parent firms and their affiliates work in concert to compete in foreign markets. We focus on the size and growth of intrafirm services trade, particularly domestic parent firms' exports to foreign affiliates. These exports support jobs at multinational parent firms' headquarters and throughout their U. S. supply chains. Using an "employment requirements" matrix developed by the Bureau of Labor Statistics (BLS) and trade data, we estimate the number of jobs thus supported. Our findings suggest that intrafirm exports of services by U. S. multinational companies support nearly 700,000 U. S. jobs.

To place these results in context, chapters 2 through 5 examine the banking, computer, logistics, and retail service industries. These sectors were selected because they feature some of the most active multinational service providers headquartered in the United States. The case studies briefly describe each industry, discuss the global dimensions of U. S. MNCs' operations, and identify the domestic employment effects associated with foreign affiliate activity.

1. ESTIMATION OF EMPLOYMENT EFFECTS

U.S. direct investment abroad[2] by services firms (excluding holding companies) totaled $1.4 trillion in 2008, or 43 percent of all such investment.[3] U. S. service firms have invested abroad because many services require their providers to be near their consumers. Outbound investment has also been driven by firms' interest in accessing new markets—especially large emerging markets—and by regulations that prohibit cross-border trade or make residence a condition of market participation.[4] Entering new markets is a means of leveraging the capital and intellectual property developed inside MNCs to develop new revenue streams and "brand" firms globally. Such investment has been facilitated by the liberalization of policies that prohibited or otherwise restricted foreign establishment. Services supplied by affiliates in 2008 ($1.1 trillion) outstripped cross-border services exports ($518 billion) by a margin of more than two-to-one.[5]

Parents of U. S. services multinationals continue to account for the majority of such firms' economic activity. In 2008, parent firms accounted for 79.4 percent of total value added[6] by U. S. services multinationals, and 74.9 percent of employment. Yet the allocation of value added and employment within services multinationals is changing. Value added by services parent firms grew at a compound annual rate of 3.5 percent between 1999 and 2008, while employment was flat. Over the same period, value added by their majority-owned foreign affiliates (MOFAs) increased at a compound annual rate of 8.2 percent, and employment grew at a compound annual rate of 4.6 percent. Sales by MOFAs became increasingly important to services multinationals over this period: such sales climbed from 14.0 percent of service multinationals' sales in 1999 to 23.9 percent in 2008.[7]

During the 1999 to 2008 period, the top ten countries by number of MOFAs was similar, although China broke into the group and Belgium dropped out of it (table 1). Value added among MOFAs increased across all industries during the period, but growth in many service industries eclipsed that in manufacturing (table 2).

Table 1. Number of U. S. majority-owned foreign affiliates, by country, 1999 and 2008

Country	1999	Country	2008
United Kingdom	2,535	United Kingdom	2,963
Canada	1,859	Canada	1,850
Germany	1,327	Germany	1,593
France	1,174	Netherlands	1,541
Netherlands	1,117	France	1,302
Mexico	802	Mexico	883
Australia	773	China	868
Italy	680	Australia	814
Japan	651	Japan	739
Belgium	542	Italy	703
Other	9,582	Other	11,729
Total	21,042	Total	24,985

Source: U. S. Department of Commerce, Bureau of Economic Analysis, "Selected Data for Foreign Affiliates in All Countries in Which Investment was Reported," 1999 and 2008.
Note: Totals exclude affiliates that were exempt from reporting requirements.

The leading countries in employment by MOFAs in 2008 largely mirrored those with the largest number of foreign affiliates (table 3), and with the exception of Germany, which saw a minimal decrease, employment grew within each of those countries during 1999-2008. Further, when measured by industry of affiliate, employment growth among MOFAs in many service industries outpaced that in manufacturing (table 4).

Table 2. Value added of U. S. majority-owned foreign affiliates by industry ($ millions), 1999 and 2008

Industry	1999	2008	CAGR 1999–2008	Growth 1999–2008
Manufacturing	316,300	517,133	5.6	63.5
Mining	38,552	221,006	21.4	473.3
Wholesale trade	76,774	157,274	8.3	104.9
Retail trade	14,499	53,323	15.6	267.8
Computer systems design and related services	16,166	36,824	9.6	127.8
Real estate and rental and leasing	5,630	29,041	20.0	415.8
Administration, support, and waste management	11,508	28,932	10.8	151.4
Insurance carriers and related activities	13,802	28,597	8.4	107.2
Transportation and warehousing	4,936	18,841	16.0	281.7
Finance, except depository institutions	11,490	17,885	5.0	55.7
All other	56,738	102,996	0.8	81.5
Total	566,395	1,211,852	8.8	114

Source: *U. S.* Department of Commerce, Bureau of Economic Analysis.

Table 3. Employment in U. S. majority-owned foreign affiliates by country (thousands of employees), 1999 and 2008

Country	1999	2008	CAGR 1999-2008	Growth 1999-2008
United Kingdom	1,060	1,174	1.1	10.8
Canada	1,004	1,064	0.6	6.0
Mexico	781	902	1.6	15.5
China	252	774	13.3	206.7
Germany	641	621	-0.3	-3.0
France	530	604	1.5	14.0
Brazil	349	486	3.7	39.3
India	62	313	19.7	403.9
Japan	207	297	4.1	43.1
Australia	253	288	1.5	14.1
All other	2,627	3,600	3.6	37.0
All countries	7,766	10,124	3.0	30.4

Source: U. S. Department of Commerce, Bureau of Economic Analysis
Note: CAGR is cumulative annual growth rate.

Table 4. Employment in U. S. majority-owned foreign affiliates by industry of affiliate (thousands of employees), 1999 and 2008

Industry	1999	2008	CAGR 1999–2008	Growth 1999–2008
Manufacturing	4,357	4,600	0.6	5.6
Retail trade	414	1,063	11.1	157.0
Administration, support, and waste management	434	873	8.1	101.0
Wholesale trade	670	797	1.9	18.9
Accommodation and food services	365	693	7.4	89.9
Computer systems design and related services	158	351	9.3	122.2
Transportation and warehousing	117	220	7.3	88.3
Mining	129	198	4.9	53.2
Insurance carriers and related activities	129	149	1.6	15.0
Internet, data processing, and other information services	([a])	130.1	([a])	([a])
All other	991.9	1,049	0.6	5.8
Total	7,765.7	10,123.9		

Source: U. S. Department of Commerce, Bureau of Economic Analysis.
[a] Data collection methods changed significantly between 1999 and 2008, obviating calculation of growth rates for the period.

Domestic Employment Effects

A number of studies have examined the relationship between MNCs' foreign activities and employment in parent companies' home country.[8] All but a few of these studies have focused on manufacturing, and most have used "firm-level" data (data collected from individual firms through surveys). These studies have found evidence of both complementarity and substitution between international activity and home country employment. Brainard and Riker (1997) found that among U. S. manufacturing multinationals, employment at affiliates substituted only modestly for U. S. employment, whereas substitution *among* affiliates in low-wage countries was stronger.[9] Desai, Foley and Hines (2008) found evidence of complementarity: among U. S. manufacturing firms, they found that 10 percent greater investment abroad was associated with 2.6 percent additional investment in the United States, and 10 percent greater foreign employee compensation was associated with 3.7 percent greater U. S. employee compensation.[10] The work of Harrison and McMillan (2006) yielded a more nuanced picture. They found that employment at affiliates in high-wage countries complemented U. S. employment, but employment in low-wage countries substituted for it.[11]

Molnar, Pain and Taglioni (2008) produced one of the few studies examining services. Using industry- level data for both goods-producing and service industries, they found that a 1 percent increase in employment at foreign affiliates is associated with a 0.1-0.2 percent increase in U. S. employment in each industry after two years, if output and wages are held constant (in contrast, they found a negative effect in Japan, although the effect is not statistically significant in all models). These results were calculated for services and manufacturing industries together. The authors also investigated the impact of outward foreign direct investment on domestic employment growth, and for these estimations they examined effects for services separately from manufacturing. They found evidence suggesting that, among member countries of the Organisation for Economic Co-operation and Development (OECD), domestic and foreign employment are substitutable in manufacturing industries with strong links to non-OECD countries, but complementary in services. Finally, Imbriani, Pittiglio, and Reganati (2010) used firm-level data from Italy to examine how "internationalization" (the change from being a purely domestic firm to having foreign affiliates) affected parents' productivity and employment. They found that outward investment strengthened productivity and employment at manufacturing parent firms but weakened them among services parent firms.[12]

We use three econometric models to explore the relationship between foreign activity and domestic employment at U. S. multinational service firms. Our models use data from the Operations of Multinational Companies database prepared by the U. S. Department of Commerce, Bureau of Economic Analysis. The data are aggregated by industry. Our dataset includes 14 service industries[13] for the years 1999–2008. The following equations illustrate our models. They are modified from models employed by Molnar, Pain and Taglioni.[14]

1. $lnL_{it} = \beta_0 + \beta_1 lnY_{it} + \beta_2 lnW_{i(t-1)} + \beta_3 lnLF_{it} + \alpha_i + \gamma_t + u_{it}$
2. $lnL_{it} = \beta_0 + \beta_1 lnY_{it} + \beta_2 lnW_{i(t-1)} + \beta_3 lnS_{it} + \alpha_i + \gamma_t + u_{it}$
3. $lnL_{it} = \beta_0 + \beta_1 lnY_{it} + \beta_2 lnW_{i(t-1)} + \beta_3 lnFDI_{it} + \alpha_i + \gamma_t + u_{it}$

L is the level of domestic employment among U. S. parent companies in service industry i in year t. Y and W are value added[15] and average wages,[16] respectively, in industry i at these U. S. parent firms. The wage variable is lagged by one year. LF, S, and FDI are alternative measures of foreign activity: employment at foreign affiliates, affiliate sales, and the U. S. outward investment stock in industry i, respectively.[17] These measures are highly correlated (table 5). α represents "fixed effects" that control for unobserved, explanatory factors specific to each industry. V represents "time fixed effects" to control for factors that are specific to each year. β_0 is a constant and u is the error term. The variables are expressed in natural logarithms to facilitate interpretation of the coefficients. The value added, wage, investment stock, and affiliate sales data are adjusted for inflation.[18]

The coefficient on value added is expected to be positive because greater output is likely to be associated with greater employment. The lagged wage variable is expected to have a negative sign because higher wage costs are likely to lead companies to employ fewer workers. The foreign activity variables will have positive signs if foreign activity and U.S. employment are complementary and negative signs if they are substitutes.

The results from our regressions appear below (table 6).

Table 5. Correlation matrix

Variables	Domestic employment	Domestic value added	Domestic wages	Foreign employment	Affiliate sales	Outward investment
Domestic employment	1.000					
Value added	0.863	1.000				
Domestic wages	-0.090	0.358	1.000			
Foreign employment	0.768	0.705	0.054	1.000		
Affiliate sales	0.596	0.732	0.390	0.883	1.000	
Outward investment	0.446	0.590	0.334	0.682	0.819	1.000

Source: Compiled by Commission staff.

Table 6. Regression results

Dependent variable: Employment at U.S. parent companies of multinational service firms t-scores in parentheses			
	1	2	3
Domestic value added	0.628*	0.637*	0.640*
	(6.29)	(6.42)	(6.54)
Domestic wages	-0.105	-0.125	-0.126
	(-0.57)	(-0.65)	(-0.63)
Foreign employment	0.118*		
	(3.27)		
Affiliate sales		0.102*	
		(2.89)	
Outward investment			0.053
			(1.23)
Constant	0.087	-0.295	0.230
	(0.04)	(-0.13)	(0.10)
Number of observations	122	122	121
Adjusted R-squared	0.990	0.990	0.989

Source: Compiled by Commission staff.
* 1 percent level significance.

In all the regressions, the coefficient on value added is significant and positive, as expected. The coefficient on wages is negative but not significant.[19] The coefficients for two of the three foreign activity variables—foreign employment and affiliate sales—are positive and significant at the 1 percent level, while the coefficient for the third, outward investment, is positive but not significant. Together, the regressions provide moderately strong evidence of a small, positive effect of foreign activity on employment at U. S. parents of multinational service companies: a 1 percent increase in foreign employment or sales at affiliates of multinationals in a given service industry is associated with a 0.1 percent increase in employment at their U. S. parents.

How does one account for this positive association between increased affiliate activity and domestic employment in U. S. multinational service firms? Intrafirm exports appear to be a key part of the answer (box 1). Such exports are conduits for the transfer of intellectual property and business services that support day-to-day operations and production of the final services sold to affiliates' local consumers. U. S. parent firms' exports of services to foreign affiliates totaled $109.1 billion in 2009, or 22.5 percent of total cross-border service exports (table 7).[20] The majority of these exports were in the form of intangible intellectual property (figure 1). Management and consulting services; research, development, and testing services; and financial services were other large sources of intrafirm export earnings.[21]

Box 1. Relationship between Cross-border Services Exports and Affiliate Sales

There is a growing body of literature that investigates the relationship between cross-border services exports and affiliate sales, with the latter sometimes proxied by foreign direct investment (FDI) stocks. There is, in general, a consensus for complementarity. Kox (2009) states that foreign affiliates require headquarters and other specialized services from MNC parents while unaffiliated firms abroad similarly require intermediary services from the home country.[a] Buch and Lipponer (2007), studying German banks, observe that higher FDI in a foreign market is strongly associated with higher financial service exports to that market, though higher country risk and lax banking supervision may dissuade investment, but not necessarily trade.[b] Fillat-Castejón, Francois, and Wörz (2009) observe aggregate services imports and inbound direct investment moving in tandem over the short term in response to trade and investment conditions. Over the long term, they see direct investment promoting trade, but not vice versa.[c] Nordås and Kox (2009) find cross-border exports and affiliate sales to be complements, although they caution that regulatory heterogeneity, by raising the cost of establishment, may discourage investment and promote cross-border trade, resulting in a substitution effect.[d]

[a] Kox, "What is Special in Services Liberalization?" 2009, 4.
[b] Buch and Lipponer, "Evidence from German Banks," 2006, 820-833.
[c] Fillat-Castejón, Francois, and Wörz, "Cross-Border Trade and FDI in Services," 2009, 9-18.
[d] Nordås and Kox, "Quantifying Regulatory Barriers to Services Trade," 2009, 20-26.

Table 7. Multinational parent firms' intrafirm exports of services ($ millions)

Industry	1999	2000	2001	2002	2003	2004	2005	2006	2007	2008	2009
Business, professional, and technical	23,794	26,680	29,443	30,947	32,177	35,022	36,033	24,027	32,630	36,176	37,320
Computer and information services	(a)	(a)	1,424	1,686	1,960	1,993	2,115	1,968	2,786	3,247	3,758
Management and consulting services	(a)	(a)	10,845	12,800	12,883	14,133	16,710	11,299	15,168	16,467	15,672
RandD and testing services	(a)	(a)	6,564	7,536	8,297	8,275	9,135	4,848	7,630	8,014	9,257
Operational leasing	(a)	(a)	2,157	2,874	2,593	3,000	3,300	1,027	1,717	1,979	2,037
Construction, architecture and engineering	(a)	(a)	(a)	(a)	(a)	(a)	(a)	685	662	814	811
Industrial engineering	(a)	(a)	(a)	(a)	(a)	(a)	(a)	367	453	419	419
Installation, maintenance and repair of equipment	(a)	(a)	(a)	(a)	(a)	(a)	(a)	456	580	847	897
Legal services	(a)	(a)	(a)	(a)	(a)	(a)	(a)	41	56	63	86
Advertising	(a)	(a)	(a)	(a)	(a)	(a)	(a)	1,937	(a)	(a)	2,110
Financial services	6,023	6,091	6,401	6,750	8,141	8,623	8,874	8,756	12,449	8,376	7,054
Intangible intellectual property	27,575	28,255	27,180	29,656	32,324	39,399	44,408	46,938	54,410	59,792	55,430
Telecommunications	(a)	(a)	(a)	(a)	(a)	(a)	(a)	1,296	2,065	2,698	3,047
Audiovisual services	(a)	(a)	(a)	(a)	(a)	(a)	(a)	4,826	5,632	5,309	6,215

Source: USDOC, BEA, *Survey of Current Business*, various issues.
[a] Not available.

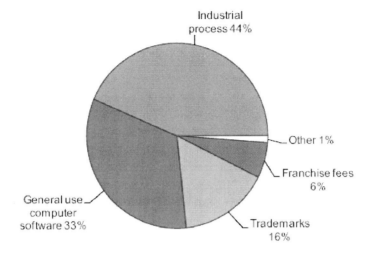

Total = $55.4 billion

Source: USDOC, BEA, *Survey of Current Business*, October 2010, 44.

Figure 1. Intrafirm exports of intangible intellectual property, by type, 2009.

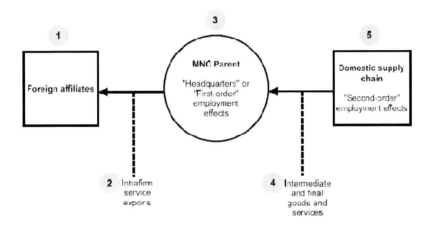

Figure 2. An increase in intrafirm exports drives first- and second-order employment effects.

Intrafirm exports support jobs at multinational parent firms' headquarters and throughout their U. S. supply chains. "Headquarters" or "first-order" job effects result from parents augmenting domestic staff to provide services demanded by foreign affiliates. "Second-order" effects occur throughout the domestic supply chain as parent firms increase production to meet affiliates' demand for services. The parent firms require greater amounts of goods and services to increase production, thus supporting jobs among their suppliers (figure 2).

We estimate the number of jobs supported by multinational service companies' intrafirm exports of services by consulting an employment requirements matrix[22] developed by the BLS. This matrix identifies the U. S. employment effects of additional demand for an industry's products, both within that industry and throughout its U. S. supply chain (box 2). We present our estimates in table 8. To generate the estimates, we multiply the number of jobs supported by $1 billion of additional demand for each service by the volume of U. S. multinationals' intrafirm exports of those services in 2008.[23] We find that almost 700,000 jobs are supported by intrafirm exports of services by U. S. multinational companies.[24] Appendix table A.1 presents our calculations in greater detail.

Table 8. Estimated number of jobs supported by intrafirm exports of services by multinational companies, 2008

Services exported by parent firms of U. S. multinational companies	Intrafirm exports of services by U. S. multinational companies ($ billions)	Jobs supported by intrafirm exports of services by U. S. multinational companies[a]
Computer and information services	3.247	23,395
Management and consulting services	16.467	153,342
RandD and testing services	8.014	58,024
Operational leasing	1.979	18,856
Construction, architectural, and engineering, services	0.814	7,280
Installation, maintenance and repair	0.847	8,371
Legal services	0.063	439
Financial services	8.376	45,799
Royalties and license fees[b]	60	367,739
Telecommunications	2.698	13,794
Totals	102.297	**697,038**

Sources: USDOC, BEA, Survey of Current Business, October 2010, 36-55; USDOC, BEA, Operations of Multinational Companies database (accessed June 16, 2011); USDOL, BLS, Employment Projections (accessed May 3, 2011).

[a] Calculated by multiplying the number of jobs supported by $1 billion of additional demand for each industry's products, as reported by BLS, by the value of intrafirm exports, as reported by BEA. Does not include jobs supported by intrafirm exports of advertising services; BEA did not disclose the value of these exports for 2008. See table A.1 for calculations.

[b] Also included in this category are newspaper, periodical, book, and directory publishing; software publishing; motion picture and video industries; sound recording industries; and radio and television broadcasts.

Box 2. Domestic Employment Requirements Matrix

The domestic employment requirements matrix used for the calculations in this paper was developed by the Bureau of Labor Statistics (BLS). The matrix is derived from input-output data, and shows the employment generated directly and indirectly across all industries by a billion dollar increase in final demand for each industry's products. The input-output matrix is developed in connection with the bureau's employment projections process. The productivity data is collected by BLS in its Current Employment Survey of enterprises and Current Employment Survey of households. Productivity data reflect technology and labor productivity figures collected in 2008, with sectors identified by 2007 North American Industrial Classification System (NAICS) codes.[a]

Each column of the employment requirements matrix shows the U. S. employment supported in each industry by a billion dollars in increased final demand. We use a version of the matrix that is adjusted to remove imports. The matrix provides employment effects for each industry as well as employment effects for each industry's entire supply chain. The employment figures are developed through a count of jobs, including full-time and part-time waged and salaried workers, self-employed workers, and unpaid family workers. Persons who hold multiple jobs can show up multiple times in the employment data.[b]

BLS is careful to note additional limitations of the matrix. To develop the matrix, BLS assumes that input-output relationships are stable overtime. Over long periods of time, changes to product mix and technology could alter these relationships, introducing error to employment effects. The relationships used in the matrix are average relationships; they may not hold on the margins, meaning the first or last unit of output may differ from the average. In addition, employment effects may be understated because investment purchases needed to increase output are excluded.[c]

For more information on the Domestic Employment Requirements matrix, see U. S. Department of Labor (USDOL), Bureau of Labor Statistics (BLS), *Employment Outlook: 2008-2018, Layout and Description for 202-Order Employment Requirements Tables: Historical 1993 through 2008*, December 2009, or visit http://www.bls.gov/emp/ ep data emp requirements.htm.

[a] USDOL, BLS, *Employment Outlook: 2008-2018* (December 2009), 3-4.
[b] USDOL, BLS, *Employment Outlook: 2008-2018* (December 2009), 4.
[c] USDOL, BLS, *Employment Outlook: 2008-2018* (December 2009), 5-6.

2. BANKING SERVICES

Summary

The recent global financial crisis had a substantial impact on the world's banking sector, with firms in developed countries generally experiencing the greatest losses. As large multinational banks seek new growth opportunities, they are increasingly looking to developing markets such as those in Asia and Latin America, where economic growth is relatively strong, emerging middle class populations have growing disposable incomes, and increasingly sophisticated banking services are in demand. The establishment of affiliate operations in such markets has the potential to create jobs in the U. S. banking industry and other industries that directly and indirectly support it. The headquarters employment effect is likely marginally positive, while job creation in a variety of services sectors in support of intrafirm trade between parent firms and their affiliates could be substantial. Our estimates indicate that intrafirm exports of financial services could result in over 45,000 new U. S. jobs across all sectors of the economy.

Industry Overview

In the context of this discussion, banking services comprise deposit taking and lending as well as fee- based commercial services to include financial management and transaction services, advisory services, custody services, credit card services, and other credit related services. While large multinational banks have increasingly expanded their service offerings to include securities, investment banking, and occasionally insurance services, this discussion focuses on the more traditional commercial banking activities that those companies provide.

Large U. S. banks tend to have affiliates outside the United States (table 10), though for some, foreign expansion has slowed in the wake of the financial crisis in order to focus on strengthening domestic operations. In 2009, for example, Bank of America elected to sell 68 percent of its overall 19 percent stake in China Construction Bank in its efforts to raise cash to cover its domestic losses.[28] However, this has been a balancing act for U. S. firms because foreign operations have also proven to be a more consistent source of revenue than domestic operations during the downturn. Despite Bank of America's pullback from the Chinese market, its international operations accounted for 20 percent of its total revenues in 2009, compared with an average of 9 percent prior to the financial crisis.[29] This increase was largely due to strong revenue growth in operations outside North America, and particularly in Asia, though U. S. revenues also grew albeit more slowly.[30] As domestic banks grow healthier they will likely seek more opportunities to establish affiliates in foreign markets, particularly developing countries, where growth opportunities may be greater.

Table 9. Top ten global banks by assets, 2009

Bank	Country of parent	Assets ($ billion)
BNP Paribas	France	2,965
Royal Bank of Scotland	United Kingdom	2,750
Credit Agricole Group	France	2,441
HSBC Holdings	United Kingdom	2,364
Barclays	United Kingdom	2,235
Bank of America	United States	2,223
Deutsche Bank	Germany	2,162
JPMorgan Chase and Co.	United States	2,032
Mitsubishi UFJ Financial Group	Japan	2,026
Citigroup	United States	1,857

Source: The Banker, Top 1000 World Banks 2010, www.thebanker.com, July 6, 2010.

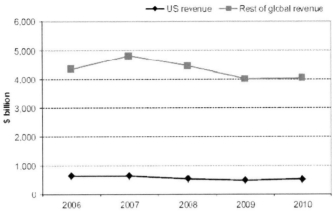

Sources: IBISWorld, *Global Commercial Banks*, January 6, 2011, 4, and IBISWorld, *Commercial Banking in the U. S.*, January 2011, 34.

Figure 3. US and global banking revenues, 2006–10.

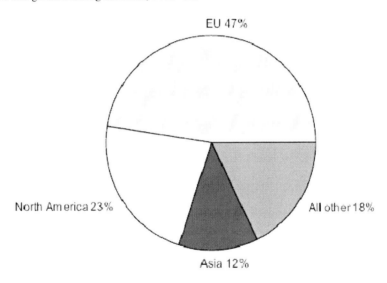

Source: IBISWorld, *Global Commercial Banks*, January 6, 2011, 4.

Figure 4. Regional share of global banking revenues, 2010.

The global banking industry, which is generally quite fragmented, has been consolidating for many years. Prior to the global financial crisis, merger and acquisition (MandA) activity was high, with larger banks in developed markets merging with smaller banks to gain market share in saturated environments, or acquiring firms in foreign countries as a method of entry into developing-country markets where economic growth is strong, disposable incomes are rising, and populations are underbanked. There were 55,279 commercial banks worldwide in 2010, of which 6,410 were U. S. banks, representing declines of 12 and 7 percent, respectively, from 2006 levels.[31]

Table 10. Assets and foreign operations of U. S. banks among the top 25 global banks, 2009

Bank	Assets ($ billion)	Number of countries
Bank of America	2,223	44
JPMorgan Chase Bank	2,032	40
Citigroup	1,857	100
Wells Fargo Bank	1,244	([a])

Sources: The Banker, Top 1000 World Banks 2010, www.thebanker.com, July 6, 2010; and individual company websites.

[a] Not available.

Expansion into developing-country markets is increasing, but emerging market banks themselves are vying for market share and may have less fallout from the financial crisis to contend with. Some of the most successful Western banks have a limited, strategic presence in a large number of countries and have been entrenched for a long time (e.g., Citigroup, Standard Chartered (UK), and HSBC (UK)) and enjoy certain advantages such as brand awareness that new Western entrants lack. Additionally, many emerging market banks themselves are becoming stronger competitors, further limiting the opportunities for foreign banks to gain market share.[32] Emerging market banks are growing much more rapidly than Western banks, reaching 53 percent of global market capitalization in 2009.[33] However, profits earned by large developed-country banks in emerging markets were equivalent to roughly one-quarter that of the local banks,[34] demonstrating the success that global banks have had in developing markets and the allure of those markets for such banks seeking new growth opportunities.

Operations of Multinational Banks and Links to Employment

Banking services can be traded cross-border or through establishment of an affiliate in a foreign market, with the latter comprising a much larger share of sales. In 2008, cross-border exports of financial services[35] totaled $60.8 billion, while foreign affiliate sales registered $175.9 billion. In commercial banking, this discrepancy is due in part to the fact that the industry relies heavily on deposit taking and lending, which require strong local branch networks.

There were 14.9 million people employed in the global banking industry in 2010, with 1.5 million of those, or nearly 10 percent of the workforce, in the United States.[36] These figures represent an overall increase in global employment of 7 percent over 2006 levels, but a 6 percent decrease in U. S. banking employment during the same period. This is consistent with the growth of banking in many developing markets, where much of that job creation likely took place, while banks in the United States and Europe contracted. However, wage growth in the sector during that same period demonstrated the opposite effect: global wages declined 6 percent while commercial banking wages in the United States grew by a modest 1 percent.[37] The decline in jobs in the United States banking industry appears to be a direct result of the financial crisis, as employment was on the rise prior to 2008. Typically, however, banks need to maintain strong workforces in order to be competitive. Even though many commercial and retail banking services have become automated, branch expansion has increased in the United States and customer service is of paramount importance for banks to retain customers and attract new ones.[38]

When multinational banks establish affiliates abroad, it is usually to develop new revenue streams and serve local clients, not to reduce the number of more costly domestic jobs.[39] In fact, significant job losses are more likely due to fluctuations in overall financial conditions, such as those seen in recent years, rather than to establishment of affiliates. Employment at affiliates tends to be complementary to U. S. employment, mirroring the types of jobs found in the headquarters and domestic branches. The "first order" or headquarters employment effects resulting from establishment of an affiliate are likely marginally positive, i.e., there would likely be a small number of jobs created at the home office to directly support the operations of the new affiliate (such as a country manager or international accounting specialist). However, a more significant employment effect results from the volume of intrafirm trade—principally U. S. bank parent firms' exports of financial services to their foreign affiliates following the establishment of such affiliates. To illustrate, if a U. S. bank were to establish an affiliate in India, the parent firm would likely export some services, such as credit intermediation, to the affiliate in support of its local operations. Those "intermediate services," along with other non-financial services such as accounting, advertising, and administrative services, bolster employment at the U. S. parent firm as well as at the firms that supply them to the parent. The BLS data suggest that a $1 billion increase in final demand for financial services (banking and securities) supported over 5,000 U. S. jobs in 2008, the majority of which were financial services jobs. When applied to the value of intrafirm exports of financial services in 2008, $8.4 billion,[40] the result is more than 45,000 U. S. jobs supported across multiple industries (see chapter 1 and Appendix table A.1 for further explanation of the BLS data and our calculations).

The BLS data enable us to examine the jobs supported per $1 billion of demand for certain banking services.[41] As expected, the majority of jobs are in the monetary authorities, credit intermediation, and related activities category. The "second-order" job effects, that is, jobs that are supported in sectors that directly or indirectly support the banking sector, also see some notable growth. The securities and investment and insurance sectors, both of which tend to have close ties to the banking sector and in many cases are also provided by large multinational banks, are both among the sectors with the greatest job effects, as are building, employment, management and business support services. Table 11 shows the number of jobs supported in various industries by additional demand for banking services. However, it should not be assumed that additional supply of services to foreign affiliates always has employment effects identical to those detailed below.

The types of jobs created within the U. S. banking sector when demand increases represent the full spectrum of responsibilities, from managers and financial analysts, to loan officers and tellers (table 12), though the scope of new jobs resulting from increased exports to affiliates may be more narrow, as location specific positions, such as loan officers, new account clerks, and tellers, would not likely be in higher demand. Growth in the number of employees in the U. S. banking industry during 2002-09 was mixed, as jobs in certain occupations such as securities, commodities, and financial service agents, loan officers, and business and financial operations increased, while the number of managers, new account clerks, financial managers and customer service representatives decreased.[42] It is unclear why employment in some occupations declined while in others it rose, but it may be that cuts to higher salaried workers, bank managers and financial managers, for example, presented a means by which to reduce costs while minimizing layoffs during the financial downturn. Further, the numbers of customer service representatives and managers may have declined as bank mergers forced closure of redundant storefronts, and more banking functions are conducted online. It should be noted, however, that wages across all the occupations in the banking sector grew consistently throughout the period.

Table 11. U. S. jobs supported by additional $1 billion of banking services[a] output, top 10 industries, 2008

Industry	Job increases
Monetary authorities, credit intermediation, and related activities	3,286
Securities, commodity contracts, and other financial investments and related activities	239
Food services and drinking places	232
Services to buildings and dwellings	150
Agencies, brokerages, and other insurance related activities	138
Retail trade	124
Employment services	120
Management of companies and enterprises	77
Investigation and security services	66
Business support services	61
All other	1,086
Total	5,579

Source: *U. S. Department of Labor, Bureau of Labor Statistics, Domestic Employment Requirements Table*, December 10, 2009.

[a] Services of monetary authorities, credit intermediation services, and related activities.

Some domestic job losses may occur as U. S. banks expand their global footprints and increase foreign revenues. Areas where jobs might be moved to lower-cost countries for the primary purpose of reducing costs could include data processing and customer service centers, though it is likely that those shifts would occur independent of affiliate growth. Further, certain trade restrictions in foreign markets may have an impact on domestic employment. For example, some countries require that foreign banks maintain all back office data operations in-country. This is typically viewed as a costly burden for foreign banks as they would typically run those operations out of consolidated, often domestic or regional data centers. By requiring those firms to establish data operations in-country, such regulations not only add considerable costs to establishment of the affiliate, but also nullify any job creation that would have occurred at the consolidated data center.

Citigroup is potentially facing the aforementioned problem in Turkey, as pending regulation would require all data functions to be done in-country. According to a Citigroup representative, not only would such regulation cost it hundreds of millions of dollars, but would actually have a negative employment effect on the datacenters where such functions for its Turkish operations are currently housed, in Warsaw and London.[43] And while this example does not affect U. S. domestic employment per se, a similar job loss could certainly occur in U. S. data centers.

Table 12. Employment and wages for certain occupations within the U. S. banking sector, 2002-09

Occupation	Employment, 2009	CAGR 2002–09 (%)	Annual mean wages, 2009 ($)	CAGR 2002–09 (%)
Business and financial operations	671,940	3.7	73,682	3.4
Customer service representatives	216,330	-0.4	33,714	2.5
Financial managers	108,650	-1.5	120,676	4.0
First-line supervisors/managers of office and administrative support workers	167,650	1.6	54,076	3.0
Loan interviewers and clerks	160,390	2.3	35,576	2.6
Loan officers	264,170	4.5	63,532	2.5
Management occupations	250,780	-4.0	125,532	3.5
New accounts clerks	76,150	-2.5	31,110	2.4
Office and administrative support occupations	1,666,980	-0.6	35,062	2.4
Sales and related occupations	215,960	0.8	61,822	2.1
Securities, commodities, and financial services sales agents	113,390	15.7	59,716	2.7
Tellers	555,060	1.4	24,784	1.8

Source: USDOL, BLS, Occupational Statistics database, accessed May 2, 2011.

Finally, there is a probable third-party employment effect that results when large multinational banks expand their affiliate networks. If these banks can more easily finance U. S. services and manufacturing firms' growth in foreign markets where they have affiliates, the resulting expansion to those companies' revenues could result in some positive first- and second-order employment effects in the United States. Further research would be required to more fully examine this issue.

3. COMPUTER SERVICES

Summary

This chapter's primary focus is the foreign activities of multinational corporations that specialize in the delivery of computer services. The rapid adoption and integration of computers into business operations have driven demand for computer services, both in the United States and abroad, leading large computer service firms to establish foreign affiliates around the globe to supply these markets. The effects on U. S. employment of international expansion by these firms are ambiguous. Employment at U. S. parent firms of computer services multinationals fell slightly in recent years, while employment grew at their majority-owned foreign affiliates. The reasons for the declines in the former are unclear. Furthermore, employment in the broader U. S. computer services industry maintained steady growth— and analysts project that this growth will continue in the next decade.

This chapter also examines intrafirm exports of computer services by the wider universe of U. S. multinational corporations. The data that we examine suggests that the foreign affiliate activities of U. S. multinational corporations, insofar as they generate intrafirm trade in computer services, likely support a moderate number of domestic jobs among computer services providers and other high-skilled, high wage occupations.

Overview

Professional computer service firms provide the expertise and technical support necessary to help businesses and consumers use technology more efficiently, offering assistance in designing, implementing, and managing information technology (IT) systems.[44] Such services include computer systems design, custom computer programming, computer facilities management services, and other computer related services.[45] Computer service providers are employed by a wide range of industries, from dedicated computer service firms to consulting firms or hardware manufacturers that offer a few or many computer services in addition to their core business activities.[46]

The economic downturn reversed a trend of steady growth in the global computer services market, weakening demand for such services in 2009 as spending contracted across many major markets.[47] From 2004 through 2008, global spending on computer services grew at an average annual rate of 6.1 percent to reach $745 billion. This growth was driven by a growing preference for end-to-end computer systems over discrete hardware and software components, for business operations in developed countries.[48] In 2009, however, spending fell 4 percent to $715 billion.[49] The decline in overall spending in 2009 was largely driven by contractions in the world's largest computer services markets—the United States and the EU. U. S. spending on computer services fell 5.4 percent to $311 billion while spending in Europe contracted 7 percent to $219 billion.[50]

The United States hosts the world's largest computer services market, so it follows that it is also home to many of the world's leading computer services firms (table 13). International Business Machines, Inc. (IBM) and Hewlett-Packard (HP), both of which initially focused solely on manufacturing, are now the largest computer service firms in the world. In 2009, IBM derived the majority of its revenues (58 percent) from service activities; HP's services segment generated 30 percent of total revenue, or approximately $34.7 billion.[51] U. S. -based Computer Sciences Corporation (CSC) is the world's largest independent computer service provider, and the third largest computer services firm in the world.[52] However, U. S. MNCs face increasing competition from providers based in developing economies, particularly India, as evidenced by Tata Consultancy Services Limited's (TCS) position among the top 10 global firms. The spread of telecommunication networks and the lower cost of computing have facilitated service provision from developing countries, allowing providers such as TCS to offer cost competitive services in the global market.

Although the U. S. market remains integral to many of these firms,[53] faced with an increasingly globalized market, the leading U. S. computer service firms all have global operations. As of 2009, IBM had subsidiaries in 62 countries, HP's subsidiaries were located in 70 countries, and CSC operated in at least 30 countries.[54] The growing importance of foreign markets for U. S. MNCs over the past ten years is illustrated by comparing U. S. parent companies to their foreign affiliates. From 1999 through 2008, assets held by affiliates of U. S. computer service firms more than tripled, growing from $82.7 billion in 1999 to $269.6 billion in 2008, or an average annual rate of 14 percent, surpassing those held by the U. S. parents (figure 5).[55] By comparison, assets held by U. S. parent companies increased from $122.4 billion to $180 billion over the same period.[56] Based on the distribution of assets, it is unsurprising that these international operations frequently account for a substantial share of company revenue. In 2009, almost two thirds of IBM's revenue and over a third of CSC's revenues were generated outside the United States.[57]

Table 13. Top ten computer systems design and related services companies, 2009[a]

Rank	Company name	Country of headquarters	Revenue from services	Services' share of total revenue
			Billions of $	%
1	International Business Machines Corporation (IBM)	U.S.	55.0	58
2	Hewlett-Packard Company (HP)[b]	U.S.	34.7	30
3	Computer Sciences Corporation (CSC)[c]	U.S.	16.1	100
4	NTT Data Corporation[d]	Japan	12.3	100
5	Capgemini	France	11.7	100
6	Science Applications International Corporation (SAIC)[e]	U.S.	10.8	100
7	Cisco Systems Inc.[f]	U.S.	7.6	19
8	Atos Origin	France	7.2	100
9	Tata Consultancy Services Limited (TCS)[d]	India	6.4	75
10	Logica PLC	UK	5.8	100

Sources: Bureau van Dijk, Orbis database (accessed December 27,2010); company Web sites, annual reports, and SEC filings.

[a] Includes only those firms for which Orbis reported computer systems design and related services as a primary industry. Ranking based on revenues from services.
[b] Revenues for the 12 months ending on October 31, 2009.
[c] Revenues for the twelve months ending April 2, 2010. May include some revenues from software licensing fees.
[d] Revenues for the twelve months ending March 31, 2010.
[e] Revenues for the twelve months ending January 31, 2010.
[f] Revenues for the twelve months ending July 31, 2010.

Over the past decade, many U. S. MNCs have focused their expansion towards opportunities presented by rapid economic growth in emerging markets. Demand for computer services in the Asia-Pacific region has grown rapidly over the past five years, rising at an average rate of 8.5 percent annually from 2004 through 2008.[58] In particular, India and China are now among the largest consumers of computer services in the region, behind only

Japan and Australia. From 2004 to 2009, spending in India rapidly grew from $3.2 billion to $5.3 billion, and in China, spending on computer services more than doubled from $10 billion to $26.2 billion.[59] Recognizing new business opportunities, many U. S. MNCs have entered these markets. In 2008 alone, IBM's revenue from the BRIC markets (Brazil, Russia, India, and China) increased 18 percent.[60]

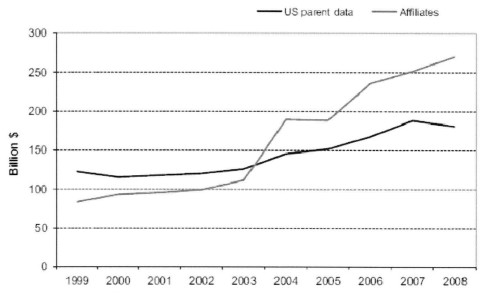

Source: USDOC, BEA, "Selected Data for Majority-Owned Foreign Affiliates," 1999–2008.

Figure 5. Total assets of computer systems design firms, by industry of parent, 1999–2008.

The recent economic downturn further underscored the value of these international operations; in 2009, many emerging markets proved more resilient than those in Western economies, as demand for computer services remained steady. The Asia-Pacific region proved the most robust as computer spending increased by 4.2 percent in 2009.[61] In Latin America and Africa, spending on computer services maintained positive, albeit slow, growth during 2009, increasing 0.3 percent and 1 percent, respectively.

Employment in Computer Services

Overall, employment in the U. S. computer services industry has maintained steady growth—a trajectory that is projected to continue, despite a slowdown in 2009. Employment increased at an average annual rate of 4.3 percent from 2002 through 2008. However, due to the weak economy in 2009, computer service firms faced lower demand from U. S. customers as IT budgets declined[62] and clients became price sensitive, resulting in price negotiations and short-term contracts.[63] As a result, employment growth slowed to 0.5 percent, reaching 1.4 million.[64] Despite this slowdown, the U. S. computer services industry is projected to be among the fastest growing areas of employment over the next decade, and almost all computer service occupations are expected to exhibit rapid growth, as firms across all industries require increasingly sophisticated computer networks as well as new computer-related security services.[65]

Among U. S. multinational computer service firms, employment by foreign affiliates has grown more rapidly than employment by U. S. parents. Employment at majority-owned foreign affiliates of U. S. firms rose at an average annual rate of 4.2 percent between 1999 and 2008.[66] In contrast, employment at U. S. parent firms fell slightly, from 394,000 in 1999, to 386,000 in 2008, representing a decline of 2 percent. As a result, from 1999 through 2008, employment at foreign affiliates of U. S. firms surpassed employment at U. S. parent firms (figure 6), demonstrating the rising importance of presence in foreign markets for U. S. computer service firms.

Regional trends in affiliate employment, which paralleled trends in computer services spending, further illustrate the importance of developing country markets for computer service providers. For example, although employment by U. S.-owned affiliates in Europe experienced very little growth between 1999 and 2008, employment by foreign affiliates in Latin America and Africa steadily increased.[67] However, the largest growth occurred in the Asia-Pacific region, where employment by U. S.-owned affiliates more than doubled, growing from 71,800 in 1999 to 185,000 in 2008.[68] As a result, during 1999 to 2008, the regional distribution of employment by U. S.-owned affiliates shifted (figure 7). The shares of employment by U. S.-owned affiliates in Europe and Canada fell from 58.7 percent and 8.5 percent, to 41.2 percent and 6.5 percent, respectively, while employment by affiliates in the Asia-Pacific region grew, accounting for the largest regional share of employment in 2008 (43.5 percent).[69]

Effects of Multinationals' Foreign Activities on U. S. Employment

Although improvement in communication technologies enables remote provision of services, the bulk of trade in computer services occurs through foreign affiliates. In 2006, export revenue for U. S. computer service firms was estimated at $7.1 billion; by comparison, in the same year U. S.-owned foreign affiliates supplied computer services worth $52.5 billion.[70]

Leading computer service providers have developed extensive operations abroad, with those in India perhaps most impressive. IBM India, a subsidiary of IBM, is currently the company's largest operation outside the United States, employing 100,000 people, making it India's second largest private sector employer.[71] In 1992, IBM entered the Indian market through a joint venture with the local firm, Tata, and five years later began operating an IBM Global Services segment there. In 1999, IBM bought out Tata's stake, and IBM India became a fully-owned subsidiary of U. S.-based IBM.

HP entered the services market through acquisition, rather than new ("greenfield") investment. In 2008, HP acquired Electronic Data Systems (EDS), which was the leading independent computer services firm at the time.[72] This acquisition not only expanded HP's services offerings, making it one of the world's largest computer service firms, but also made HP the second largest IT multinational in India.[73] In 2007, over half of EDS' 41,000 foreign workers were located in India.[74]

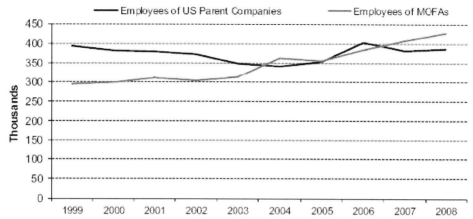

Source: USDOC, BEA, "Majority-owned Foreign Affiliates," and "U.S. Parent Companies," 1999-2008.

Figure 6. Employees of MOFAs of U. S. computer systems design firms exceeded employment at U. S. parent companies in 2008.

Available employment data for IBM and HP demonstrate that these firms' U. S. employment has declined over the past five to ten years. In 2002, IBM's 137,000 U. S. employees accounted for 43 percent of IBM's global workforce; by 2008, U. S. employment declined to 115,000, or 29 percent of the global workforce.[75] Similarly, available data for HP report that in 2002 (the earliest year available), U. S. employment totaled 67,352, or 48 percent of HP's total workforce. In 2007 (the most recent data available) U. S. employment had fallen to 53,519, or 31 percent of HP's total workforce.[76] However, although the numbers of U. S. workers have declined, in both cases, employment is relatively commensurate to regional revenue; for both IBM and HP, the United States accounted for roughly a third of global revenue in 2008 and 2007, respectively.[77]

Even with these employment figures, it is not possible to isolate the effects on U. S. employment of computer services multinationals' foreign activities. For example, although IBM's U. S. employment reportedly declined to 105,000 in 2010,[78] these data may not capture the use of fixed-term contractors, a common practice among computer service firms, but one which is not captured in full time employment figures. Further, it is difficult to isolate the effects of international expansion from the effects of other factors affecting employment by U. S. MNCs, such as disruptive technology. For example, innovation has reportedly led to workforce reductions at HP's data centers, as much of the work can be automated through the use of software, and the number of data centers overall is falling as more powerful computer hardware, such as servers, have increased processing capacity, which allows fewer machines to handle more work.[79] Given the steady growth of total U. S. employment in the computer services industry, it is likely that international expansion by these firms supports at least a small number of jobs at the U. S. headquarters, but the specific employment effects of foreign investment by IBM, HP, and similar companies on the domestic workforce remain ambiguous.

Using data from the U. S. Department of Labor (USDOL), Bureau of Labor Statistics (BLS), we can examine a separate, but related question: the effects on U. S. employment of intrafirm exports of computer services by U. S. parent firms across all industries to their foreign affiliates. The BLS estimates employment effects, or jobs supported, based on an increase in final demand for a given service. These estimates provide information on the volume and types of U. S. jobs supported by a $1 billion increase in final demand for computer services. Using the BLS estimates of employment effects in conjunction with data on the volume of intrafirm exports of computer and data processing services, we estimate the number of U. S. jobs supported by intrafirm exports of computer services by U. S. multinational companies.[80] However, it must be noted that it cannot be assumed that demand generated by foreign affiliates will result in effects corresponding exactly to those caused by domestic demand.

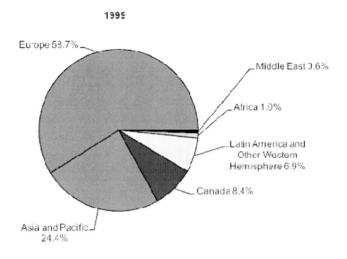

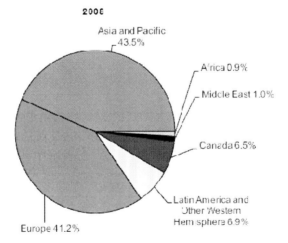

Source: USDOC, BEA, "Majority-Owned Foreign Affiliates," 1999-2008.

Figure 7. Employment by majority-owned foreign affiliates of U. S. computer service firms in Asia and Pacific surpassed such employment in Europe in 2008.

Table 14. U. S. jobs supported by an additional $1 billion of computer services output, top 10 industries, 2008

Industry	Job increases
Computer systems design and related services	3,831
Employment services	592
Wholesale trade	344
Food services and drinking places	236
Data processing, hosting, related services and other information services	228
Management, scientific, and technical consulting services	187
Services to buildings and dwellings	163
Architectural, engineering, and related services	147
Management of companies and enterprises	142
Software publishers	134
All others	366
Total	8,387

Source: United States Department of Labor, BLS, Domestic Employment Requirements Table, December 10, 2009.

The BLS estimated that, in 2008, each additional $1 billion of computer services output supported 8,387 U. S. jobs, of which roughly half were in industries related to computers. Of those, 3,831 were jobs in the computer systems design industry (table 14).[81] When applied to the $2.8 billion of computer and data processing services exported by U. S. parent firms to their foreign affiliates in 2008, these figures suggest that intrafirm exports of computer services supported 23,484 U. S. jobs, of which the largest share were in the computer systems design industry.[82]

The large distribution of jobs supported in the computer systems design industry (hereafter computer services industry) is notable, because occupations within this industry tend to require highly educated and highly skilled workers.[83] In 2009, 55 percent of employment in the U. S. computer services industry was made up of professional computer service jobs, such as computer software engineering, computer programming, or computer systems analysis.[84] Due in part to the high percentage of professionals in the industry, on average, U. S. computer service workers earn higher annual wages than the average U. S. worker—$80,050 in 2009, compared to the economy-wide average of $43,460.[85] Within the industry, mean annual wages ranged from $47,850 for computer support specialists to $106,230 for computer and information research scientists.

Beyond the direct effects of jobs in the computer services industry, jobs are supported in a wide variety of industries. The second largest employment effect, following computer services, was among jobs in the employment services industry. Employment service firms include employment placement agencies, professional employer organizations, and temporary help services.[86] Employment services allow firms, such as computer service providers, to meet temporary or fixed-period employment needs without incurring adjustment costs, such as those associated with hiring or firing workers.[87] High-skilled workers, such as computer service employees, are accounting for a growing share of temporary workers; computer and mathematical occupations are among the fastest growing in employment services, rising over 41.2 percent from 2004 through 2008.[88] Demand for computer services also supports jobs in other computer-related industries, although to a lesser degree, such as software publishing and data processing, hosting, and other information services. Other industries that are supported by increased computer services output include wholesale trade, and food services and drinking places.

Many of the secondary employment effects (or effects outside the computer services industry) are in high-skilled industries, such as management and consulting services; architecture, engineering, and construction; and management. Perhaps surprisingly, a $1 billion increase in demand for computer services has a relatively small effect on industries related to hardware, such as computer and peripheral manufacturing, where only 14.5 jobs were supported. This disparity in employment effects may be due to the labor intensive nature of many professional services, such as management consulting and engineering; capital intensive industries, such as manufacturing, may not require as much additional labor to meet increased demand.

Conclusions

Over the past decade the computer services industry has undergone significant change. U. S. multinationals have followed business strategies focused on geographic expansion, and as a result foreign affiliates have experienced tremendous growth. Concurrently, domestic U. S. employment among computer service workers has also continued to grow, albeit at slower rates. Demand for computer services has risen as businesses across all industries continue to incorporate increasingly sophisticated and complex technology into all aspects of their business operations. Yet the specific effects of international expansion by individual U. S. computer service firms on domestic employment remain ambiguous. Employment at some of the largest U. S. computer services multinationals has declined in recent years, but the reasons for these declines are unclear.

Within the broader universe of multinational companies, the employment effects of intrafirm exports of computer services are clearer. Increased demand for computer services appears to support a moderate number of jobs, many of which are in high-skilled, high wage industries.

4. LOGISTICS SERVICES

Summary

This chapter covers the logistics industry with a focus on large multinational "global integrators" such as FedEx and UPS that supply an array of shipping services, transport management services, and supply chain management services.[89] The international expansion of global integrators in recent decades was both a cause and a consequence of increased volumes of international commerce and efficiency gains in transporting information and goods. Global integrators expand abroad by constructing assets like air freight hubs and warehousing facilities, and establishing or purchasing affiliates like truck delivery services. These investments increase the scope and efficiency of international shipping operations, allowing global integrators to offer lower prices and faster delivery times to a greater number of countries.

Global integrators employ a variety of personnel at home and abroad (box 3), and foreign investment by these firms affects domestic employment in subtle ways. Building facilities abroad increases the overall capacity of the international logistics network, which requires expanding domestic hubs in order to process the greater volume of international shipments. Capacity-building employment effects can be reflected both in job growth at companies' headquarters and in increased purchases of inputs such as fuel, information technology, and aircraft repair services, as well as complementary logistics services provided by independent contractors. There are also additional employment effects on firms that rely on fast and cost-effective international logistics services to import and export goods. Finally, international expansion may be necessary for global integrators to remain competitive. International operations account for a substantial portion of global integrators' revenue (for example, 26 percent of UPS's 2010 revenue[90] and 44 percent of FedEx Express's 2010 revenue[91]), and a counterfactual scenario in which these firms did not invest abroad could result in their ceasing to exist.

Box 3. Employment Categories for Courier and Messenger Service Providers

According to the Bureau of Labor Statistics (BLS), firms that fall within the "couriers and messengers" subsector include those that provide interurban and local delivery services for documents and parcels, but that do not operate under a universal service obligation. Such firms include express delivery service providers. In general, courier and messenger service firms carry out the collection, pick-up, sorting, and delivery of items; for courier firms, these activities are often performed using established IT and transportation networks. Where possible, sorting and transportation activities are mechanized to minimize labor costs. The table below provides a breakdown of BLS' occupational data series on "couriers and messengers" for the United States.

BLS data series on couriers and messengers, 2009[a]		
Sub-categories	Employment	Annual mean wage
Couriers and messengers	26,010	$25,230
Customer service representatives	9,860	$36,680
Dispatchers (except police, fire, and ambulance)	6,190	$39,900
First-line supervisors/ managers of transportation and material-moving machine and vehicle operators	8,950	$60,880
Laborers, and freight, stock, material movers, hand[b]	152,580	$24,560
Truck drivers, light, or delivery services	147,930	$44,440

[a] USDOL, BLS, "Industries at a Glance: Couriers and Messengers; NAICS 492." (accessed April 13, 2011).
[b] Refers to laborers who move items manually.

Laborers, and freight, stock, and material movers are the single largest employment category within the courier and messengers subsector.[a] According to BLS data, a large number of workers in this category are employed through "employment services" agencies (see table below).[b] Courier and messenger services firms therefore hire a significant proportion (53 percent) of "laborers, and freight, stock, and material movers" through employment agencies. In addition, 54 percent of "first-line supervisors/ managers of transportation and material-moving machine and vehicle operators"— a much smaller proportion of the total workforce in the courier and messenger services industry— are retained through employment agencies.

BLS data series on employment services, 2009[a]		
Sub-categories	Total number employed through employment services firms	Percentage contracted out to courier and messenger firms
Couriers and messengers	480	NA
Customer service representatives	85,020	12
Dispatchers (except police, fire, and ambulance)	2,670	43
First-line supervisors/ managers of transportation and material-moving machine and vehicle operators	16,460	54
Laborers, and freight, stock, material movers, hand[b]	288,460	53
Truck drivers, light, or delivery services	17,500	12

[a] USDOL, BLS, "Occupational Employment Statistics: May 2009 National Industry-Specific Occupational Employment and Wage Estimates; NAICS 561300—Employment Services" (accessed April 18, 2011). In 2009, 11 percent of material movers were employed through the employment services industry as temporary or contract workers.

[a] USDOL, BLS, "Occupational Outlook Handbook: 2010–11 Edition; Material Moving Occupations" (accessed April 14, 2011). BLS places these jobs under the umbrella name "material moving occupations." There are more than ten occupational subcategories related to the movement of materials. These occupations are classified into two groups: laborers, or those that move materials by hand; and operators, or those that move materials using machinery. Of the 4.6 million jobs held by material movers in the United States in 2008, 2.3 million, or 50 percent of jobs fell within the subcategory "laborers, and freight, stock, and material movers, hand," and 41,000, or less than 1 percent, were classified as "material moving workers, all other."

[b] Refers to laborers who move items manually.

Industry Overview

The logistics industry provides coordinated transport of goods between suppliers, intermediaries, and consumers. Raw materials, intermediate inputs, and finished goods are transported globally by logistics providers via road, rail, sea, and air, forming long and often time-sensitive supply chains. Heavy goods are generally moved by road, rail, and water, while light, high-value goods are generally moved by air. While some companies have in-house logistics capacities, many such services are supplied by third-party logistics (3PL) providers. In addition to supply chain consulting and transportation management, logistics services may also include payment collection, product repair, transport insurance, telecommunications, trade finance, and other peripheral service activities.[92]

The growth of the global logistics market has been driven by increasing international trade volumes, particularly imports from and exports to emerging markets; the adoption of just-in-time global supply chains, which require small, frequent, and reliable deliveries of intermediate inputs; and improved information technology, including Internet commerce, which drives demand for quick delivery of small packages to end-users. Strong logistics links between countries cause, and are caused by, increased trade: it is easier and less expensive to ship to and from countries with strong logistics markets, which lowers the total costs of imports and exports, and thereby encourages other types of investment.[93] Fast-growing, high-tech industries such as pharmaceuticals, medical devices, biotech, semiconductors, and electronics are especially reliant on global logistics systems.

Logistics networks are usually developed in a "hub-and-spoke" pattern, in which dispersed delivery and pickup points are connected to a few central nodes. The hubs have an enormous capacity to collect, sort, and transfer packages, and are positioned to minimize fuel costs and transit times. Customers typically take packages to drop-off points (such as a company-branded retail outlet or the U.S. post office) or use the Internet to schedule package pickups. Packages are given a tracking number and shipped by truck to a regional sorting facility. They are then usually shipped by plane to a main sorting hub (such as Memphis for FedEx or Louisville for UPS) where they are sorted by destination, shipped from the hub to the appropriate regional sorting facility, and then loaded onto trucks for delivery. This process relies heavily on information technology, including software that plans optimal routes for delivery trucks and determines the optimal placement of packages within trucks, as well as communication systems that provide information on estimated delivery times to customers.[94]

The 3PL industry[95] had an estimated $507 billion in global revenue in 2009,[96] while the express delivery industry had an estimated $175 billion in global revenue in 2008.[97] The large multinational logistics firms most directly comparable to each other are FedEx, UPS, DHL, and TNT (table 15). These firms had a total of $159 billion in revenue in 2009, down from $186 billion in 2008. DHL, UPS, FedEx, and TNT respectively accounted for 40 percent, 28 percent, 22 percent, and 9 percent of that revenue. Their average 2009 profit margin was 2 percent (down from 3 percent in 2008), reflecting a range of total profits from $363 million (DHL) to $2.1 billion (UPS). These four firms combined had about 1,252,000 employees in 2009.[98]

The growth of 3PL providers in the United States was facilitated by the deregulation of the domestic transportation industry starting in the late 1970s. In the following years, transportation prices decreased and annual ton-miles of shipped air freight increased steadily, from 4.5 billion in 1980 to 13.8 billion in 2008.[99] Integrated logistics services have expanded to the point where they are available to many small, rural U.S. communities. The widespread availability of logistics services in the United States (and other developed countries) illustrates the maturity of those logistics markets relative to rapidly developing markets in emerging economies. This has consequences for employment trends, as mature logistics markets may have less potential than emerging markets for high growth rates that could drive future job creation.

Table 15. Financial profile of top 4 global logistics firms, 2009

	Revenue ($ millions)	Revenue growth over previous year (%)	Net income ($ millions)	Employees
DHL	64,168	-15.2	363	436,651
UPS	45,297	-12.0	2,152	408,000
FedEx	35,497	-6.5	98	247,908
TNT	14,447	-6.7	390	159,663

Source: Company annual reports. DHL and TNT figures calculated using exchange rates of $1 = 0.683 EU (2008) and $1 = 0.720 EU (2009). FedEx employment includes independent contractors.

Table 16. FedEx and UPS: Number of foreign subsidiaries and employees[a]

Country/Region	Number of FedEx subsidiaries	Number of FedEx employees	Number of UPS subsidiaries	Number of UPS employees
Canada	9	[b]8,227	5	[b]10,000
Asia	9	[c]14,000	12	([d])
Europe	62	[c]13,800	35	[b]36,939
Latin America	12	[c]3,400	18	[b]1,751
Africa and the Middle East	1	[c]>1,000	8	([d])
Total	93	40,427	78	48,690

Source: BvDEP, ORBIS database (accessed November 1, 2010), and FedEx company website.

[a] Latest available data.
[b] ORBIS database.
[c] FedEx company website.
[d] Not available. UPS' 2009 annual report indicates that the company employs 68,000 workers overseas, suggesting that roughly 20,000 UPS employees are dispersed among Asia, Africa, and the Middle East.

Operations of MNCs in the Logistics Industry

Logistics providers add value by providing broad international coverage. This allows them to offer a similar collection of transportation and supply chain management services to customers in foreign markets as they do at home. Logistics firms' extensive international presence also makes it easier and less expensive for domestic exporters to access foreign markets. Large global integrators typically operate in 200 countries or more, establishing air hubs as well as warehousing and storage facilities in many of them.[100] They also invest in trucking fleets and retail outlets, and enter into partnerships with local postal providers.[101]

According to BEA data, U. S. courier and messenger services firms (used here as a proxy for logistics firms) invested nearly $4.0 billion in foreign markets in 2008. Countries in which U. S. courier firms invested the largest amounts include Canada ($556 million), France ($333 million), the Netherlands ($80 million), Switzerland ($34 billion), and Brazil ($33 million).[102] Company-specific information for FedEx and UPS indicate that both have the highest number of foreign subsidiaries in Europe (62 and 35 respectively), and the second highest number of foreign subsidiaries in Latin America (12 and 18) (table 16). FedEx and UPS have had substantial operations in Europe since the 1980s; at that time logistics services were demanded and supplied largely within national borders, but the companies anticipated that regional integration and movement towards a single currency would increase demand for cross-border logistics services.[103] Canada ties for second place among FDI recipient countries for FedEx, where the company has established 9 subsidiaries, and ranks third for UPS (5 subsidiaries).

Overall Employment Trends

According to the ILO, in 2007 there were at least 72 million people employed globally in the transport, storage, and communications sector (the most specific employment category for which data were available).[104] The transportation and warehousing industry, which includes couriers and messengers, employed an estimated 4.2 million Americans in 2009, down from 4.5 million in 2007 but still representing an average 1 percent growth per annum since 1990.[105] The decrease in overall employment reflects the negative impact of the 2008-2009 economic downturn.

UPS, FedEx, DHL, and TNT have seen steady employment growth over the past decade. For these four companies, 2008 employment was on average 44 percent higher than 1998 employment.[106] However, the recession affected these firms as well, and their employment dropped by an average of 2 percent from 2008 to 2009.[107] Uniquely among these companies, TNT increased its employees from 2008 to 2009, but that increase was primarily caused by TNT's acquisition of LIT Cargo and Aracatuba; otherwise, 1,448 employees left TNT Express in 2009.[108] The past decade also yielded productivity gains for these firms, as average revenue per employee increased from $83,000 in 1998 to $137,000 in 2008.[109] Among these companies, year-on-year growth in revenue per employee averaged 6.2 percent from 1998 to 2008, which compares favorably to productivity growth in the broader category of couriers and messengers in the United States. Year-on-year growth in output per employee averaged 3.5 percent for the U.S. courier and messenger industry over this period.[110]

Employment growth at these companies is partly driven by international expansion, which increases the total capacities of their logistics networks and hence requires additional hiring. Company representatives at UPS estimated that for every 22 packages per day that UPS transports across international borders, the company creates a job for one full-time equivalent employee (not necessarily in the United States).[111] Expansion also drives purchases of inputs, including real estate, IT and communications services, and air and ground fleets. In 2009, TNT Express spent $31 million replacing the Mercurio fleet in Brazil and $6 million on a new facility for its Middle East road network,[112] DHL invested $183 million in IT equipment and $231 million in software,[113] and UPS added 300 compressed natural gas vehicles.[114] Fleet investments can be very large; UPS operates an air fleet of 510 aircraft and a ground fleet of 101,900 vehicles,[115] and FedEx owns or leases more than 600 aircraft and 100,000 ground vehicles.[116] Aircraft and related equipment accounted for 55 percent of FedEx's total 2010 expenditures, followed by facilities and sorting equipment (22 percent), information technology investments (10 percent), and ground vehicles (8 percent).[117] These input purchases are an important source of second-order job growth. One study estimates that the global express services industry supports 1.3 million direct jobs, as well as an additional 910,000 indirect jobs in aerospace, air transportation, automotive, information technology, petroleum, and professional services industries.[118]

International Employment

Employees located overseas account for a significant part of logistics firms' workforces. For example, among UPS's 408,000 employees in 2009, 340,000 were located in the United States while 68,000 were located abroad.[119] UPS's China operations alone have reportedly grown from less than 200 employees in 2000 to 5,500 employees in 2010, with most of the new hires being Chinese nationals. FedEx has expanded its overseas express operations largely by acquiring local firms, which suggests that such operations mostly comprise local personnel, enabling FedEx to maintain the in-house expertise of the acquired firm. Similarly, one UPS official estimated in 2003 that less than 0.1 percent of UPS employees located abroad were U. S. nationals, and noted: "We've learned that everyone wins when we put international business operations into the hands of the people who know their local cultures."[120] When UPS employs U. S. personnel abroad, they are often working in such areas as cargo security and customs, and their positions are often short- or medium-term relocation assignments.[121]

International expansion by U. S. logistics firms may also result in increased employment of foreign nationals in the United States. For example, when securing a contract to provide logistics services during the Beijing Olympics in 2009 (which stimulated growth in freight shipments to and from Beijing), UPS estimated that it would increase the number of Asian nationals hired to work at its U. S. headquarters.[122] As a company expands into new regions it can access a wider pool of potential employees, matching their skills with the company's needs in all of its countries of operation.

Employment in the United States

The domestic employment effects of foreign investment by logistics firms are difficult to estimate. In part, this is because multinational logistics firms tend to think of themselves as global networks, and hence measure factors affecting total employment and throughput (e.g., package delivery) more carefully than they measure specific relationships between operations in one region and employment in another.[123] An additional challenge is that different logistics firms have different employment models: UPS truck drivers are largely UPS employees whereas FedEx truck drivers are independent contractors. Therefore, an increase in domestic employment for UPS may appear as growth in the firm's U. S. workforce (i.e., a direct employment effect), whereas a similar increase for FedEx may correlate with the firm's purchases of transportation services from third-party providers (i.e., an indirect employment effect) (box 4).

Box 4. Contingent Workers, Independent Contractors, and FedEx

According to the Bureau of Labor Statistics (BLS), independent contractors accounted for an estimated 7.4 percent of the total U. S. workforce in 2005.[a] Many independent contractors are contingent workers who are employed on a temporary or non-permanent basis.[b] Contingent work schedules present certain advantages to both employers and employees; for instance, contingent arrangements permit employers to adjust the number of workers they employ depending on cyclical or seasonal changes in demand. At the same time, employees have greater flexibility regarding when or how many hours they work. However, contingent workers generally receive lower wages and fewer employee benefits (e.g., healthcare and pensions) than permanent workers, placing the former at an economic disadvantage. For their part, employers may in some cases prefer contingent over permanent work arrangements because of the potential to reduce labor costs.[c]

Express delivery and logistics firms like FedEx may use contingent workers, in particular independent contractors, to carry out ground delivery operations. In general, independent contractors use their own trucks, determine their own routes, and hire their own employees. FedEx employs approximately 15,000 independent contractors in its ground delivery operations. However, FedEx is currently involved in several disputes with independent contractors regarding their employment status.[d] In some states, independent contractors that work for FedEx have sued the express provider claiming that they are in fact direct employees of FedEx—relying on the company for route assignments, using the FedEx logo on their trucks, and wearing the FedEx uniform. As employees of FedEx, independent contractors would be entitled to certain benefits that they do not currently receive.[e]

FedEx has taken measures to address disputes with its independent contractors (or owner-operators, as they are referred to by FedEx). For example, the company has implemented a new Independent Service Provider model that requires contractors in certain states, such as Maryland and New Hampshire, to serve multiple routes within a geographic area rather than just a single route (hence avoiding single route reliance by contractors). FedEx also requires that contractors register as corporate entities under state law, and that they treat their own workers as employees. In addition, contractors must negotiate independent agreements with FedEx, rather than sign standard contracts.[f]

---

[a] USDOL, BLS, "Contingent and Alternative Employment Arrangements, February 2005," USDL 05–1433, released July 27, 2005; United States Government Accountability Office (GAO), "Employment Arrangements," GAO–06–656, July 2006, 1. Independent contractors are responsible for building their own customer base, and may have employees that work for them (e.g., real estate agents).

[b] GAO defines contingent workers as those workers who "are not wage and salary workers working at least 35 hours a week in permanent jobs."

[c] USDOL, Office of the Secretary "V. Contingent Workers," Special Report, n.d. http://www.dol.gov/sec/media/reports/dunlop/section5.htm (accessed April 13, 2011); GAO, "Employment Arrangements: Improved Outreach Could Help Ensure Proper Worker Classification," GAO–06–656, July 2006, 3. In addition, contingent workers may not be protected under labor laws designed to ensure, among other things, that employees are not discriminated against in the workplace, and that work environments meet certain safety standards. The protections granted under these labor laws apply largely to individuals who work for an employer, and therefore do not extend to independent contractors who are self-employed.

[d] Litvak, Anya, "FedEx Changes Model for Independent Contractors in NH," *Pittsburgh Business Times*, January 9, 2009. http://bizjournals.com/pittsburgh/ stories/2009/01/05/daily64.html?s=print (accessed April 13, 2011).

[e] Speizer, Irwin, "The Independent Contractor Question," *Workforce Management Online*, July 2007. http://www.workforce.com/section/recruiting-staffing/feature/independent-contractor-question/index.html (accessed April 12, 2011). In 2002, a lawsuit brought by independent contractors against a local express delivery firm in California was settled in favor of the express firm. According to one attorney, the case resulted in several guidelines that may assist other companies to determine whether or not the independent contractors that work for them are correctly classified: (1) independent contractors must be permitted to work for other companies; (2) they must be allowed to refuse assignments from a company; (3) they must be allowed to hire others to perform work; and (4) they must have managerial control over their own operations.

[f] *FedEx Annual Report, 2010*, 22. In addition to Maryland and New Hampshire, FedEx plans to implement the ISP model in Illinois, Massachusetts, Minnesota, Rhode Island, Tennessee, and Vermont.

In 2007 the U. S. courier and messenger services industry comprised about 13,000 employer firms (with 560,000 paid employees) and 191,000 non-employer firms.[124] According to BLS data, in 2008 a $1 billion increase in final demand for courier and messenger services supported 11,800 jobs across all U. S. industries. The top ten industries affected by demand for courier and messenger services are listed in table 17.

The BLS data show the rates at which U. S. courier and messenger firms expand their domestic workforces to manage overall increases in production. "Couriers and messengers" account for the majority of jobs created, suggesting that an increase in the total number of packages shipped globally requires more U. S. couriers and messengers to pick up and deliver such packages within the United States. "Employment services," which accounted for the second- highest number of jobs created, include both temporary help and human resources management services. The latter category, along with "management of companies and enterprises," are among jobs that tend to be carried out at firms' headquarters regardless of the geographic source of demand. Other industries in which employment effects are noted reflect cross-industry partnerships: for example, courier and messenger services firms often collaborate with postal services to deliver packages, and rely on third-party as well as in-house warehousing and storage firms. While courier and messenger services firms spend a significant amount of money on commodities such as fuel and manufactures (including aerospace products), these expenditures do not result in high rates of average job creation according to BLS data. However, the category "scenic and sightseeing transportation and support activities for transportation" includes servicing and repairing existing aircraft.

Previous econometric research and company information also indicate the scope and magnitude of the U. S. employment effects of logistics firms. For instance, in a FedEx-sponsored study entitled *Global Impacts of FedEx on the New Economy* (2001), employment multipliers were calculated for each of the industries in which FedEx operates, based on input-output data from BEA. Such calculations estimated that for every 1 job created by FedEx in the United States in the year 2000, approximately 3.4 U. S. jobs were created in air transportation services; 2.9 jobs in trucking and courier services (except by air); 2.7 jobs in warehousing and storage services; and 2.8 jobs in freight forwarding and other transportation services.[125] These numbers, like the BLS data, do not illustrate a direct relationship between foreign activity and domestic job creation, but they do show the ability of successful multinational logistics firms to create "ripple effects" by generating jobs in the wider U. S. economy.

Employment at Firms that Rely on Logistics Networks

In addition to the above-mentioned employment effects, large logistics firms like FedEx and UPS may promote job growth at companies that rely on low-cost international deliveries. The importance of minimizing the cost and time of shipments is apparent in the number of firms that establish operations near logistics hubs. For example, FedEx has reportedly attracted 130 firms from 22 countries to its Memphis hub, resulting in an estimated 17,000 local jobs. The expansion of UPS' hub in Louisville has resulted in an additional 14,000 direct and indirect jobs in the Louisville metropolitan area. Similarly, a new hub constructed by DHL in Leipzig, Germany has added approximately 2,000 direct jobs in the area, with an estimated 7,000 direct and indirect jobs to be created in the future. Most new workers will likely come from nearby regions.[126]

Access to relatively low-cost international logistics networks helps companies maintain competitiveness, enter new markets, and expand their workforces. Illustratively, in 2004, UPS and Toshiba formed a partnership in which UPS personnel became responsible for repairing as well as shipping Toshiba's laptops, which reduced total laptop repair time from an estimated 14 to 4 days.[127] Toshiba employs over 20,000 people in North America.[128] In addition, On-X Life Technologies, a medical device manufacturer, uses FedEx's shipping software and electronic trade documents to process its exports. Currently, the manufacturer exports to 80 countries and employs 100 people.[129] When international logistics services improve in quality and decrease in price, businesses that purchase those services as inputs can become more profitable and increase their output.

Conclusion

Available data from the Bureau of Labor Statistics point to some effects on job creation in both logistics industries and non-logistics related industries, such as employment services, when U. S. logistics firms expand their operations abroad. Other industries in which one might anticipate logistics firms to create substantial amounts of indirect employment—e.g., the aerospace and automotive industries—may be sufficiently productive as to absorb the relatively small employment effects created by demand for logistics services. Apart from BLS data, other research studies regarding the employment effects of large logistics firms indicate that such effects are most substantial at the location of the logistics firms' primary hubs. Both FedEx and UPS have created employment around their major U. S. hubs, as customers and suppliers of these firms locate facilities near these hubs.

Table 17. U. S. job supported by an additional $1 billion of courier and messenger services output, top 10 industries, 2008

Industry	Job increases
Couriers and messengers	8,805
Employment services	467
Services to buildings and dwellings	197
Scenic and sightseeing transportation and support activities for transportation	190
Wholesale trade	159
Postal services	158
Management of companies and enterprises	151
Retail trade	131
Consumer goods rental and general rental centers	107
Warehousing and storage	102
All others	1,333
Total	**11,798**

Source: United States Department of Labor, BLS, Domestic Employment Requirements Table, December 10, 2009.

There are some quantitative estimates that point towards the domestic employment effects of foreign investment by logistics firms. The BLS estimates that $1 billion in increased final demand for courier and messenger services was correlated with the creation of 11,800 domestic jobs in 2008. Additionally, one economic impact study found that each job created by FedEx in the United States in 2000 was correlated with the creation of 11.8 jobs throughout all industries. Finally, UPS representatives estimate that one full-time equivalent position is created for every 22 international packages per day that UPS transports. These estimates do not draw a straight line from a quantity of foreign investment to a quantity of domestic employment, but they do illustrate and indirectly suggest the scale of the relationship between U. S. employment and the foreign activities of U. S. logistics firms.

5. Retail Services

Summary

Over the past decade, sales and employment grew rapidly at U. S. multinational retailers' foreign affiliates, whereas employment at U. S. parent firms grew only modestly. However, our research suggests that increased foreign affiliate activity may create a small number of jobs within multinational retailers' U. S. parent firms and more among their U. S. -based suppliers. It is possible that retailers' foreign expansion could also have negative effects on some workers. As retailers expand, they can demand lower prices from their suppliers in exchange for higher- volume contracts, which the suppliers might "pass on" to workers as job or wage cuts. However, we encountered no specific evidence of such effects.

Overview: An Increasingly International Business

The retail industry comprises businesses that sell merchandise in small quantities to the public.[130] Retailers sell through fixed locations as well as non-store media (e.g., catalogs or the Internet). Establishments may specialize in selling a particular type of merchandise (e.g., groceries, clothing, or hardware) or a variety of goods.

The global financial crisis and subsequent economic downturn caused global retail sales to decrease in 2009. The industry's sales revenues totaled $14.0 trillion, down 3.4 percent from 2008. This marked a sharp reversal from the previous three years, during which annual growth of sales averaged 9.9 percent.[131] The "G7" countries (the United States, Japan, France, Germany the United Kingdom, Italy, and Canada) accounted for 45.9 percent of global retail sales in 2009, down from 55.9 percent in 2004, while the share of the "BRIC" countries (Brazil, Russia, India, and China) rose from 13.7 percent to 21.7 percent over the same period (figure 8). These statistics illustrate developing countries' emergence as the locus of growth in the global retail industry. Developing countries' share of global retail revenues has increased on the strength of economic growth exceeding that in developed countries.[132] Their increasingly affluent consumers are spending more and demanding greater access to modern stores.[133]

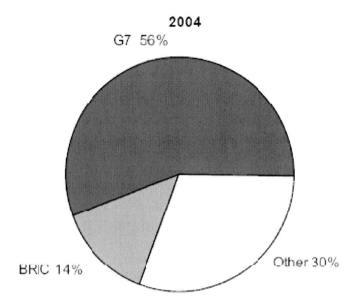

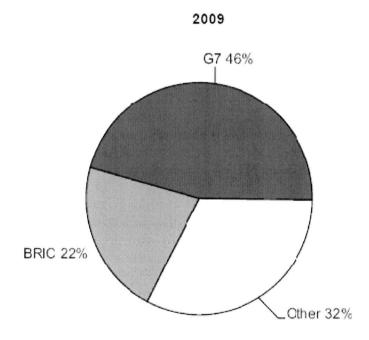

Source: Planet Retail Database (accessed September 28–29, 2010).

Figure 8. Global retail sales, by country group, 2004 and 2009.

Table 18. Top 10 retailers, by global retail sales, 2009

Rank	Company	Country[a]	Global retail sales (US$ billions)[b]	Number of countries[c]
1	Wal-Mart	United States	405.0	15
2	Carrefour	France	119.9	35
3	Metro	Germany	90.9	33
4	Tesco	United Kingdom	90.4	14
5	Schwarz Group	Germany	77.2	25
6	Kroger	United States	76.7	1
7	Costco	United States	69.9	9
8	Aldi	Germany	[d]67.7	18
9	Home Depot	United States	66.2	5
10	Target	United States	63.4	1

Sources: Deloitte, "Leaving Home," January 2011; Planet Retail Database (accessed September 28-29, 2010).

[a] Country represents location of headquarters.
[b] Some figures are adjusted from those reported by companies to exclude non-retail sales.
[c] Hong Kong counted within China. Puerto Rico counted within the United States. Taiwan counted as a separate country.
[d] Estimate.

In 2009, all of the world's top 10 retailers were headquartered in the United States, Western Europe, or Japan (table 18). Wal-Mart is by far the world's largest retailer: its sales in 2009 exceeded those of the next three largest retailers combined. Larger retailers are more likely to operate outside their home markets,[134] but two of the global top 10, the United States' Kroger and Target, operated only in their home country.

Table 19. Top 10 retailers in the United States, 2009

Rank	Company	Headquarters	U.S. retail sales (US$ billions)	Number of countries[a]
1	Wal-Mart	Bentonville, AR	304.9	15
2	Kroger	Cincinnati, OH	76.7	1
3	Target	Minneapolis, MN	63.4	1
4	Walgreens	Deerfield, IL	63.3	1
5	The Home Depot	Atlanta, GA	59.2	4
6	Costco	Issaquah, WA	56.5	9
7	CVS Caremark	Woonsocket, RI	55.4	1
8	Lowe's	Mooresville, NC	47.2	2
9	Sears Holdings	Hoffman Estates, IL	44.0	2
10	Best Buy	Richfield, MN	37.3	15

Sources: Kantar Retail, "2010 Top 100 Retailers," July 2010; Planet Retail Database (accessed September 29, 2010).

[a] Hong Kong counted within China. Puerto Rico and Guam counted within the United States. Taiwan counted as a separate country.

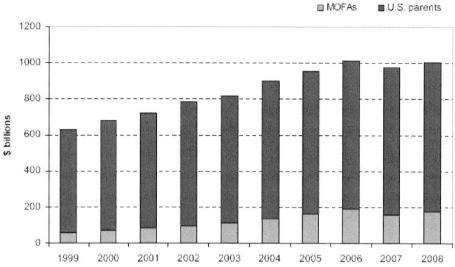

Source: USDOC, BEA, Operations of Multinational Companies Database (accessed April 1, 2011).

Figure 9. U. S. multinational retailers, sales by parent companies and by majority-owned foreign affiliates, 1999–2008.

Large U. S. retailers are less internationally-oriented than their counterparts in Europe. Four of the United States' top ten retailers in 2009 (Kroger, Target, Walgreens, and CVS) operated only in the United States, and only three were present in five or more countries. (table 19).

However, international operations have grown increasingly important for U. S. multinational retailers in recent years. Sales by their majority-owned foreign affiliates tripled between 1999 and 2008, growing from $59.2 billion to $179.0 billion. Meanwhile, U. S. parent firms' sales grew by only 44 percent, from $572 billion to $824 billion (figure 9).

Wal-Mart exemplifies this trend. The company opened its first non-U.S. store in Mexico in 1991, but international sales remained small through most of the 1990s. In 1997, the company described its international operations as "immaterial to total company operations," and international sales for that fiscal year were less than five percent of all sales.[135] By 2010, one-quarter of the company's sales, one-third of its employees, and almost half of its stores were outside the United States.[136]

Some observers have predicted that slower growth and weak consumer demand in the United States will compel more U. S. retailers to expand abroad.[137] There are signs that this is already happening. For example, in January 2010, Target announced that it would likely open stores in Canada, Mexico, or elsewhere in Latin America in the next decade.[138]

Employment in the Retail Industry

Workers in the U. S. retail industry earn less and work fewer hours per week than the average U. S. worker. In January 2011, retail employees earned an average of $15.65 per hour and worked 31.3 hours per week, compared to economy-wide averages of $22.86 and 34.2.[139] Leading occupations include cashiers, retail salespersons, stock clerks and order fillers, and first-line supervisors.[140] Cashiers and retail salespersons were the largest occupations in the U. S. private sector in May 2009; together, they accounted for almost 7 percent of total private sector employment.[141]

During the past decade, employment growth in retail was slightly lower than in the U. S. economy as a whole but followed a similar trajectory (figure 10). Retailers employed an average of 11.4 percent of workers between 2000 and 2011, and a total of 14.5 million as of March 2011. While there was no evidence of a major shift in the industry's importance as an employer vis-à-vis other industries, its share of overall employment decreased slightly over the period—from a high of 11.6 percent in April 2000 to 11.1 percent in March 2011.[142]

During the same time period, employment increased sharply among foreign affiliates of U. S. multinational retailers. These affiliates employed 538,900 people in 2000 and 960,200 in 2008, an increase of 78 percent. Growth was particularly impressive in the Asia-Pacific region, where employment increased from 37,900 in 2000 to 178,700 in 2008. Meanwhile, employment by U. S. parent firms of retail multinationals increased by a modest 4.7 percent, to just over 4 million.[143] Again, Wal-Mart's experience is illustrative. Between 1998 and 2008, Wal-Mart's workforce grew both outside and within the United States, although employment outside the United States grew faster. The trends diverged between 2008 and 2010, as Wal-Mart's U. S. workforce shrunk by 20,000 while its non-U.S. workforce grew by 65,000 (figure 11).[144]

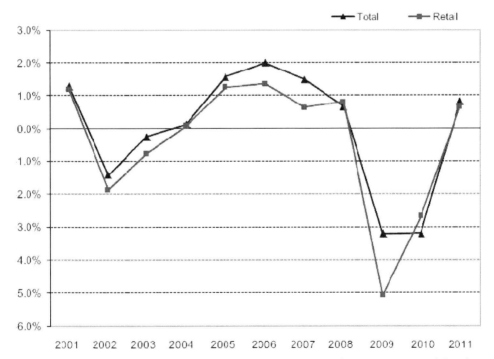

Source: *U. S.* Department of Labor, Bureau of Labor Statistics, Employment, Hours, and Earnings – National Database. Seasonally adjusted data. Growth is calculated as year-on-year change in employment as measured in January of each year.

Figure 10. Growth of employment within the United States, 1999–2009.

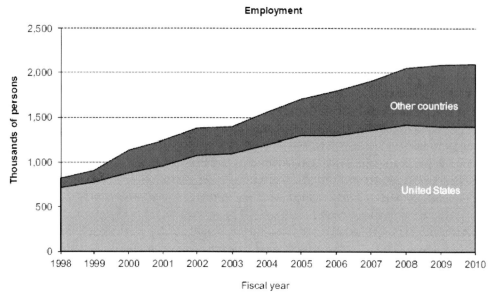

Source: Wal-Mart, Form 10-K reports, 1998–2010.

[a] Wal-Mart's fiscal year ends January 31. Employment data are for the last date of each fiscal year. Employment for "other countries" is for Wal-Mart's International business segment, as defined in each year's 10-K filing. Figures for the United States include data for the Wal-Mart U. S. and Sam's Club business segments. Each part-time employee is counted as one worker. The employment figures are described as approximations in the 10-K filings.

Figure 11. Wal-Mart employment, by location, 1998–2010[a].

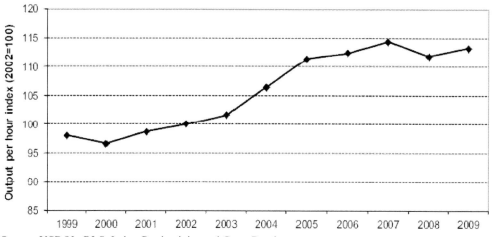

Source: USDOL, BLS, Labor Productivity and Costs Database.

Figure 12. Labor productivity (output per hour), U. S. supermarkets and other grocery (except convenience) stores, 1999–2009.

Rising productivity may have played a role in the slow growth of U. S. retail employment over the past decade (figure 12).[145] These productivity gains may have been due to the adoption of new in-store technologies, such as self-checkout scanners, as well as computerized systems for supply chain management.

Operations of Multinational Retailers and U. S. Employment

Multinational retailers enter new markets via new ("greenfield") investments or acquisitions. Affiliates' legal forms and their parent firms' stakes in them vary, due both to host country regulations and individual companies' preferences. For example, Costco, a U. S. operator of wholesale clubs, owns 50 percent of a joint venture in Mexico but majority stakes of affiliates in six other countries.[146] In contrast, Swedish home-furnishings retailer IKEA operates in 38 countries via franchise agreements.[147] A small but growing number of retailers also enter new markets via cross-border Internet sales. For example, in 2010, U. S. clothing retailer Gap Inc. began selling via the Internet to customers in dozens of countries where it did not have brickand-mortar stores.[148]

In this paper, we use the term "first-order employment effects" to describe jobs created at a multinational company's U. S. parent firm to support operations abroad. It is difficult to make sweeping statements about the magnitude of these effects among retailers because the division of labor between retail parent companies and their foreign affiliates varies. Many functions must, by necessity, be fulfilled by staff of the affiliates or local contractors, such as in-store sales, operation of distribution centers, and local transport of merchandise. But others can be assigned to headquarters, the affiliates, or some combination of both.

For example, Wal-Mart's Bentonville headquarters employs more than 11,000 people.[149] Of those, fewer than 200 work in Wal-Mart's International Division, which oversees the company's operations outside the United States.

Some employees in other divisions, such as Information Systems and Tax, also work on international operations. Wal-Mart reserves certain functions for headquarters, such as decisions on real estate acquisition, and delegates others exclusively to affiliates, such as merchandising. Still other functions, such as legal services, are performed by teams at headquarters as well as affiliates.[150]

"Second-order" effects occur when U. S. suppliers of goods and services to the retail industry create jobs in order to meet demand from retailers' foreign affiliates. Like first-order effects, second-order effects are difficult to estimate precisely, but data from the U. S. Bureau of Labor Statistics suggest which industries might experience the largest effects. In the United States in 2008, each additional billion dollars of retail services output supported over 14,000 jobs, of which about one-fifth were in industries other than retail (table 20).[151] Jobs were created in industries across the economy, including employment services (e.g., temporary help agencies and human resource management), wholesale trade, warehousing, finance, construction, and manufacturing (notably printing and motor vehicle parts manufacturing).

It cannot be assumed that additional output by foreign affiliates has employment effects identical to those summarized above.

However, some retailers draw substantially on U. S. firms to supply goods and services to foreign affiliates. For instance, numerous suppliers of merchandise have entered new markets via Wal-Mart's foreign affiliates, while others have used those affiliates to expand sales in markets where the suppliers already had a presence. Examples include canned peaches from California, cheese from Wisconsin, and tea manufactured by Harris Tea Company. Harris has added production capacity in the United States in order to meet demand from Walmart's stores in Japan.[152] Box 5 describes the experience of one of Wal-Mart's largest suppliers of merchandise, Proctor and Gamble.

Box 5. Proctor and Gamble Expands Global Sales through Wal-Mart[a]

Proctor and Gamble (PandG) is one of the world's leading producers of consumer goods, such as cleaning supplies, personal care products, and pet food. In fiscal year 2010, the company had sales of $78.9 billion in roughly 180 countries. Almost 60 percent of its sales came from outside North America.[b]

Wal-Mart is PandG's largest single distributor. It distributes over 10 percent of PandG's products in the United States and 7 to 8 percent abroad. According to one company representative, "PandG does best where Wal-Mart is." Mexico is an example of a location where Wal-Mart has greatly expanded PandG's sales. Wal-Mart expanded rapidly in Mexico after the North American Free Trade Agreement (NAFTA) came into effect in January 1994. Wal-Mart's expansion there transformed PandG's distribution model in the country: the company moved from selling through small "tiendas" to superstores. The efficiency gains and sales growth that PandG experienced—largely through the expansion of Wal-Mart—caused the company to view retail liberalization as its single largest benefit from NAFTA.

PandG employed 50,000 people in the United States in 2008. Forty thousand of these employees worked in Ohio, the site of PandG's headquarters. A company representative said that one in five of PandG's U.S. employees works on the company's international business, and two in five in Ohio. The company representative described their work as "good headquarters jobs," in fields such as marketing, finance, and logistics.[c] Using the company representative's estimates, one might associate 700 to 800 U.S. jobs at PandG with sales that the company realizes through international distribution via Wal-Mart.[d]

[a] Unless indicated otherwise, the source for this textbox is PandG company representative, interview by authors, January 11, 2011.
[b] Proctor and Gamble, "2010 Annual Report (online version)," 2010; Proctor and Gamble, Company Web site, http://www.pg.com/en US/company/global structure operations/index.shtml (accessed February 4, 2011). The sales figures quoted here are for the period of July 1, 2009–June 30, 2010.
[c] PandG described the impact of its international operations on U.S. employment similarly in Business Roundtable, *International Engagement*, 2008, 98.
[d] To derive this estimate, we multiply Wal-Mart's share of the international distribution of PandG products (7–8 percent) times the number of PandG's U.S. jobs focused on international business (10,000).

Another channel through which Wal-Mart may support a substantial number of jobs is procurement of materials to build and operate stores outside the United States. Company representatives described numerous links between Wal-Mart operations abroad and "green jobs" in the United States. For example, in 2008, Wal-Mart de México agreed to purchase wind energy generated by 27 wind turbines manufactured in Iowa by Clipper Windpower. In Guatemala City, Guatemala, Wal-Mart made store parking lots brighter using LED lights manufactured by General Electric in Hendersonville, North Carolina. And Schneider Electric is supplying electrical switching gear manufactured in Indiana and Iowa to every country where Wal-Mart has affiliates. U. S. suppliers of services also support Wal-Mart's international operations, in industries such as logistics and legal services.[153]

Table 20. U. S. jobs supported by an additional $1 billion of U. S. retail services output, 2008, top ten industries

Industry	Job increases
Retail trade	11,474
Employment services	175
Wholesale trade	140
Warehousing and storage	139
Food services and drinking places	131
Services to buildings and dwellings	122
Real estate	113
Monetary authorities, credit intermediation, and related activities	94
Management of companies and enterprises	74
Business support services	73
All others	1667
Total	14,192

Source: *U. S. Department of Labor, Bureau of Labor Statistics, Employment Requirements Table,* December 10, 2009.

It is also possible that international expansion by multinational retailers is associated with some negative effects on U. S. employment. As retailers grow larger—internationally or domestically— they gain leverage vis-à-vis suppliers with respect to prices. For example, Costco grew rapidly over the past decade[154] and was the world's seventh-largest retailer in 2009. In November of that year, it temporarily stopped restocking Coca-Cola products in an effort to compel Coca-Cola to supply those products at lower prices.[155] Such demands place downward pressure on suppliers' margins, which the suppliers could pass on to workers in the form of wage or job cuts. On the other hand, suppliers may need to hire more workers to meet the greater demand associated with larger sales contracts. The net effects are ambiguous *a priori.*

Wal-Mart provides another example. In January 2010, the company announced that it would "leverage its global scale" to reduce the costs of merchandise. The company planned to increase its use of direct contracts with producers for goods marketed under its store brands.[156] Observers reported that the company was seeking to reduce its dependence on intermediaries (such as produce wholesalers) and consolidate purchases by the company's various foreign affiliates.[157] It is possible that this strategy could negatively affect the financial performance, and ultimately employment, at intermediary firms. However, it is also possible that job losses at wholesalers could be matched or exceeded by gains among suppliers. Additional empirical evidence is needed to assess the net employment effects of this and other initiatives by multinational retailers to cut supply chain costs.

Directions for Future Research

The data examined in this chapter suggest that international expansion by multinational retailers may create jobs within the United States—a modest number within the retailers' U. S. parent firms and more among U. S. suppliers of their foreign affiliates. But the exact balance of job gains and losses is unclear, particularly among suppliers. Additional research could help clarify the relationship between retailers' foreign activities and U. S. employment. Useful directions for this research include:

- Examining, via a survey or case studies, the extent to which multinational retailers employ headquarters staff to manage foreign affiliates, and the extent to which the retailers procure U. S. -produced goods and services for their affiliates.
- Interviewing or surveying additional suppliers about the effects of multinationals' international activities on the suppliers' production and employment decisions.
- Analyzing firm-level data on retailers' employment in the United States and abroad. Econometric techniques could prove useful for this analysis.

CONCLUSION

Our research indicates that the foreign activities of U. S. multinational services companies have varying effects on domestic employment when examined on an industry-by-industry basis, but in aggregate result in net job creation. Much of the support for domestic employment results from increased exports of services from parent firms to the affiliates in support of their foreign operations. We estimate that U. S. multinationals' intrafirm exports of services in 2008 supported nearly 700,000 U. S. jobs, including jobs at U. S. parent firms as well as these firms' suppliers.

However, this figure likely underestimates the job effects of services multinationals' foreign activities. It does not account for intrafirm exports of goods, which are significant even among services firms. In addition, it does not account for a possible "third-order" employment effect among unrelated U. S. MNCs operating in the same foreign markets as the services multinationals. The services provided by the affiliates of U. S. services multinationals may enable other U. S. MNCs to expand abroad more rapidly, thereby boosting their own U. S. headquarters employment. We have not attempted to quantify such third-order employment effects in this paper, but discussions with industry representatives suggest that they could be substantial.

In examining the banking, computer services, logistics, and retail services sectors, we found a number of factors and compelling trends that support our data and econometric analyses presented in chapter 1. Key findings include:

Banking

- In the wake of the global financial crisis, U. S. multinational banks are increasingly looking to grow affiliate operations in developing markets where economic activity

is more robust, disposable incomes are increasing, and demand for more sophisticated banking services is high.
- Employment at bank affiliates tends to complement that of the parent firms, and likely provides a small positive effect on headquarters employment, as well as a more substantial positive effect throughout the domestic supply chain.
- Intrafirm exports of services from U. S. banks to their foreign affiliates likely supported over 45,000 jobs across a variety of sectors in 2008.

Computer Services

- The widespread adoption and integration of technology into business operations has generated global demand for computer services, driving U. S. computer service multinationals to establish foreign affiliates around the world, particularly in emerging markets, to supply this growing demand.
- Although it is likely that international expansion by U. S. computer service multinationals supports at least a small number of jobs at U. S. headquarters, U. S. employment by these firms has followed a slight downward trend over the past decade. However, it is not clear to what degree this is attributable to foreign expansion rather than shifting employment patterns or technological disruption.
- More broadly, intrafirm exports of computer services by all U. S. multinational firms appears to support a moderate number of high-skilled, high wage domestic jobs – roughly 23,500 in 2008.

Logistics

- Logistics firms often invest abroad to expand their international coverage and increase their total network capacity. The domestic employment effects of these investments are difficult to measure given the global nature of logistics firms' operations, as well as their use of different employment models and the lack of employment data that capture such effects.
- As logistics firms grow and expand, the areas surrounding their U.S hubs tend to experience employment gains due to customers and suppliers of these firms locating facilities near such hubs.
- Quantitative estimates that suggest the scale of the relationship between U. S. employment and the foreign activities of U. S. logistics firms (while not directly measuring this relationship) include:
    - The U. S. Bureau of Labor Statistics estimated that a $1 billion increase in final demand for courier and messenger services likely supported 11,800 domestic jobs in 2008;
    - One economic impact study found that each job created by FedEx in the United States in 2000 was correlated with the creation of 11.8 jobs throughout all industries; and

- UPS representatives estimate that one full-time equivalent position is created for every 22 international packages per day that UPS transports.

Retail Services

- Developing countries have emerged in recent years as the locus of growth in the global retail industry, with their share of global retail revenues increasing on the strength of economic growth exceeding that in developed countries. Their increasingly affluent consumers are spending more and demanding greater access to modern stores.
- Over the past decade, sales and employment grew rapidly at U. S. multinational retailers' foreign affiliates, whereas employment at U. S. parent firms grew only modestly. Our research suggests that increased foreign affiliate activity may create a small number of jobs within multinational retailers' U. S. parent firms and more among their U. S.-based suppliers.

Further Research

There is a great deal of additional research that needs to be done in order to better understand and quantify the wider domestic employment effects of establishing services affiliates abroad. Some potential research avenues include:

- A more detailed examination of the second-order employment effects throughout services MNCs' supply chains
- The extent to which third-order effects generate increased domestic employment
- Whether first- and second-order domestic employment effects change with the duration of affiliate operations.

APPENDIX

Table A.1. Estimated number of jobs supported by intrafirm exports of services by multinational companies, 2008: detailed calculations

Services exported by parent firms of U.S. multinational companies	Corresponding BEA International Surveys Industry (ISI) codes[a]	Corresponding BLS categories[b]	NAICS codes covered by BLS categories	Jobs supported per $1 billion of demand, 2008	Intrafirm exports of services by U.S. multinational companies ($ billions), 2008	Jobs supported by intrafirm exports of services by U.S. multinational companies[c]
Computer and information services	5415	Computer systems design and related services	5415	8,387	3.247	23,395
	5182, 5191	Data processing, hosting, related services, and other information services	518, 519	6,023		
Management and consulting services	5416	Management, scientific, and technical consulting services	5416	9,312	16.467	153,342
RandD and testing services	5417	Scientific research and development services	5417	7,240	8.014	58,024
	5321	Automotive equipment rental and leasing	5321	6,984		
	5329	Consumer goods rental and general rental centers	5322, 5323	14,069		
Operational leasing	5329	Commercial and industrial machinery and equipment rental and leasing	5324	7,531	1.979	18,856
Construction, architectural, and engineering, services	5413	Architectural, engineering, and related services	5413	8,943	0.814	7,280
	8110	Electronic and precision equipment repair and maintenance	8112	8,787		
Installation, maintenance and repair	Commercial and industrial machinery and equipment (except automotive and electronic) repair and maintenance		8113	9,603	0.847	8,371
	Personal and household goods repair and maintenance		8114	11,260		
Legal services	5411	Legal services	5411	6,973	0.063	439
Advertising	5418	Advertising and related services	5418	8,303	not available[d]	

Table A.1. Continued

Services exported by parent firms of U.S. multinational companies	Corresponding BEA International Surveys Industry (ISI) codes[a]	Corresponding BLS categories[b]	NAICS codes covered by BLS categories	Jobs supported per $1 billion of demand, 2008	Intrafirm exports of services by U.S. multinational companies ($ billions), 2008	Jobs supported by intrafirm exports of services by U.S. multinational companies[c]
	5221	Monetary authorities, credit intermediation, and related activities	521,522	5,579		
Financial services	5231	Securities, commodity contracts, and other financial investments and related activities	523	5,357	8.376	45,799
	5331	Lessors of nonfinancial intangible assets (except copyrighted works)	533	2,166		
Royalties and License Fees	5111	Newspaper, periodical, book, and directory publishers	5111	8,248	60	367,739
	5112	Software publishers	5112	5,283		
	5121 5122 industries	Motion picture, video, and sound recording	512	7,718		
	5151	Broadcasting (except internet)	515	7,336		
Telecommunications	517	Tele-communications	517	5,113	2.698	13,794
Total						697,038

Source: USDOC, BEA, Survey of Current Business, (October 2010), 36-55; and USDOL, BLS, Employment Projections, http://www.bls.gov/emp/ep_data_emp_requirements.htm (accessed May 3, 2011).

[a] International Surveys Industry classifications are used by respondents to BEA surveys on foreign direct investment and services. ISI codes are adapted from the 2007 North American Industry Classification System (NAICS).

[b] BLS classifications do not have exact matches among the BEA ISI codes in all cases. In cases where the BLS codes are broader than the corresponding ISI codes, employment effects may be overstated.

[c] To calculate the values in this column, we multiply the jobs supported by an additional $1 billion of demand for each service in 2008 by intrafirm exports of that service in 2008. For services with more than one corresponding category in the BLS data, we multiply the value of intrafirm exports by the simple average of the jobs supported by $1 billion of demand for each category. For example, intrafirm exports of computer and information services totaled $3.247 billion in 2008. We multiply this by the average of the number of jobs supported by $1 billion of demand for computer systems design and related services (8,387) and data processing, hosting, related services, and other information services (6,023): (8,387+6,023)/2 x 3.247 = 23,395. Averaging is done to account for the fact that the exports are composed of some combination of the services named in the corresponding BLS categories (the exact composition is not specified in the available export data).

[d] Data not released by BEA.

BIBLIOGRAPHY

[1] Armstrong and Associates. "Global 3PL Market Size Estimates." http://www.3plogistics.com/3PLmarketGlobal.htm (accessed October 8,).

[2] *The Banker.* Top 1000 World Banks 2010. July 6, 2010. www.thebanker.com.

[3] Beinhocker, Eric D; Diana Farrell and Adil S. Zainulbhai. "Tracking the Growth of India's Middle Class." *The McKinsey Quarterly, 3,* (2007): 51–61.

[4] Brainard, S. Lael. and David Riker. "*Are U. S. Multinationals Exporting U. S. Jobs?*" National Bureau of Economic Research Working Paper 5958, March 1997. http://www.nber.org/papers/w5958.pdf?new window=1.

[5] Buch, Claudia M. and Alexander Lipponer. "FDI versus Exports: Evidence from German Banks." *Journal of Banking and Finance 31*, no., *3,* (2007), 805-826

[6] Bureau van Dijk. Orbis Companies Database. http://orbis.bvdep.com (accessed various dates).

[7] Business Roundtable. *International Engagement: How American Workers and Businesses Succeed in the Worldwide Economy.* Washington: Business Roundtable, 2008.

[8] Cathers, Dylan. "*Industry Surveys–Computers–Commercial Services.*" Standard and Poor's, May 6, 2010. http://www.netadvantage. standardandpoors.com/NASApp/ NetAdvantage/servlet/login?url=/N ASApp/NetAdvantage/index.do (subscription required).

[9] Clipper Windpower. "*Clipper Windpower and EDF EN Sign Strategic Agreement for Long-term Supply of Liberty Wind Turbines for Projects in Mexico.*" News release, August 5, 2008. http://www.clipper wind.com/pr080508.html.

[10] Computer Sciences Corporation (CSC). *Annual Report 2009.* Falls Church, VA: CSC, 2010. http://www.csc.com/investorrelations/ds/ 32578-financialreports.

[11] Costco. *2010 Annual Report.* Issaquah, WA: Costco, December 13, 2010. http://phx.corporateir.net/External.File?item=UGFyZW50SUQ9 NzU1MjR8Q2hpbGRJRD0tMXxUeXBlPTM=andt=1.

[12] Cosmas, Alex and Bastien, Martini. "*UPS and FedEx Air Hubs.*" Cambridge, MA: Massachusetts Institute of Technology (MIT), December 14, 2007. http:// ardent.mit.edu/airports/ASPexercises/ASP% 20matl%20for %20posting%202007/ UPS%20and%20FedEx%20Hub% 20Operations%20Cosmas%20Martini.pdf (accessed May 11, 2011).

[13] CSRwire. "*U.S. Businesses Must Take Sustainable Approach to International Business Development.*" June 18, 2003. http://www.csrwire.com/pressreleases/24319-U-S-Businesses-Must-TakeSustainable-Approach-to-International-Business-Development-U PS-Exec-Says.

[14] Deloitte. *Emerging from the Downturn: Global Powers of Retailing 2010.* London: Deloitte, January 2010. http://www.deloitte.com/assets/ Dcom-Global/Local%20Assets/ Documents/Consumer%20Business/dtt globalpowersofretailing2010.pdf.

[15] Deloitte. *Feeling the Squeeze: Global Powers of Retailing 2009.* London: Deloitte, January 2009. http://public.deloitte.com/media/ 0460/2009GlobalPowersofRetail FINAL2.pdf.

[16] Deloitte. *Leaving Home: Global Powers of Retailing 2011.* London: Deloitte, January 2011. https://www.deloitte.com/assets/Dcom-Global/ Local%20Assets/Documents/Consu mer%20Business/GlobPow DELOITTE 14%20Jan.pdf.

[17] Desai, Mihir; C. Fritz Foley and James, R. Hines. "*Domestic Effects of the Foreign Activities of U. S. Multinationals.*" May 2008. http://www.people.hbs.edu/ffoley/fdidomestic.pdf.

[18] Deutsche Post DHL. "Annual Report 2009." Bonn, Germany: Deutsche Post DHL, March 16, 2010.

[19] Economist. "*World Banks: The Bigger and Bigger Picture,*" May 13, 2010. www.economist.com.

[20] ———. "*World Banks: We Lucky Few,*" May 13, 2010. www.economist.com.

[21] Economist Intelligence Unit (EI U). *Country Finance: United States of America.* New York: EI U, November 2010. www.eiu.com (subscription required).

[22] Enright, Allison. "Gap Goes Global." *Internet Retailer,* August 12, 2010. http://www.internetretailer.com/2010/08/12/gap-goes-global.

[23] The Federal Reserve Board. "Summary: April 15, 2009." *The Beige Book*, April 15, 2009. http://www.federalreserve.gov/fomc/beigebook/ 2009/20090415/default.htm.

[24] FedEx. "Annual Report, 2010." Memphis: FedEx, 2011. http://ir.fedex.com/annuals.cfm

[25] ——— . "*Acquisition History.*" http://ir.fedex.com/acquisitions.cfm (accessed November 4, 2010).

[26] ——— . Company Information, "*Regional Facts.*" http://about.fedex.designcdt.com/ourcompany/companyinformation/regionalfacts (accessed September 24, 2010).

[27] ——— . "FedEx Expands Leadership in Asia Pacific with Plan to Build Region's Largest Air Cargo Hub in Guangzhou, China." *FedEx Global Newsroom,* July 13, 2005. http://news.vanfedex.com/node/5160 (accessed August 30, 2010).

[28] ——— . "FedEx Express Supports European Trade Growth with Hub Expansions in France, Germany." *FedEx Global Newsroom,* June 3, 2008. http://news.van.fedex.com/node/10917/print (accessed September 24, 2010).

[29] ——— . "FedEx Timeline." http://fedex.com/us/about/today/history/ timeline.html (accessed October 12, 2010).

[30] ——— . "FedEx Welcomes the World to China." *FedEx Global Newsroom*, July 5, 2007. http://news.van/fedex.com/node/693/ (accessed September 24, 2010).

[31] Fillat-Castejón, Carmen, Joseph F. Francois, and Julia Wörz. "*Cross-Border Trade and FDI in Services.*" Vienna Institute for International Economic Studies, Working Paper - 50, February 2009.

[32] Harrison, Ann, and Margaret McMillan. "*Outsourcing Jobs? Multinationals and US Employment.*" NBER Working Paper No. W12372, July 2006. http://www.nber.org/papers/w12372.

[33] Hewlett-Packard (HP). *2003 HP Global Citizenship Report.* Palo Alto, CA: HP, 2003. http://h30261.www3.hp.com/phoenix.zhtml?c=71087and p=irol-reportsAnnual.

[34] ———. *2007 Annual Report.* Palo Alto, CA: HP, 2008. http:// h30261.www3.hp.com/phoenix.zhtml?c=71087andp=irol-reportsAnnual.

[35] ———. *2009 Annual Report.* Palo Alto, CA: HP, 2010. http:// h30261.www3.hp.com/phoenix.zhtml?c=71087andp=irol-reportsAnnual.

[36] ———. *HP FY07 Global Citizenship Report.* Palo Alto, CA: HP, 2008. http://www.hp.com/hpinfo/globalcitizenship/downloadreport.html.

[37] ———. "HP Global Citizenship – HP Operations." http://www.hp.com/hpinfo/globalcitizenship/environment/hplistofmajoroperations.html (accessed October 27, 2010).

[38] IBISWorld. "Commercial Banking in the US: 52211." *Ibis World Industry Report,* January 2011. www.ibisworld.com (subscription required).

[39] ———. "Global Commercial Banks: J5511-GL." *Ibis World Industry Report,* January 6, 2011. www.ibisworld.com (subscription required).

[40] International Business Machines Corp. (IBM). *Annual Report 2008.* Armonk, NY: IBM, 2009.

[41] ———. *Annual Report 2009.* Armonk, NY: IBM, 2010.

[42] ———. "*Computer Services and Management Consulting: Opportunities in the World Trade Organization.*" June 2006. http://www.ibm.com/ibm/governmentalprograms/computerservicesandmanagementconsultin g.pdf.

[43] ———. *Corporate Responsibility Report 2002.* Armonk, NY: IBM, 2003.

[44] ———. "*IBM Worldwide Banking Center of Excellence.*" http://www03.ibm.com/systems/services/bankingcoe/ (accessed January 24, 2011).

[45] ———. "*The IBM Worldwide Banking Center of Excellence,*" March 2007. http://public.dhe.ibm.com/common/ssi/ecm/en/zsb03015usen/ZSB 03015USEN.PDF.

[46] ———. "*Understanding Our Company–An IBM Prospectus.*" Armonk, NY: IBM, March 2005. ftp://ftp.software.ibm.com/annualreport/2004/ 2004ibmprospectus.pdf.

[47] IKEA. "*Facts and Figures.*" http://www.ikea.com/ms/enCN/aboutikea/ facts and figures/facts figures.html (accessed March 31, 2011).

[48] Imbriani, Cesare, Rosanna Pittiglio, and Filippo Reganati. "*Outward FDI and Home Country Performance: Evidence from Italian Manufacturing and Service Firms.*" Paper presented at the 6th International Scientific Conference, Vilnius, Lithuania, May 13–14, 2010. http://www.vgtu.lt/ leidiniai/leidykla/BUSANDMANA2010/FinanceEngineering/075- 082 Imbriani Pittiglio Reganati.pdf.

[49] International Monetary Fund (IMF). *World Economic Outlook Database* (accessed April 26, 2011). http://www.imf.org/external/pubs/ft/weo/ 2011/01/weodata/index.aspx.

[50] Kantar Retail. "*2010 Top 100 Retailers.*" *Stores,* July 2010. http://www.stores.org/2010/Top-100- Retailers.

[51] Kletzer, Lori G. and J. Bradford Jensen. "Tradable Services: Understanding the Scope and Impact of Services Offshoring."*Brookings Trade Forum*, 2005.

[52] Kox, Henk. "*What is Special in Services Internationalisation?*" Paper presented at a conference of the German Institute for Economic Research, Berlin, June 2009.

[53] Kulkarni, Vishwanath. "*EDS Buy Gives HP Services, India Edge.*" Livemint.com, May 14, 2008.

[54] Litvak, Anya. "FedEx Changes Model for Independent Contractors in NH." *Pittsburgh Business Times*, January 9, 2009. http://bizjournals.com/pittsburgh/stories/2009/01/05/daily64.html?s= print (accessed April 13, 2011).

[55] Lounsbury, John. "*IBM Stops Reporting U. S. Employment Numbers.*" *The Street*, March 19, 2010.

[56] Luo, Tian, Amar Mann and Richard Holden. "*The Expanding Role of Temporary Help Services from 1990 to 2008.*" U. S. Department of Labor. Bureau of Labor Statistics. *Monthly Labor Review* August 2010, 3–16.

[57] Maestri, Nicole. "Update 3—Target Seeks Growth from Small Stores, Overseas." *Reuters,* January 21, 2010. http://www.reuters.com/article/ 2010/01/21/target-idUSN2120840620100121.

[58] McDonald, Mark. "*Innovation Marching On – McKinsey Top 10 Trends and What They Mean for IT.*" *Mark McDonald* (blog), September 8, 2009. http://blogs.gartner.com/markmcdonald/2009/09/08/innovation-marching-on-mckinsey-top10-trends-a nd-what-they-mean-for-it/.

[59] Mildenberg, David. "Bank of America, Li Ka-Shing Reduce China Bank Stakes." *Bloomberg,* January 7, 2009. http://www.bloomberg.com/apps/ news?pid= newsarchiveandsid=aKSEI9jAvfHYandrefer=home

[60] Molnar, Margit, Nigel Pain and Daria Taglioni. Globalisation and Employment in the OECD. *OECD Economic Studies* No. 44, 2008/1, 2008. http://www.oecd.org/dataoecd/40/24/42503843.pdf.

[61] Nordås, Hildegunn K. and Henk Kox, "*Quantifying Regulatory Barriers to Services Trade.*" OECD Trade Policy Working Papers No. 85, February 2009.

[62] Ono, Yukako. "Why Do Firms Use Temporary Workers?" *Chicago Fed Letter* no. 260 (March 2009).

[63] Organization of Economic Co-operation and Development (OECD). "*The Impact of the Crisis on ICT and ICT-Related Employment.*" Paris: OECD, October 2009. http://www.oecd.org/dataoecd/47/22/ 43969700.pdf.

[64] Ortutay, Barbara. "*Hewlett-Packard to Cut 9K Jobs in Services Unit.*" signonsandiego.com, June 1, 2010. http://www.signonsandiego.com/ news/2010/jun/ 01/hewlett-packard-to-cut-9k-jobs-inservices-unit/.

[65] Oxford Economics. "*The Impact of the Express Delivery Industry on the Global Economy.*" September 2009. http://www.global-express.org/ assets/files/Oxford%2 0Economics%20Study%20Report.pdf.

[66] Pearce, Brian. "*Industry Financial Forecast.*" IATA Economic Briefing, December 2007. http://www.iata.org/whatwedo/economics/Documents/ FinancialForecastBriefing Dec 07.pdf (accessed May 11, 2011).

[67] Planet Retail. *Planet Retail Database* (accessed various dates). www.planetretail.net (subscription required).

[68] Public Broadcasting Service. "*The Rise of Wal-Mart.*" November 16, 2004. http://www.pbs.org/wgbh/pages/frontline/shows/Wal-Mart/ transform/cron.html.

[69] Reda, Susan. "Markets with Muscle: Three Hot Countries Retailers Need to Watch." *Stores,* November 2009. http://www.stores.org/stores-magazine-november-2009/markets-muscle (accessed March 30, 2011).

[70] Speizer, Irwin, "The Independent Contractor Question." *Workforce Management Online,* July 2007. http://www.workforce.com/ section/recruiting-staffing/feature/independent-contractorquestion/ index.html (accessed April 12, 2011).

[71] SRI International. "Macro Impacts of FedEx on the U. S. and Global Economies." Chap. 7 in *Global Impacts of FedEx in the New Economy.* 2001. http://www.sri.com/policy/ csted/reports/economics/fedex/.

[72] Stambor, Zak. "Wal-Mart Creates a Global E-commerce Unit, Reorganizes U. S. Web Operations." *Internet Retailer,* January 29, 2010. http://www.internetretailer.com/2010/01/29/wal-martcreates-a-global-e-commerce-unit-reorganizes-u-s-web.

[73] *Standard and Poor's.* "Hewlett-Packard – Business Summary." www.netadvantage.standardandpoors.com (accessed October 5, 2010) (subscription required).

[74] *Supply Chain Digest.* "*Wal-Mart to Centralize Global Sourcing, Reduce Use of Middlemen,*" January 6, 2010. http://www.scdigest.com/assets/ newsviews/10-01-06-1.pdf.

[75] Tejaswi, Mini Joseph and Sujit John. "*IBM is India's Second Largest Pvt Sector Employer.*" Times of India, August 18, 2010.

[76] Tharpe, Jim. "For UPS Executive, Olympics a Marathon," *Atlanta Business News*, November 30, 2009. http://www.ajc.com/business/for-ups-executive-olympics-218964.html (accessed July 5, 2011).

[77] Thibodeau, Patrick. "IBM Stops Disclosing U. S. Headcount Data." *Computerworld*, March 12, 2010.

[78] Timberlake, Cotten and Duane Stanford. "Costco Stops Restocking Coca-Cola Products in Dispute (Update 1)." *Bloomberg,* November 16, 2009. http://www.bloomberg.com/apps/news?pid=newsarchiveandsid=ai1bI8TKizU.

[79] TNT. "Annual Report 2009." Hoofddorp, Netherlands: TNT, 2010. http://group.tnt.com/annualreports/annualreport09/index.html.

[80] United Nations Conference on Trade and Development. *Information Economy Report 2007–2008: Science and Technology for Development; The New Paradigm of ICT.*" New York: United Nations, 2007.

[81] United Nations Economic and Social Commission for Asia and the Pacific (UNESCAP). "The Relationship between Liberalization in the Logistics Sector and Trade Facilitation." *Asia-Pacific Trade and Investment Review,* Vol. 2, No. 2, December 2006.

[82] UPS. "*Annual Report 2010.*" Atlanta: UPS, 2011. http://www.investors.ups.com/phoenix.zhtml?c=62900andp=irol-reportsannual.

[83] U.S. Agricultural Export Development Council. "*Success Story.*" April 15, 2010. http://www.usaedc.org/success.cfm.

[84] U.S. Census Bureau. "2007 NAICS Definition: Sector 44–45; Retail Trade." *North American Industry Classification System* [NAICS]*: United States, 2007.* http://www.census.gov/cgibin/sssd/naics/naicsrch?code=44andsearch= 2007%20NAICS%20Search

[85] ———. "2007 NAICS Definition: Sector 54; Professional, Scientific, and Technical Services; Computer Systems Design and Related Services." *North American Industry Classification System* [NAICS]*: United States, 2007.* http://www.census.gov/cgi-bin/sssd/naics/naicsrch? code=54151andsearch=2007%20NAICS%20Search.

[86] ———. U. S. Census Bureau. "*Industry Statistics Sampler– NAICS 5613, Employment Services.*" http://www.census.gov/econ/industry/ hierarchy/i5613.htm (accessed April 11, 2011).

[87] ———. "NAICS 4921: Couriers." http://www.census.gov/econ/ industry/hierarchy/i4921.htm (accessed March 25, 2011).

[88] —. *Services Annual Survey 2009.* "Table 6.5," 2005–09. http://www.census.gov/services//

[89] U.S. Department of Commerce (USDOC). Bureau of Economic Analysis (BEA). *Guide to Industry Classifications for International Surveys 2007*. BE-799. Revised December 2007.

[90] ———. Operations of Multinational Companies Database (accessed various dates). http://www.bea.gov/international/index.htm.

[91] ———. *Survey of Current Business* 90, no. 8 (August 2010).

[92] ———. *Survey of Current Business* 90, no. 10 (October 2010).

[93] ———. U. S. *Direct Investment Abroad: Balance of Payments and Direct Investment Position Data.* "U.S. Direct Investment Abroad on Historical Cost Basis," 1997–2009. http://www.bea.gov/international/di1usdbal.htm.

[94] ———. *U. S. Direct Investment Abroad: Financial and Operating Data for U. S. Multinational Companies.* "Majority-Owned Foreign Affiliates, Employment," 1999–2008. http://www.bea.gov/international/di1usdop.htm.

[95] ———. U. S. *Direct Investment Abroad: Financial and Operating Data for U. S. Multinational Companies.* "Selected Data for Majority-Owned Nonbank Foreign Affiliates and Nonbank U. S. Parents in All Industries," 1999–2008. http://www.bea.gov/international/di1usdop.htm (accessed April 26, 2011).

[96] ———. U. S. *Direct Investment Abroad: Financial and Operating Data for U. S. Multinational Companies.* "Selected Data for Foreign Affiliates in All Countries in Which Investment Was Reported," 1999 and 2008. http://www.bea.gov/international/di1usdop.htm (accessed June 30, 2011).

[97] ———. U. S. *Direct Investment Abroad: Financial and Operating Data for U. S. Multinational Companies.* "U.S. Parent Companies, Employment," 1999–2008.

[98] ———. U. S. *International Services.* "Table A. Services Supplied to Foreign and U. S. Markets Through Cross-Border Trade and Through *Affiliates,"* 1986–2009. http://www.bea.gov/international/international services.htm.

[99] ———. U. S. *International Services.* "Table 9.a: Services Supplied to Foreign Persons by U. S. MNCs Through their MOFAs," 2006–08. http://www.bea.gov/international/internationalservices.htm.

[100] U.S. Government Accountability Office (GAO). "*Employment Arrangements: Improved Outreach Could Help Ensure Proper Worker Classification.*" GAO–06–656, July 2006. http://www.gao.gov/ new.items/d06656.pdf.

[101] U.S. Department of Labor (USDOL). Bureau of Labor Statistics (BLS). "Computer Systems Design and Related Services." *Career Guide to Industries, 2010–11 Edition.* (accessed March 22, 2011). http://www.bls.gov/oco/cg/

[102] ———. "Computer Systems Design and Related Services: Total Employment, 2002–09." *Occupational Employment Statistics Survey*, May 2009.

[103] ———. "*Contingent and Alternative Employment Arrangements, February 2005.*" USDL 05–1433, July 27, 2005.

[104] ———. *Employment, Hours and Earnings—National Database* (accessed April 22, 2011). http://data.bls.gov.

[105] ———. *Employment Outlook: 2008-2018; Layout and Description for 202-Order Employment Requirements Tables—Historical 1993 through 2008.* December 2009. ftp://ftp.bls.gov/pub/special.requests/ ep/emp.requirement/erdesc.pdf.

[106] ———. *Employment Projections*. "Nominal Dollar Based Domestic Employment Requirements" table for 2008. http://www.bls.gov/emp/ epdataemprequirements.htm (accessed May 3, 2011).

[107] ———. "*Industries at a Glance: Couriers and Messengers; NAICS 492.*" http://www.bls.gov/iag/tgs/iag492.htm (accessed April 13, 2011).

[108] ———. *Labor Productivity and Costs Database* (accessed April 25, 2011). http://data.bls.gov.

[109] ———. Occupational Employment Statistics Database (accessed various dates). http://data.bls.gov.

[110] ———. "*Occupational Employment Statistics: May 2009 National Industry-Specific Occupational Employment and Wage Estimates; NAICS 561300—Employment Services.*" http://www.bls.gov/oes/ current/naics4561300.htm (accessed April 18, 2011).

[111] ———. "*Occupational Employment and Wages by Ownership.*" News release, July 27, 2010. http://www.bls.gov/news.release/ocwag2.htm.

[112] ———. "*Occupational Outlook Handbook: 2010–11 Edition; Material Moving Occupations.*" http://www.bls.gov/oco/ocos243.htm (accessed April 14, 2011).

[113] U.S. Department of Labor (USDOL). Office of the Secretary. "*V. Contingent Workers.*" Special report, n.d. http://www.dol.gov/sec/ media/reports/dunlop/section5.htm (accessed April 13, 2011).

[114] U.S. Department of Transportation (DOT), Bureau of Transport Statistics (BTS). "*Freight Transportation.*" 2010. http://www.bts.gov (accessed October 8, 2010).

[115] ———. "*National Transportation Statistics.*" http://www.bts.gov (accessed October 8, 2010).

[116] U.S. International Trade Commission (USITC). *Logistic Services: An Overview of the Global Market and Potential Effects of Removing Trade Impediments*, USITC Publication 3770. Washington, DC: USITC, May 2005.

[117] Wal-Mart. *2010 Annual Report* (online edition). http://Wal- Martstores.com/sites/annualreport/2010/worldwidelocations.aspx.

[118] ———. "About Us." http://Wal-Martstores.com/AboutUs/9505.aspx (accessed February 2, 2011).

[119] ———. "*Fact Sheets.*" http://Wal-Martstores.com/pressroom/Fact Sheets/ (accessed January 26, 2011).

[120] ———. Form 10-K. Washington: Securities and Exchange Commission, April 21, 1997. http://investors.Wal-Martstores.com/phoenix.zhtml?c= 112761andp=irol-sec.

[121] ———. Form 10-K. Washington: Securities and Exchange Commission, April 23, 1998. http://investors.Wal-Martstores.com/phoenix.zhtml?c =112761andp=irol-sec.

[122] ———. Form 10-K. Washington: Securities and Exchange Commission, April 19, 1999. http://investors.Wal-Martstores.com/phoenix.zhtml?c =112761andp=irol-sec.

[123] ———. Form 10-K. Washington: Securities and Exchange Commission, April 17, 2000. http://investors.Wal-Martstores.com/phoenix.zhtml?c= 112761andp=irol-sec.

[124] ———. Form 10-K. Washington: Securities and Exchange Commission, April 10, 2001. http://investors.Wal-Martstores.com/phoenix.zhtml?c= 112761andp=irol-sec.

[125] ———. Form 10-K. Washington: Securities and Exchange Commission, April 15, 2002. http://investors.Wal-Martstores.com/phoenix.zhtml?c= 112761andp=irol-sec.

[126] ———. Form 10-K. Washington: Securities and Exchange Commission, April 15, 2003. http://investors.Wal-Martstores.com/phoenix.zhtml?c=112761andp=irol-sec.

[127] ———. Form 10-K. Washington: Securities and Exchange Commission, April 09, 2004. http://investors.Wal-Martstores.com/phoenix.zhtml?c=112761andp=irol-sec.

[128] ———. Form 10-K. Washington: Securities and Exchange Commission, March 31, 2005. http://investors.Wal-Martstores.com/phoenix.zhtml?c=112761andp=irol-sec.

[129] ———. Form 10-K. Washington: Securities and Exchange Commission, March 29, 2006. http://investors.Wal-Martstores.com/phoenix.zhtml?c=112761andp=irol-sec.

[130] ———. Form 10-K. Washington: Securities and Exchange Commission, March 27, 2007. http://investors.Wal-Martstores.com/phoenix.zhtml?c=112761andp=irol-sec.

[131] ———. Form 10-K. Washington: Securities and Exchange Commission, March 31, 2008. http://investors.Wal-Martstores.com/phoenix.zhtml?c=112761andp=irol-sec.

[132] ———. Form 10-K. Washington: Securities and Exchange Commission, April 1, 2009. http://investors.Wal-Martstores.com/phoenix.zhtml?c=112761andp=irol-sec.

[133] ———. Form 10-K. Washington: Securities and Exchange Commission, March 30, 2010. http://investors.Wal-Martstores.com/phoenix.zhtml?c =112761andp=irol-sec.

[134] ———.Organizational Change Memo Regarding E-commerce from Eduardo Castro-Wright." January 28, 2010. http://Wal-Martstores.com/pressroom/9629.aspx.

[135] ———."Puerto Rico Fact Sheet." 2009. http://www.docstoc.com/ docs/ 21396711/Puerto-Rico-FactSheet.

[136] ———. "*Wal-Mart Leverages Global Scale to to Lower Costs of Goods*, Accelerate Speed to Market, Improve Quality of Products." News release, January 28, 2010. http://walmartstores.com/ pressroom/news/9621.aspx.

[137] Woods, Rose A. "*Employment Outlook: 2008–2018; Industry Output and Employment Projections to 2018.*" U. S. Department of Labor. Bureau of Labor Statistics. *Monthly Labor Review* November 2009, 52–81.

[138] World Information Technology and Services Alliance (WITSA). *Digital Planet 2010*, October 2010.

[139] Yeaple, Stephen. "The Complex Integration Strategies of Multinationals and Cross Country Dependencies in the Structure of Foreign Direct Investment." *Journal of International Economics*.

End Notes

[1] This paper represents solely the views of the authors and is not meant to represent the views of the U. S. International Trade Commission or any of its commissioners. Please direct all correspondence to Lisa Alejandro, Office of Industries, U. S. International Trade Commission, 500 E Street, SW, Washington, DC 20436, telephone: 202-205- 3486, fax: 202-205-2359, email: lisa.alejandro@usitc.gov.

[2] U. S. direct investment abroad, or outbound investment, reflects investment by U. S. parent companies in foreign-based affiliate companies, where the U. S. parent owns or controls, directly or indirectly, 10 percent or more of the voting securities of an incorporated foreign business enterprise, or the equivalent interest in an unincorporated foreign business enterprise. Unless otherwise noted, this paper refers to majority-owned foreign affiliates (MOFAs), for which the combined ownership of all U. S. parents exceeds 50 percent. In 2008, majority-owned affiliates accounted for 85.2 percent of the employment of all foreign affiliates. U. S. Department of Commerce (USDOC), Bureau of Economic Analysis (BEA), *Survey of Current Business*, August 2010, 205-06.

[3] Holding companies are service providers, but in many cases they hold the equity of goods-producing firms. Holding companies accounted for $1.2 trillion in direct investment abroad in 2008. USDOC, BEA, "U.S. Direct Investment Abroad on a Historical Cost Basis," 1997-2009.

[4] The desire to relocate specific stages of production to lower-cost locations ("vertical" FDI) has also motivated some investments, such as those of some computer services firms in India. However, the distinction between vertical and horizontal multinational firms is rarely clear, as many firms pursue "complex integration" strategies to both access new markets and economize on production costs. Yeaple, "The Complex Integration Strategies of Multinationals," 2003.

[5] USDOC, BEA, "Table A. Services Supplied to Foreign and U. S. Markets Through Cross-Border Trade and Through Affiliates," October 2010. One caveat applies to comparison of service exports and affiliate sales: BEA records cross-border trade data by the type of service delivered, but classifies the affiliate sales data by the primary industry of the affiliate (regardless of the nature of the service delivered).

[6] Value added is "The portion of the goods and services sold or added to inventory or fixed investment by a firm that reflects the production of the firm itself" (USDOC, BEA, Operations of Multinational Companies Database, accessed June 14, 2011). We analyze value added here instead of sales because it illuminates how multinational firms distribute value-creating production processes.

[7] USDOC, BEA, Operations of Multinational Companies Database (accessed June 21, 2011). Activities of holding companies are excluded from the calculations in this paragraph. Our calculations do not take into account any sales from foreign affiliates in which U. S. parents do not hold majority stakes.

[8] A comprehensive review of this literature appears in Molnar, Pain, and Taglioni, "Globalisation and Employment in the OECD," December 2008.

[9] Brainard and Riker, "Are U. S. Multinationals Exporting U. S. Jobs?" March 1997.

[10] Desai, Foley, and Hines, "Domestic Effects of the Foreign Activities of U. S. Multinationals," May 2008.

[11] Harrison and McMillan, "Outsourcing Jobs?" July 2006.

[12] Imbriani, Pittiglio, and Reganati, "Outward FDI and Home Country Performance," May 13–14, 2010.

[13] The industries are accommodation; broadcasting and telecommunications; computer systems design and related services; construction; finance (except depository institutions) and insurance; food services and drinking places; health care and social assistance; motion picture and sound recording; professional, scientific, and technical services; real estate, rental, and leasing; retail trade; transportation and warehousing; utilities; and wholesale trade.

[14] Their equations use rates of change rather than levels. They also include additional lagged variables.

[15] Value added is "The portion of the goods and services sold or added to inventory or fixed investment by a firm that reflects the production of the firm itself... measured as gross output minus intermediate inputs; alternatively, it can be measured as the sum of the costs incurred (except for intermediate inputs) and the profits earned in production." USDOC, BEA, Operations of Multinational Companies Database (accessed June 24, 2011).

[16] We calculated the wages by dividing total U. S. compensation costs by the total number of employees (full-time and part-time).

[17] The parent company data and the data on affiliate sales and employment are aggregated according to the industry of the U. S. parent company. The data on outward investment stock are aggregated by the industry of the affiliate. The two methods of aggregation do not always yield identical results. For example, a U. S. multinational parent company might be a retailer, but it might have one or more non-retail affiliates. This distinction should be kept in mind when comparing the results generated using the outward investment variable to those using foreign employment and affiliate sales.

[18] As a robustness check, we also ran the regressions with these variables expressed in nominal terms. Doing so produced no significant changes in the results.

[19] The wage term's insignificance may be caused by offsetting effects on labor demand and supply. Higher wages cause firms to demand fewer workers, but the higher wages also attract more people to work.

[20] USDOC, BEA, Survey of Current Business, October 2010, 36-55.

[21] Management and consulting services are diverse, including human resources consulting, compensation and benefit consulting, biological and environmental consulting, administrative and general management consulting, marketing consulting, and process, distribution, and logistics consulting. RandD and testing services provide new knowledge, products, or processes by conducting original research on biology, environment, industrial processes, physical sciences, and social sciences. Financial services include banking, other credit intermediation services, securities and commodity intermediation and brokerage, and insurance underwriting and brokerage. USDOC, BEA, Guide to Industry Classifications for International Surveys, 2007, BE-799 (REV. 12/2007).

[22] The employment requirements matrix can be found at USDOL, Employment Projections, "Nominal Dollar Based Domestic Employment Requirements" table for 2008 (http://www.bls.gov/emp/ep data emp requirements.htm).

[23] It is likely that some of these intrafirm exports of services happened within multinationals specializing in the production of goods. However, a substantial share of such trade may happen between MNCs' subsidiaries in

the U. S. specializing in services and the MNCs' foreign affiliates. For example, Ford Motor Company, a vehicle manufacturer, owns Ford Motor Credit Company, which specializes in automotive finance. BEA defines a "parent company" as all U. S. operations of a U. S. MNC, so any services exports of Ford Credit would be recorded by BEA as coming from Ford Motor Company's (goods-producing) corporate parent.

[24] These estimates do not account for intrafirm exports of goods by multinational companies, which are substantial even among service multinationals. For example, in 2006, U. S. multinationals in the professional, scientific, and technical services industries exported $5.2 billion in goods to their foreign affiliates. USDOC, BEA, Operations of Multinational Companies database (accessed June 16, 2011).

[25] IBISWorld, *Global Commercial Banks*, January 6, 2011, 4.

[26] IBISWorld, *Global Commercial Banks*, January 6, 2011, 4, and IBISWorld, *Commercial Banking in the U. S.*, January 2011, 34.

[27] IBISWorld, *Commercial Banking in the U. S.*, January 2011, 11-12.

[28] Bloomberg, David Mildenberg, "Bank of America, Li Ka-Shing Reduce China Bank Stakes," January 7, 2009.

[29] Average taken from international revenues during 2004-08, Bloomberg database.

[30] Revenue growth for Bank of America's operations outside North America registered 568 percent from 2004-08, with Asian revenues growing 1358 percent, Latin American revenues growing 50 percent, and European, Middle Eastern, and African revenues rising 540 percent during that period. By comparison, U. S. revenues increased by 110 percent. These figures include revenue from all of Bank of America's business lines, and it is likely that some portion of that growth resulted from Bank of America's acquisitions of Merrill Lynch and Countrywide. Revenue figures from Bloomberg database.

[31] IBISWorld, *Global Commercial Banks*, January 6, 2011, 4, and IBISWorld, *Commercial Banking in the U. S.*, January 2011, 34.

[32] Economist, "World Banks: We Lucky Few," May 14, 2010.

[33] China accounted for roughly half of this share. Economist, "World Banks: The Bigger and Bigger Picture," May 14, 2010.

[34] Economist, "World Banks: The Bigger and Bigger Picture," May 14, 2010.

[35] Financial services trade data include a wider range of activities such as securities services that are not the focus of this chapter. BEA, *Survey of Current Business*, October 2010.

[36] IBISWorld, *Global Commercial Banks*, January 6, 2011, 4, and IBISWorld, *Commercial Banking in the U. S.*, January 2011,34.

[37] This wage shift is likely a reflection of an increase in banking employment in developing countries, where wages are lower, driving down average global wages. IBISWorld, *Global Commercial Banks*, January 6, 2011,4, and IBISWorld, *Commercial Banking in the U. S.*, January 2011, 34.

[38] IBISWorld, *Commercial Banking in the U. S.*, January 2011.

[39] This is not to say that certain functions such as those performed in customer services centers are not subject to outsourcing, but such decisions are not likely linked to establishment of an affiliate.

[40] This figure includes exports of banking as well as securities and other financial services, but excludes insurance. USDOC, BEA, *Survey of Current Business*, October 2010, 36-55; and USDOL, BLS, Employment Projections, http://www.bls.gov/emp/epdataemprequirements.htm, accessed May 3, 2011.

[41] The banking services included in the BLS data are services performed by monetary authorities, credit intermediation services, and related activities. US Department of Labor, Bureau of Labor Statistics, Domestic Employment Requirements Table, December 10, 2009.

[42] USDOL, BLS, Occupational Statistics database, accessed May 2, 2011.

[43] Industry representative, meeting with Commission staff, Washington, DC, April 2, 2010.

[44] Cathers, "Industry Surveys," May 6, 2010.

[45] For the purposes of this analysis, the scope is limited to professional computer services, which roughly correspond to NAICS code 5415: Computer Systems Design and Related Services. U. S. Census Bureau, "2007 NAICS Definition: Sector 54," 2007.

[46] Bureau van Dijk, Orbis Companies Database, n.d. (accessed January 26, 2011).

[47] World Information Technology and Services Alliance (WITSA), *Digital Planet 2010*, October 2010, 26.

[48] United Nations Conference on Trade and Development, *Information Economy Report 2007–08*, xxvi; IBM, "Computer Services and Management Consulting," 1, June 2006.

[49] Figures for computer services expenditure include outsourced services, both offshore and domestic, including IT consulting, systems integration, custom software development, web page design, network systems and systems integration, office automation, facilities management, equipment maintenance, web hosting, computer disaster recovery, and data processing services. WITSA, *Digital Planet 2010*, October 2010, 20.

[50] WITSA, *Digital Planet 2010*, October 2010, 26.

[51] IBM, *Annual Report 2009*, 2010, 26; HP, *2009 Annual Report*, 2010, 158.

[52] CSC derives 100 percent of its revenues from computer services, unlike firms such as IBM and HP, which both operate in other industries.

[53] The United States was the only country to account for more than 10 percent of HP's net revenue in 2009, representing 36 percent of HP's total consolidated net revenue. HP, *2009 Annual Report*, 2010, 158.

[54] IBM, *Annual Report 2009*, 2010, 6; HP Company Web site, "HP Global Citizenship" (accessed October 27, 2010).
[55] Data on assets held by U. S. parents and their foreign affiliates are presented in lieu of sales figures due to data limitations. Data on sales by U. S. computer services parents and their foreign affiliates are suppressed by the BEA for much of the past decade to avoid disclosure of data from individual firms. USDOC, BEA, "Selected Data for Majority-Owned Nonbank Foreign Affiliates and Nonbank U. S. Parents in All Industries," 1999–2008 (accessed April 26, 2011).
[56] USDOC, BEA, "Selected Data for Majority-Owned Nonbank Foreign Affiliates and Nonbank U. S. Parents in All Industries," 1999–2008 (accessed April 26, 2011). These data are classified based on NAICS industry of the U. S. parent. As a result, they do not capture firms that provide computer services but are classified under a NAICS code other than 5415, such as HP.
[57] In 2009, foreign markets accounted for 64.3 percent of IBM's and 38.3 percent of CSC's. IBM, *Annual Report 2009*, 2010, 125; CSC, *Annual Report 2009*, 2010, 108.
[58] Author calculations based on data from WITSA, *Digital Planet 2010*, October 2010, 26.
[59] WITSA, *Digital Planet 2010*, October 2010, 26.
[60] IBM, *Annual Report 2008*, 2009, 11.
[61] WITSA, *Digital Planet 2010,* October 2010.
[62] McDonald, Mark, "Innovation Marching On," September 8, 2009; The Federal Reserve Board, "Summary: April 15, 2009," April 15, 2009.
[63] The Federal Reserve Board, "Summary: April 15, 2009," April 15, 2009; OECD, "The Impact of the Crisis on ICT and ICTRelated Employment," October 2009, 15.
[64] Author calculations using data from USDOL, BLS, "Computer Systems Design and Related Services," May 2009.
[65] Woods, Rose A., "Employment Outlook: 2008–2018," *Monthly Labor Review*, November 2009, 56.
[66] Data for 2008 are the most recent available. Author calculations based on data from USDOC, BEA, "Majority-Owned Foreign Affiliates," and "U.S. Parent Companies," 1999–2008.
[67] In Latin America, foreign affiliate employment rose from 20,400 in 1999 to 29,400 in 2008. Over the same period, employment by foreign affiliates in Africa nearly doubled, albeit from a much smaller base, increasing from 2,800 to 4,000.
[68] Author calculations based on data from USDOC, BEA, "Majority-Owned Foreign Affiliates," and "U.S. Parent Companies," 1999–2008.
[69] Author calculations based on data from USDOC, BEA, "Majority-Owned Foreign Affiliates," 1999–2008.
[70] 2006 is the most recent year for which comparable data are available. Figures reporting services supplied by foreign affiliates of U. S. firms in 2007 and 2008 were suppressed by the BEA to avoid disclosure of data for individual firms. Export revenue figures are for computer systems design and related services (NAICS 5415) and are based on reporting by employer firms. U. S. Census Bureau, "Table 6.5.," 2005–09; USDOC, BEA, "Table 9.a," 2006–08.
[71] Tejaswi and John, "IBM is India's Second Largest Pvt Sector Employer," August 18, 2010.
[72] Cathers, "Industry Surveys," May 6, 2010, 3.
[73] Kulkarni, "EDS Buy gives HP Services, India Edge," May 14, 2008.
[74] Cathers, "Industry Surveys," May 6, 2010, 10.
[75] IBM, *Corporate Responsibility Report* 2002, 2003, 15; IBM, *Annual Report 2008*, 2009, 53.
[76] HP, *2003 HP Global Citizenship Report*, 2003, 23; HP, *HP FY07 Global Citizenship Report*, 2007, 134.
[77] IBM *Annual Report 2008*, 2009, 119; HP, *2007 Annual Report*, 2008.
[78] This figure is reported from congressional testimony; it was reported in 2010 that IBM would no longer report U. S. employment figures, instead providing global employment figures. IBM, *Annual Report 2008*, 11; IBM, *Understanding our Company*, March 2005, 29; Lounsbury, "IBM Stops Reporting U. S. Employment Numbers," March 19, 2010; Thibodeau, "IBM Stops Disclosing U. S. Headcount Data," March 12, 2010.
[79] Ortutay, "Hewlett-Packard to Cut 9K Jobs in Services Unit," June 1, 2010.
[80] For a more detailed discussion of the method used, see chapter 1.
[81] Computer services output is defined using NAICS code 5415 Computer Systems Design and Related Services. USDOL, BLS, Domestic Employment Requirements table, December 10, 2009.
[82] The USDOC, BEA reported that in 2008, U. S. parent firms provided $2.8 billion of computer and data processing services to their foreign affiliates. See chapter 1 for estimates of total jobs supported by demand for computer and information services, which includes computer and data processing services, as well as database and other information services.
[83] USDOL, BLS, "Computer Systems Design and Related Services," (accessed March 22, 2011).
[84] Professional computer services occupations comprise computer and information scientists, research; computer programmers; computer software engineers, both applications and systems software; computer support specialists; computer systems analysts; database administrators; network and computer systems administrators; network systems and data communications analysts; and other computer specialists. USDOL, BLS, "Computer systems design and related services" May 2009.

[85] USDOC, BLS, Occupation Employment Statistics Query System, May 2009 (accessed April 25, 2011 and May 2, 2011).
[86] US Census Bureau, "Industry Statistics Sampler" April 11, 2011.
[87] Ono, "Why Do Firms Use Temporary Workers?" March 2009.
[88] Luo, Mann, and Holden, "The expanding role of temporary help services," August 2010, 3–16.
[89] U. S. Census Bureau, "NAICS 4921: Couriers." http://www.census.gov/econ/industry/hierarchy/i4921.htm (accessed March 25, 2011). Logistic service providers may be affiliated with a range of industry classification codes, including those pertaining to air, maritime, road and rail transport services; freight forwarding services; business management and consultancy services; and postal services, among others. However, for the purposes of this paper, logistic services are identified under the broad industry code NAICS 492, "couriers and messengers." This industry code includes express delivery services and air courier services.
[90] UPS, *Annual Report 2010*, 5.
[91] FedEx, *Annual Report 2010*, 63.
[92] USITC, *Logistic Services: An Overview of the Global Market and Potential Effects of Removing Trade Impediments*, Inv. No. 332-463, May 2005, 1-3.
[93] UNESCAP, "The Relationship between Liberalization in the Logistics Sector and Trade Facilitation," 2006.
[94] Cosmas and Martini, "UPS and FedEx Air Hubs," December 14, 2007, 4.
[95] This industry is primarily composed of freight forwarders, intermodal marketing companies, distributors, and other non-asset-based companies that contract with vehicle- and equipment-owners. ("Asset-based" refers to whether a company owns the trucks, warehouses, distribution centers, or other assets used in supply chain management.)
[96] Armstrong and Associates, "Global 3PL Market Size Estimates," retrieved October 8, 2010. $107 billion of that revenue was in the United States.
[97] Oxford Economics, "The Impact of the Express Delivery Industry on the Global Economy," September 2009, 5.
[98] Company annual reports, USITC calculations. This number includes Fed Ex's independent contractors.
[99] Bureau of Transport Statistics, "National Transportation Statistics," retrieved October 8, 2010.
[100] For example, FedEx operates 9 air hubs overseas, with the largest in Paris, France and Subic Bay in the Philippines. In 2009, the company opened a new hub at Guangzhou Baiyun International Airport, located in southern China, intended to replace Subic Bay as the company's main hub in the Asia-Pacific region. In 2010 FedEx built a new facility in Cologne, Germany, which now serves as the Express segment's primary hub for operations in central and eastern Europe.
[101] These investments may take the form of wholly owned subsidiaries, joint ventures, or strategic alliances, depending on how logistics firms balance the desire for control over foreign operations against the value of local relationships provided by partners. For example, DHL has formed partnerships with Polar Air and Blue Dart (the latter provides domestic ground transport services in India), while FedEx purchased U.K. express company ANC Holdings in 2006, allowing the former to operate within the U.K. domestic market. FedEx followed this acquisition with the 2007 purchases of its joint venture express partner in China, DTW, and its air freight service provider in India, Prakash Air. Logistics firms also expand internationally by adding shipping routes or increasing the frequency of flights: in 1994, FedEx began express service in the U. S. - China market by taking over the Chinese air service rights of U. S. cargo carrier, Evergreen International; and in 2007, UPS added six daily flights from the United States to Nagoya (Japan) and later extended those flights further to connect with Shanghai. See Deutsche Post DHL, "Annual Report 2009," 55; "FedEx Timeline," FedEx company website. http://fedex.com/us/about/today/history/timeline.html (accessed October 12, 2010); "Acquisition History," FedEx company website. http://ir.fedex.com/acquisitions.cfm (accessed November 4, 2010); and UPS, "Annual Report 2009," 15.
[102] BEA, "U.S. Direct Investment Abroad on Historical Cost Basis," 2008.
[103] CSRwire, "U.S. Businesses Must Take Sustainable Approach to International Business Development," June 18, 2003.
[104] International Labor Organization LABORSTA database (accessed October 13, 2010). This category includes a number of industries outside of logistics, such as telecommunications and audiovisual services.
[105] Bureau of Labor Statistics databases (accessed October 6, 2010).
[106] Bloomberg databases (accessed November 10, 2010). This calculation does not include FedEx's independent contractors.
[107] Annual reports, USITC calculations
[108] TNT, *Annual Report 2009*, 33.
[109] Bloomberg databases (accessed November 10, 2010); FedEx annual reports. These calculations include Fed Ex's independent contractors.
[110] BLS Labor Productivity and Costs database, accessed April 28, 2011.
[111] UPS company representatives, interview with Commission staff, Washington, DC, December 17, 2010.
[112] TNT, *Annual Report 2009*, 22.
[113] Deutsche Post DHL, *Annual Report 2009*, 39.
[114] UPS, *Annual Report 2009*, 5.

[115] UPS, *Annual Report 2009*, 13.
[116] *FedExAnnual Report, 2010*, 26. http://www.fedex.com/us/investorrelations/(accessed September 8, 2010).
[117] *FedExAnnual Report, 2010*, 26. http://www.fedex.com/us/investorrelations/(accessed September 8, 2010).
[118] Oxford Economics, *The Impact of the Express Delivery Industry on the Global Economy*, September 2009, 7–8.
[119] U PS, *Annual Report 2009*, 20.
[120] CSRwire, "U.S. Businesses Must Take Sustainable Approach to International Business Development," June 18, 2003.
[121] UPS company representatives, interview with Commission staff, Washington, DC, December 17, 2010.
[122] Tharpe, "For UPS Executive, Olympics a Marathon," November 30, 2009.
[123] UPS company representatives, interview with Commission staff, Washington, DC, December 17, 2010.
[124] U. S. Census Bureau American Factfinder, retrieved April 28, 2011.
[125] SRI International, Macro Impacts of FedEx on the U. S. and Global Economies, 2001, 114. http://www.sri.com/policy/csted/reports/economics/fedex/chapter5.pdf (accessed March 25, 2011).
[126] Oxford Economics, *The Impact of the Express Delivery Industry on the Global Economy*, September 2009, 31–32.
[127] UPS website, accessed April 28, 2011.
[128] Toshiba website, accessed April 28, 2011.
[129] FedEx website, accessed April 28, 2009.
[130] U. S. Census Bureau, "2007 NAICS Definition: Sector 44–45." Retailing is one type of distribution service. Retailers typically purchase merchandise for resale rather than manufacturing the items themselves. Wholesaling, the other principal distribution service, occurs when a firm purchases merchandise that it then sells to industrial or institutional users, retailers, or other wholesalers.
[131] Planet Retail, Planet Retail Database (accessed September 28, 2010).
[132] Between 2004 and 2008, real GDP growth in economies categorized by the International Monetary Fund (IMF) as "emerging and developing" averaged 7.6 percent per year, compared to 2.4 percent in "advanced" economies. IMF, World Economic Outlook Database.
[133] Beinhocker, Farrell, and Zainulbhai, "Tracking the Growth of India's Middle Class," 2007, 58; Reda, "Markets with Muscle," November 2009.
[134] Deloitte, *Feeling the Squeeze,* January 2009, G26.
[135] Wal-Mart, Form 10-K, April 21, 1997, 26–27. Wal-Mart's fiscal year ends January 31, so fiscal year 1997 extended from February 1, 1996 to January 31, 1997.
[136] Number of retail units from Wal-Mart, *2010 Annual Report* (online edition). Sales and employment data from Wal-Mart, Form 10-K report, 2010. Wal-Mart's fiscal year ends January 31. Sales data for 2010 are for February 1, 2009–January 31, 2010. Employment data are for the last date of the fiscal year.
[137] Deloitte, *Emerging from the Downturn,* January 2010, G11.
[138] Maestri, "Update 3—Target Seeks Growth from Small Stores, Overseas," January 21, 2010.
[139] USDOL, BLS, Employment, Hours, and Earnings– National Database.
[140] USDOL, BLS, Occupational Employment Statistics Database.
[141] USDOL, BLS, "Occupational Employment and Wages by Ownership," July 27, 2010.
[142] USDOL, BLS, Employment, Hours, and Earnings– National Database.
[143] USDOC, BEA, Operations of Multinational Companies database (accessed March 31, 2011).
[144] Wal-Mart, Form 10-K reports, 1998–2010.
[145] The data necessary to conduct a similar analysis of productivity in affiliates were not available.
[146] Costco, *2010 Annual Report,* December 13, 2010, i.
[147] IKEA, "Facts and Figures."
[148] Enright, "Gap Goes Global," August 12, 2010.
[149] Wal-Mart, "About Us."
[150] Company representatives, interviews with authors, Bentonville, Arkansas, September 13–14, 2010.
[151] USDOL, BLS, *Employment Projections* (accessed May 3, 2011).
[152] Company representatives, interviews with authors, Bentonville, Arkansas, September 13–14, 2010. The example of canned peaches is corroborated by U. S. Agricultural Export Development Council, "Success Story," April 15, 2010.
[153] Clipper Windpower, "Clipper Windpower and EDF EN," August 5, 2008; Company representatives, interviews with authors, Bentonville, Arkansas, September 13–14, 2010.
[154] Costco's operating revenue more than doubled between 2001 and 2008. Bureau van Dijk, Orbis database (accessed August 4, 2011).
[155] Timberlake and Stanford, "Costco Stops Restocking Coca-Cola Products," November 16, 2009.
[156] Wal-Mart, "Walmart Leverages Global Scale," January 28, 2010.
[157] *Supply Chain Digest*, "Walmart to Centralize Global Sourcing," January 6, 2010.

CHAPTER SOURCES

The following chapters have been previously published:

Chapter 1 - This is an edited, reformatted and augmented version of United States International Trade Commission, Publication No. 4243, dated July 2011.

Chapter 2 – This is an edited, reformatted and augmented version of United States International Trade Commission, No. ID-29, dated August 2011.

INDEX

A

ABA, 111, 112
academic performance, 52
access, 15, 31, 50, 62, 66, 67, 76, 91, 117, 121, 123, 161, 163, 167, 178, 189
accessibility, 60
accommodation, 189
accounting, 4, 11, 13, 14, 18, 19, 22, 28, 30, 36, 67, 71, 79, 86, 115, 116, 117, 147, 153, 156
acquisitions, 80, 82, 127, 129, 173, 182, 190, 192
adjustment, 156
administrative support, 149
administrators, 191
adults, 67
advertisements, 125
aerospace, 92, 163, 165, 166
affiliate transactions, vii, 1, 4, 9, 11, 12, 37, 46, 58, 72, 73, 74, 76, 85, 115
Africa, 31, 41, 63, 69, 76, 86, 96, 107, 124, 131, 152, 153, 161, 191
age, 33, 34
agencies, 9, 49, 57, 90, 124, 156, 159, 173
aggregation, 189
aging population, 43, 75
airports, 31, 181
Albania, 101, 122
alcohol consumption, 125
American Recovery and Reinvestment Act, 43, 69, 124
American Recovery and Reinvestment Act of 2009, 43, 69
ANC, 192
annual rate, 7, 22, 38, 40, 41, 46, 51, 62, 80, 83, 89, 129, 134, 150, 151, 152, 153
annuals, 182
arbitrage, 92
arbitration, 128, 129

Argentina, 127
Armenia, 10
arthritis, 125
ASEAN, 1, 60
Asia, 6, 8, 15, 30, 34, 35, 39, 40, 41, 48, 56, 58, 59, 60, 64, 76, 77, 78, 82, 84, 86, 105, 106, 109, 110, 113, 126, 127, 129, 130, 131, 143, 144, 151, 152, 153, 155, 161, 171, 182, 185, 192
Asian countries, 7, 51
assessment, 52, 120
assets, 93, 96, 144, 150, 152, 157, 180, 181, 182, 184, 185, 191, 192
Association of Southeast Asian Nations, 1, 60, 75
asymmetry, 19, 64
at-risk populations, 64
audit, 13, 14, 115, 116
Australasia, 105, 126
authorities, 147, 148, 175, 180, 190
authority, 59
automate, 36
automation, 120, 190
autonomy, 60
average revenue, 162
awareness, 68, 146
Azerbaijan, 10

B

balance of payments, 11, 58
ban, 31
banking, vii, viii, 1, 82, 115, 116, 121, 133, 134, 139, 143, 144, 145, 146, 147, 148, 149, 176, 177, 189, 190
banking industry, 144, 145, 146, 147
banking sector, 143, 147, 149
bankruptcies, 129
bankruptcy, 35, 39, 127, 128

banks, 15, 139, 143, 144, 145, 146, 147, 148, 149, 176, 177
barriers, 7, 31, 39, 40, 42, 49, 50, 51, 60, 75
barriers to entry, 42
base, 89, 164, 191
behaviors, 116
Beijing, 84, 128, 163
Belarus, 10
Belgium, 32, 127, 134, 135
benefits, 5, 19, 35, 36, 92, 164
blogs, 99, 184
Bologna Process, 104, 123
Brazil, 55, 63, 64, 76, 82, 86, 90, 97, 109, 110, 112, 114, 127, 129, 131, 136, 152, 161, 162, 167
breakdown, 158
Broadband, 45, 98, 121
Bulgaria, 119
Bureau of Economic Analysis, vii, 1, 9, 37, 46, 71, 85, 91, 93, 95, 97, 101, 103, 104, 108, 113, 133, 135, 136, 137, 186, 188
Bureau of Labor Statistics, vii, 1, 95, 97, 101, 114, 116, 118, 120, 130, 133, 134, 143, 148, 154, 158, 164, 166, 171, 175, 184, 186, 188, 190, 192
business costs, 9, 77
business management, 192
business model, 91
Business Roundtable, 174, 181
businesses, 15, 44, 120, 150, 157, 166, 167

C

Cameroon, 31
campaigns, 52
cancer, 67
capital expenditure, 44
capital flows, 77
capital intensive, 92, 115, 116, 157
capital markets, 82, 128
cardiovascular disease, 67, 125
Caribbean, 45, 108, 125
case studies, 100, 134, 176
case study, 99
cash, 56, 144
casting, 31, 120
categorization, 91
category a, 142, 158
category d, 23
Census, 80, 81, 91, 101, 114, 120, 127, 185, 190, 191, 192, 193
certification, 127
Chad, 107
challenges, vii, 2, 3, 9, 34, 77, 90, 91, 92
cheese, 174

Chicago, 53, 94, 104, 130, 184
Chile, 67, 101, 104, 125, 127
chronic diseases, 62, 67, 76, 124, 125
chronic illness, 8, 61, 67
cities, 31, 68, 130
citizens, 12, 44, 75, 125
City, 44, 45, 95, 99, 130, 175
class size, 56
classes, 56
classification, 85, 192
cleaning, 174
clients, 6, 40, 42, 43, 45, 49, 50, 79, 80, 82, 85, 86, 89, 90, 92, 120, 128, 147, 152
closure, 148
clothing, 167, 173
Cloud computing, 44
collaboration, 45, 77
colleges, 52, 58, 103
Colombia, 101, 127
color, iv
commerce, 77, 157, 160, 185, 188
commercial, 8, 11, 12, 39, 43, 49, 79, 80, 82, 84, 115, 117, 127, 128, 129, 144, 145, 146
commercial bank, 144, 145, 146
commodity, 37, 148, 180, 189
communication, 43, 71, 72, 120, 121, 153, 160
communication systems, 160
communication technologies, 43, 71, 72, 120, 153
communities, 75, 160
comparative advantage, 20, 91, 92
compatibility, 34
compensation, 132, 137, 189
competition, 5, 7, 19, 31, 42, 51, 52, 61, 116, 150
competitive advantage, 8, 61
competitive conditions, 9
competitiveness, 2, 8, 9, 77, 84, 90, 115, 166
competitors, vii, 2, 43, 49, 146
complement, 60, 177
complementarity, 137, 139
complexity, 64
complications, 67
composition, 180
computer software, 19, 156, 191
computer systems, 4, 5, 22, 25, 40, 41, 42, 46, 49, 50, 116, 117, 120, 121, 122, 150, 151, 152, 154, 156, 180, 189, 191
computing, 7, 40, 42, 44, 45, 50, 51, 98, 99, 121, 150
conference, 95, 102, 183
confidentiality, 91
conflict, 50
congress, iv, 66, 94, 122, 124
consensus, 5, 139
consolidation, 56

Index 199

constituents, 8, 61, 123
construction, 6, 28, 30, 42, 70, 115, 116, 117, 118, 157, 173, 189
consulting, 5, 25, 26, 42, 43, 51, 99, 117, 120, 139, 140, 142, 150, 156, 157, 160, 179, 189, 190
consumer goods, 174
consumers, vii, 1, 11, 13, 15, 19, 29, 33, 34, 37, 43, 45, 51, 64, 72, 75, 76, 114, 117, 134, 139, 150, 151, 159, 167, 178
consumption, 12, 13, 39, 71, 75
cooperation, 30, 62
cooperative agreements, 132
copyright, iv, 31, 119
coronary bypass surgery, 126
correlation, 84
cosmetic, 67, 71, 126
cost, 6, 8, 21, 28, 29, 32, 33, 34, 35, 36, 39, 43, 44, 45, 61, 64, 66, 68, 71, 73, 75, 79, 83, 92, 96, 115, 119, 123, 124, 125, 127, 139, 148, 150, 158, 165, 166, 189
counsel, 82, 85, 90, 112, 129
covering, 91
CPC, 101, 113
credentials, 60
creep, 5
CRM, 100
Croatia, 101
cross-border trade, vii, 1, 2, 3, 4, 5, 7, 9, 11, 12, 13, 14, 25, 37, 45, 46, 47, 49, 51, 52, 57, 71, 72, 76, 85, 87, 115, 117, 126, 134, 139, 189
CSS, 97
CT, 125
CT scan, 125
cultural differences, 34
cultural influence, 31
cultural values, 28
currency, 30, 118
current account, 115
curricula, 52, 61
customer service, 45, 147, 148, 190
customers, 13, 45, 49, 147, 152, 160, 161, 166, 173, 177
Czech Republic, 74, 127

D

damages, iv
data availability, 32
data center, 42, 148, 154
data collection, 71, 91
data communication, 191
data processing, 7, 13, 19, 26, 40, 42, 44, 45, 46, 47, 48, 49, 91, 116, 117, 120, 121, 136, 148, 155, 156, 157, 180, 190, 191
data set, 90
database, 37, 42, 45, 46, 72, 100, 120, 121, 124, 126, 137, 142, 149, 151, 161, 190, 191, 192, 193
DCI, 96, 119
deaths, 67
deficit, 4, 13, 45
delegates, 173
Democratic Republic of Congo, 31
Denmark, 109, 127
dental care, 67, 68
Department of Commerce, 93
Department of Labor, 156, 166, 190
Department of Transportation, 187
depository institutions, 135, 189
depth, vii, 2, 116
deregulation, 5, 19, 160
designers, 45
detection, 67, 125
developed countries, vii, 1, 11, 12, 14, 43, 49, 56, 62, 66, 67, 69, 80, 128, 143, 150, 160, 167, 178
developing countries, vii, 1, 5, 8, 21, 35, 42, 61, 63, 67, 69, 82, 144, 150, 167, 190
developing economies, 69, 117
diabetes, 67, 76, 125
dialysis, 70, 74
digital cameras, 31
direct cost, 66
direct investment, 8, 12, 46, 75, 77, 86, 89, 134, 139, 188, 189
directors, 31
disaster, 120, 190
disclosure, 37, 50, 74, 88, 116, 117, 122, 191
discs, 33, 39, 117
diseases, 67, 76, 108, 125
displacement, 20, 21, 117
disposable income, 143, 145, 177
distortions, 64, 124
distribution, 6, 28, 30, 31, 33, 36, 37, 38, 39, 117, 118, 151, 153, 156, 173, 174, 189, 192, 193
diversity, 7, 51, 123
division of labor, 173
doctors, 69, 123
Doha, 60
DOL, 95, 97, 101, 114, 116, 118, 119, 120, 130
domestic demand, 155
domestic economy, 19, 21
domestic markets, 66
DOT, 187
drugs, 67

E

earnings, 20, 34, 139
Eastern Europe, 30, 34, 35
e-commerce, 185
economic activity, 134, 176
economic crisis, 105
economic development, 3
economic disadvantage, 164
economic downturn, 2, 3, 4, 6, 8, 13, 19, 28, 29, 30, 33, 36, 40, 41, 43, 46, 49, 56, 61, 62, 66, 71, 76, 77, 79, 82, 84, 86, 127, 150, 152, 162, 167
economic efficiency, 19
economic growth, 5, 21, 29, 35, 39, 60, 62, 82, 115, 116, 127, 143, 145, 151, 167, 178
economic recession, vii, 1, 14, 15, 18, 132
economics, 184, 193
education, vii, 1, 2, 3, 4, 7, 9, 13, 15, 18, 19, 21, 23, 25, 51, 52, 55, 56, 57, 58, 59, 60, 61, 69, 92, 103, 116, 117, 123
education industry, 60, 123
educational services, 13, 117
Egypt, 30, 42, 118
elderly population, 124
electronic trade, 166
e-mail, 45, 58, 72, 85, 117, 121
emergency, 64, 71
emerging markets, 3, 30, 40, 77, 89, 134, 146, 151, 152, 160, 177
employee compensation, 137
employees, 4, 9, 11, 18, 21, 22, 23, 24, 43, 64, 76, 79, 80, 81, 83, 84, 115, 117, 124, 128, 130, 136, 147, 154, 156, 160, 161, 162, 163, 164, 165, 170, 173, 174, 189
employers, 64, 68, 164
employment growth, 19, 20, 22, 135, 137, 152, 162, 171
employment levels, 130
employment status, 164
end-users, 160
energy, 18, 175
enforcement, 119
engineering, 18, 19, 20, 27, 28, 92, 115, 116, 117, 123, 140, 142, 156, 157, 179
enrollment, 51, 55, 57, 69
environment, 35, 49, 183, 189
environments, 145
epidemic, 76
equipment, 13, 118, 119, 120, 140, 162, 179, 190, 192
equity, 6, 28, 39, 70, 84, 128, 130, 189
equity market, 128
Estonia, 32, 74

EU, 14, 16, 17, 18, 34, 42, 60, 75, 99, 122, 150, 161
Europe, 4, 7, 8, 15, 33, 34, 36, 38, 39, 41, 43, 46, 47, 49, 56, 59, 60, 61, 62, 66, 67, 71, 77, 78, 82, 84, 86, 88, 89, 94, 95, 100, 109, 110, 119, 122, 124, 127, 130, 131, 146, 150, 153, 155, 161, 170, 192
European Central Bank, 105, 125, 126
European Commission, 50, 98, 99, 105, 107, 121, 122, 124
European market, 36, 77, 89, 127
European Parliament, 98, 122
European Union, 7, 34, 42, 50, 51, 58, 59, 99, 107, 122
evidence, 21, 73, 137, 139, 167, 171, 175
exchange rate, 125, 161
exercise, 59
expenditures, 8, 43, 52, 59, 61, 66, 71, 72, 82, 162, 165
expertise, 2, 8, 61, 120, 150, 163
export market, 36, 47, 71, 73, 86, 92, 131
exporter, vii, 2, 3, 11, 49
exporters, 11, 38, 46, 61, 79, 80, 81, 92, 161

F

face-to-face interaction, 49
families, 55
faster delivery, 158
FDI, 137, 139, 162, 181, 182, 183, 189
fear, 19
fears, 56
Federal Reserve, 94, 95, 104, 125, 126, 182, 191
Federal Reserve Board, 182, 191
fiber, 34
fillers, 170
films, 29, 30, 31, 33, 34, 35, 36, 37, 38, 117, 118, 119
financial, 4, 6, 7, 13, 14, 20, 33, 36, 40, 43, 51, 52, 56, 66, 79, 116, 117, 121, 122, 123, 124, 139, 143, 144, 145, 146, 147, 148, 149, 167, 175, 176, 180, 190
financial condition, 147
financial XE "financial" crisis, 66, 124, 143, 144, 145, 146, 167, 176
financial firms, 6, 40, 79
financial performance, 175
financial resources, 122
financial support, 56, 123
firm size, 80, 128
flavor, 52
flexibility, 164
flight, 125
flights, 117, 192
fluctuations, 30, 147

FMC, 93
food, 115, 136, 157, 174, 189
food services, 136, 157, 189
Ford, 129, 190
forecasting, 51
foreign affiliate activity, viii, 133, 167, 178
foreign affiliates, vii, 1, 4, 6, 8, 12, 17, 27, 47, 49, 50, 61, 73, 74, 75, 85, 88, 115, 116, 121, 130, 131, 133, 134, 135, 136, 137, 139, 142, 147, 149, 150, 153, 155, 156, 157, 167, 170, 171, 173, 175, 176, 177, 178, 188, 189, 190, 191
foreign banks, 146, 148
foreign companies, 12
foreign direct investment, vii, 86, 133, 137, 139, 180
foreign firms, 4, 6, 7, 8, 16, 27, 28, 35, 40, 50, 61, 70, 72, 73, 74, 75, 89, 126
foreign investment, 7, 40, 46, 49, 70, 75, 92, 154, 158, 163, 167
foreign nationals, 163
France, 7, 18, 29, 30, 32, 33, 36, 39, 41, 51, 53, 59, 63, 64, 66, 67, 73, 74, 84, 86, 89, 96, 110, 111, 118, 122, 124, 127, 128, 135, 136, 144, 151, 161, 167, 169, 182, 192
franchise, 173
free trade, 89, 132
freezing, 83
funding, 52, 56, 123
funds, 56, 60, 61, 76, 126

G

GAO, 95, 116, 164, 186
GATS, 1, 11, 12, 49, 50, 60, 75, 97, 103, 126
GDP, 1, 4, 5, 7, 11, 15, 18, 22, 24, 62, 117, 123, 124, 128, 193
General Agreement on Trade in Services, 1, 11, 12, 49, 60, 75, 91, 94
general election, 118
general practitioner, 125
Georgia, 10, 49
Germany, 11, 14, 18, 25, 26, 29, 30, 32, 33, 36, 43, 47, 49, 53, 55, 61, 63, 66, 67, 78, 80, 84, 86, 89, 110, 122, 124, 127, 128, 135, 136, 144, 165, 167, 169, 182, 192
global competition, 92
global demand, 4, 8, 61, 69, 76, 177
global economy, vii, 2, 71
global leaders, 42
global markets, 6, 30
global recession, 122
global scale, 175
global trade, vii, 2, 14, 37, 71
globalization, 9, 90, 91

God, 106, 126
goods and services, 18, 29, 91, 115, 116, 123, 128, 142, 173, 176, 189
government budget, 7, 51, 76
government policy, 3
governments, 31, 34, 36, 39, 43, 55, 56, 60, 61, 62, 63, 64, 66, 67, 69, 70, 76, 91, 123, 124, 126
graduate program, 55, 60
grants, 35, 52
graph, 105
gross domestic product, 11, 21, 23, 115, 120
Gross Domestic Product, 1, 22, 101, 108
growth rate, 11, 17, 18, 23, 36, 53, 57, 66, 71, 79, 84, 85, 88, 130, 131, 136, 160
Guangzhou, 182, 192
Guatemala, 175
guidelines, 119, 164

H

health, 18, 43, 61, 62, 64, 65, 66, 68, 69, 70, 75, 104, 107, 123, 124, 125, 126, 189
health care, 43, 189
health insurance, 61, 62, 64, 66, 68, 75, 124, 125, 126
health services, 64, 70
Henry Ford, 126
heterogeneity, 50, 139
higher education, 52, 58, 60
hiring, 7, 51, 57, 83, 132, 156, 162
Hispanics, 104
history, 52, 64, 182, 192
Hong Kong, 39, 53, 84, 89, 97, 101, 169
host, 11, 12, 17, 50, 51, 53, 54, 64, 114, 173
hotels, 31, 45
House, 111, 130
hub, 160, 165, 192
human, 117, 126, 165, 173, 189
human capital, 117
human resources, 117, 165, 189
Hungary, 74, 119, 127
hypertension, 67

I

Iceland, 42
ID, 97, 98
imagery, 32
images, 100
IMF, 2, 111, 115, 121, 128, 183, 193
immigrants, 7, 55, 58, 126
immigration, 51, 75
import penetration, 116

Index

imports, vii, 1, 3, 5, 6, 7, 8, 10, 11, 12, 13, 14, 15, 16, 25, 26, 28, 36, 38, 40, 45, 46, 48, 49, 57, 58, 59, 68, 70, 71, 73, 77, 84, 85, 86, 87, 91, 116, 126, 131, 139, 143, 160
incidence, 8, 61, 62, 67, 76, 124, 125
income, 11, 12, 35, 45, 91, 120, 124, 161
income tax, 35
increased competition, 70
incumbents, 19
indirect effect, 4
individuals, 65, 66, 67, 68, 70, 71, 72, 115, 116, 120, 122, 126, 164
Indonesia, 86
inflation, 56, 76, 138
information technology, 42, 91, 120, 150, 158, 160, 162
infrastructure, vii, 1, 2, 4, 5, 7, 8, 18, 19, 22, 23, 24, 38, 40, 44, 45, 61, 69, 70, 82, 114, 115, 116, 124
infrastructure service industries, vii, 1
injury, iv, 128
institutions, 7, 49, 51, 52, 56, 58, 123
integration, 46, 51, 61, 75, 120, 149, 177, 189, 190
integrators, 157, 158, 161
intellectual property, 6, 28, 36, 37, 50, 128, 134, 139, 140, 141
intellectual property rights, 28, 36, 37
intermediaries, 15, 159, 175
international competition, 53, 117
international investment, 80
international law, 89, 132
International Monetary Fund, 2, 111, 115, 183, 193
international trade, 6, 11, 28, 51, 56, 61, 66, 77, 80, 90, 120, 160
internationalization, 137
interoperability, 34
intrafirm exports, vii, 133, 134, 140, 141, 142, 144, 147, 150, 154, 156, 157, 176, 177, 179, 180, 189, 190
investment, vii, 1, 2, 12, 28, 31, 32, 33, 49, 66, 75, 77, 79, 82, 86, 89, 92, 115, 116, 122, 131, 133, 134, 137, 138, 139, 143, 144, 147, 153, 160, 167, 188, 189
investment bank, 92, 144
investments, 34, 35, 44, 51, 64, 80, 82, 86, 128, 129, 148, 157, 162, 173, 177, 180, 189, 192
investors, 34, 70, 185, 187, 188
Iowa, 175
IPO, 2, 80, 129
Ireland, 14, 17, 25, 26, 32, 35, 42, 98
Israel, 86, 131
issues, 9, 50, 61, 74, 88, 89, 90, 105, 118, 140
Italy, 7, 29, 30, 33, 51, 59, 63, 127, 135, 137, 167

J

Japan, 4, 11, 14, 15, 16, 17, 18, 25, 26, 29, 30, 32, 33, 34, 35, 36, 41, 49, 53, 55, 56, 58, 60, 63, 64, 84, 86, 89, 96, 97, 101, 102, 110, 118, 119, 122, 123, 127, 128, 131, 135, 136, 137, 144, 151, 152, 167, 169, 174, 192
job creation, 144, 146, 148, 160, 165, 166, 176
joint ventures, 132, 192
Jordan, 107
jurisdiction, 89, 132

K

Kazakhstan, 10
Korea, 7, 29, 35, 36, 39, 50, 51, 54, 55, 58, 60, 89, 90, 97, 114, 120, 122, 127, 131, 132
Kyrgyzstan, 10

L

labor force, 20, 123
labor market(s), 117
language proficiency, 122
languages, 92
laptop, 166
Latin America, 8, 30, 38, 41, 45, 60, 77, 82, 86, 89, 118, 131, 143, 152, 153, 161, 162, 170, 190, 191
Latvia, 32
law enforcement, 50
laws, 50, 132, 164
lawyers, 19, 77, 79, 83, 89, 90, 127
layoffs, 19, 56, 83, 84, 148
lead, 31, 49, 55, 56, 138
leadership, 92
learning, 60
learning outcomes, 60
LED, 175
legal issues, 79, 89
legal protection, 119
legislation, 56, 69
leisure, 29, 33
lending, 144, 146
level of education, 123
liberalization, 12, 20, 75, 116, 134, 174
Liberia, 31
license fee, 4, 13, 28, 142
light, 158, 159
Lion, 32
Lithuania, 183
litigation, 79, 127, 128, 129
locus, 167, 178

logistic services, 117, 192
logistics, vii, viii, 1, 133, 134, 157, 158, 159, 160, 161, 162, 163, 164, 165, 166, 167, 174, 175, 176, 177, 189, 192
lower prices, 84, 158, 167, 175
low-interest loans, 52
Luo, 184, 192

M

machinery, 159, 179
magazines, 125
magnitude, 165, 173
majority, 10, 12, 13, 17, 27, 33, 55, 63, 66, 68, 73, 75, 85, 88, 116, 124, 125, 131, 134, 135, 136, 139, 147, 149, 150, 153, 155, 165, 170, 173, 188, 189
Malaysia, 42, 45, 57, 61, 70, 75, 86, 106
management, 5, 19, 25, 40, 42, 43, 46, 116, 117, 120, 144, 147, 150, 157, 160, 161, 165, 173, 189, 190, 192
manufactured goods, 4, 13, 14, 15
manufacturing, vii, 4, 24, 46, 91, 133, 134, 135, 136, 137, 149, 150, 157, 173, 193
market access, 49
market capitalization, 146
market concentration, 116
market failure, 64
market segment, 6, 28
market share, 8, 30, 32, 43, 61, 77, 78, 127, 145, 146
marketing, 9, 43, 44, 52, 77, 84, 117, 174, 189, 192
Maryland, 92, 164
masking, 118
materials, 36, 159, 174
mathematics, 92, 123
matrix, 134, 138, 142, 143, 189
matter, iv
measurement, 60
media, 9, 104, 105, 110, 164, 167, 181, 187
median, 34, 116
mediation, 129
Medicaid, 64, 124
medical, 21, 62, 66, 67, 68, 69, 70, 71, 72, 75, 117, 123, 124, 126, 160, 166
medical care, 66, 124
medical reason, 72
Medicare, 64, 68, 124, 127
Mediterranean, 124
merchandise, 4, 13, 14, 15, 167, 173, 175, 193
mergers, 80, 82, 127, 129, 148
messages, 85
messengers, 158, 159, 162, 165, 166, 192

Mexico, 8, 16, 55, 59, 61, 66, 68, 69, 71, 73, 75, 97, 101, 104, 106, 107, 108, 118, 120, 125, 126, 127, 131, 135, 136, 170, 173, 174, 181
Miami, 44, 45, 99
Microsoft, 43, 44, 45, 99, 100, 121, 122
middle class, 64, 66, 143
Middle East, 8, 41, 64, 69, 76, 77, 82, 86, 89, 106, 118, 124, 129, 130, 131, 161, 162, 190
migration, 56, 122
military, 115
Minneapolis, 169
missions, 115
models, 31, 132, 137, 163, 177
Moldova, 10
momentum, 60
monopoly, 33
mortality, 62, 67, 76, 125
mortality rate, 62, 67
Multilateral, 39, 44, 49, 59, 75, 89
multinational companies, 92, 133, 134, 142, 155, 157, 179, 180, 190
multinational corporations, 149, 150
multinational firms, 92, 177, 189

N

NAFTA, 174
national borders, 12, 85, 162
National Health Service, 2, 66
national income, 123
nationality, 118
natural gas, 162
negative effects, 167, 175
negotiating, 91
Nepal, 55
Netherlands, 118, 122, 127, 135, 161, 185
New York, iv
New Zealand, 33, 35, 39, 131
NHS, 2, 66, 70
Nigeria, 29, 31
nodes, 160
non-OECD, 137
nonprofit organizations, 123, 124
North Africa, 60, 76, 106
North America, 6, 8, 34, 36, 40, 42, 43, 61, 66, 73, 77, 101, 113, 120, 127, 143, 144, 166, 174, 180, 185, 190
North American Free Trade Agreement, 174
Norway, 42, 101, 127
nurses, 69, 76, 105, 123
nursing, 69, 123
nutrition, 44, 123, 125

O

obesity, 76
obstacles, 42
OECD, 2, 5, 45, 94, 95, 98, 100, 103, 105, 111, 116, 121, 122, 137, 184, 189, 191
Office of the United States Trade Representative, 2
officials, 50, 56
offshoring, 19, 20, 21, 35, 91, 92, 117
OH, 169
olympics, 185
operating system, 121
operations, viii, 16, 42, 50, 57, 61, 64, 91, 92, 115, 118, 120, 133, 134, 139, 144, 146, 147, 148, 149, 150, 152, 153, 157, 158, 162, 163, 164, 165, 166, 170, 173, 174, 176, 177, 178, 190, 192
opportunities, vii, 1, 8, 35, 62, 70, 74, 75, 82, 90, 92, 143, 144, 146, 151
Organization for Economic Cooperation and Development, 45, 69
Organization of American States, 93
outpatient, 64, 71, 74
outsourcing, 14, 19, 20, 35, 42, 91, 121, 129, 190
overlap, 12, 127
overtime, 143
ownership, 188
ox, 11, 21, 45, 142

P

Pacific, 6, 8, 40, 41, 48, 59, 64, 76, 77, 78, 84, 86, 106, 110, 127, 129, 130, 131, 151, 152, 153, 155, 171, 182, 185, 192
Pakistan, 69
parent firms, vii, 17, 27, 133, 134, 137, 139, 140, 142, 144, 147, 149, 153, 154, 156, 167, 170, 171, 173, 176, 177, 178, 179, 180, 191
parents, vii, 47, 49, 121, 122, 133, 137, 139, 142, 151, 153, 188, 189, 191
Parliament, 56
participants, 9, 90, 92, 128, 130
pathways, 58
payroll, 117
peace, 115
permission, iv
permit, 75, 98, 132, 164
Peru, 101
petroleum, 163
Petroleum, 114, 129
pharmaceutical, 125
pharmaceuticals, 160
Philadelphia, 95, 111, 130
Philippines, 35, 192
physical inactivity, 125
physical sciences, 189
physicians, 69, 75, 76, 127
piracy, 6, 28, 30, 31, 36
plastic surgeon, 125
platform, 121
Poland, 73, 74, 119, 127
police, 158, 159
policy, 3, 28, 55, 60, 103, 184, 193
policy issues, 28
policymakers, 92
pools, 35
population, 20, 34, 36, 66, 67, 68, 92, 124, 126
portability, 75
positive relationship, 116
postal service, 85, 165, 192
predictability, 77, 90
preparation, iv, 117
President, 93
prevention, 125
principles, 122
private education, 60
private firms, 62, 70
private sector, 4, 5, 13, 22, 24, 70, 82, 115, 125, 153, 171
privatization, 75
procurement, 174
producers, 28, 29, 31, 35, 36, 174, 175
production costs, 31, 189
productivity growth, 19, 21, 25, 162
professional service firms, vii, 1
professionals, 19, 69, 72, 75, 76, 84, 85, 123, 128, 129, 130, 156
profit, 31, 92, 130, 160
profit margin, 160
programming, 19, 42, 46, 150, 156
project, 60, 149
proliferation, 6, 28, 39
property rights, 28
protection, 28, 36, 42, 50, 119, 122
public education, 59
public financing, 30
public health, 75
public sector, 16, 17, 27, 34, 61, 115
publishing, 46, 142, 157
Puerto Rico, 169, 188

Q

qualifications, 56
quality assurance, 60
quality control, 119
quality of life, 67, 69

query, 95
quotas, 6, 28, 39, 98

R

radio, 142
real estate, 162, 164, 173, 189
recession, vii, 1, 14, 15, 18, 19, 22, 29, 44, 51, 124, 132, 162
recognition, 52
recommendations, iv
recovery, 4, 100, 120, 190
recreation, 115
recruiting, 52, 57, 69, 164, 184
reform(s), 8, 19, 60, 61, 67, 76, 86, 104, 125, 127
refugees, 58
regional integration, 75, 162
regulations, 7, 19, 50, 51, 56, 60, 64, 75, 89, 134, 148, 173
reimburse, 124, 126
reinsurance, 4, 16
reliability, 119
repair, 13, 140, 142, 158, 160, 166, 179
reputation, 52, 53
requirements, 18, 34, 39, 42, 56, 122, 134, 135, 142, 143, 180, 189
resale, 115, 193
researchers, 5, 21, 60, 90, 117
reserves, 173
resilience, vii, 1, 14
resistance, 40
resource management, 173
resources, 57, 66, 79, 100, 114, 121, 123
response, vii, 2, 6, 28, 33, 46, 64, 67, 83, 139
restaurants, 31
restoration, 100
restrictions, 6, 7, 28, 39, 51, 60, 70, 77, 89, 132, 148
retail, viii, 115, 116, 133, 134, 147, 160, 161, 167, 168, 169, 170, 171, 173, 174, 175, 176, 178, 189, 193
retail industries, viii, 133
retirement, 75
revenue, 28, 29, 30, 32, 33, 34, 35, 36, 37, 39, 41, 44, 57, 65, 77, 79, 80, 81, 84, 117, 118, 127, 128, 129, 134, 144, 147, 151, 152, 153, 154, 158, 160, 162, 190, 191, 192, 193
rights, iv, 28, 37, 50, 76, 192
risk(s), 2, 13, 33, 67, 77, 125, 139
risk factors, 67, 125
Romania, 119, 127
root, 36
routes, 160, 164, 192
ruble, 30

rules, 99, 122
Russia, 10, 30, 118, 127, 129, 152, 167

S

SaaS, 45, 99
safety, 164
salaried workers, 143, 148
saturation, 39
Saudi Arabia, 11, 55, 69, 82, 86, 89, 112, 114, 129, 132
savings, 75, 123, 126
school, 7, 52, 57, 69
science, 92, 123
scope, 39, 59, 75, 82, 126, 147, 157, 165, 190
scripts, 35
seasonal changes, 164
securities, 115, 116, 144, 147, 188, 189, 190
security, 148, 153, 163
security services, 148, 153
self-employed, 120, 130, 143, 164
semiconductors, 43, 160
Serbia, 119
servers, 42, 121, 154
service firms, vii, 1, 9, 12, 80, 133, 134, 137, 138, 139, 149, 150, 152, 153, 154, 155, 156, 157, 158
service industries, vii, 1, 2, 3, 4, 5, 8, 9, 11, 13, 19, 20, 21, 22, 23, 25, 77, 115, 133, 134, 135, 137
service provider, 4, 8, 12, 18, 19, 36, 45, 119, 120, 134, 150, 153, 156, 158, 189, 192
service quality, 60
shortage, 69, 75, 76, 120, 125
shortfall, 76
signs, 39, 43, 138, 170
Silicon Valley, 128
Singapore, 35, 57, 75, 89, 112, 113, 114, 119, 127, 129, 131, 132
single currency, 162
skilled workers, 18, 156
small businesses, 118
small firms, 42, 80, 130
social network, 90
social sciences, 189
software, 6, 21, 40, 41, 42, 43, 44, 45, 46, 51, 119, 120, 121, 142, 150, 151, 154, 157, 160, 162, 166, 183, 190, 191
solution, 69
South Africa, 31, 36, 131
South America, 127
Southeast Asia, 30, 73, 75
SP, 119
Spain, 7, 29, 30, 33, 51, 59, 63, 64, 67, 127
special education, 52

specialists, 50, 69, 70, 72, 120, 127, 156, 191
specifications, 119
spending, 6, 7, 15, 29, 39, 40, 42, 51, 61, 62, 63, 65, 66, 71, 72, 74, 76, 82, 91, 107, 111, 112, 120, 123, 124, 126, 150, 152, 153, 167, 178
staffing, 82, 164, 184
stakeholders, 60
Star Wars, 119
state, 31, 38, 39, 52, 56, 70, 76, 84, 123, 164
states, 35, 68, 117, 120, 123, 130, 139, 164
statistics, 12, 37, 68, 71, 72, 90, 105, 120, 121, 129, 167
statutes, 50
stimulus, 43
stock, 137, 170, 189
storage, 44, 161, 162, 165, 166, 175
structural changes, 84
structure, 117, 118, 174
student enrollment, 7, 51, 57
student populations, 123
sub-Saharan Africa, 45, 69
substitutes, 138
substitution, 137, 139
substitution effect, 139
Sudan, 100, 121
supervisors, 139, 149, 158, 159, 171
supplier, 12, 28, 72, 74
suppliers, 3, 11, 25, 39, 44, 55, 86, 114, 142, 159, 166, 167, 173, 175, 176, 177, 178
supply chain, vii, 43, 133, 134, 142, 143, 157, 159, 160, 161, 173, 175, 177, 178, 192
support services, 56, 109, 118, 147, 148, 175
suppression, 17, 116
surplus, vii, 1, 2, 3, 4, 5, 6, 7, 8, 11, 13, 14, 25, 28, 37, 51, 57, 58, 61, 70, 72, 76, 84, 87, 115, 116
Sweden, 74, 127
Switzerland, 42, 50, 53, 97, 161

T

Taiwan, 36, 55, 97, 101, 127, 169
Tajikistan, 10
talent, 32
Tanzania, 31
target, 184
tax breaks, 35
tax credits, 33, 35
tax incentive, 28
taxation, 84
taxes, 39, 115
teams, 173
technical support, 150
techniques, 35, 176

technological advancement, 9
technological advances, 90
technological change, 90
technologies, 35, 36, 120
technology, 3, 19, 31, 33, 34, 35, 36, 51, 90, 100, 116, 119, 123, 143, 150, 154, 157, 163, 177
telecommunications, vii, 1, 15, 19, 49, 115, 116, 160, 189, 192
telephone, 85, 115, 127, 188
television stations, 117
tellers, 147
testing, 26, 117, 120, 139, 140, 142, 179, 189
Thailand, 55, 67, 118
threats, 36
time periods, 115
tobacco, 125
total costs, 160
total revenue, 30, 41, 43, 121, 128, 144, 150, 151
toys, 118
trade agreement, 39, 49
trade deficit, 4, 7, 11, 13, 16, 40, 45, 47
trade liberalization, 39, 116
trading partners, 9, 73
training, 69, 115, 116, 120
trajectory, 73, 76, 152, 171
transactions, vii, 1, 4, 9, 10, 11, 12, 13, 16, 17, 26, 27, 28, 37, 46, 58, 72, 73, 74, 76, 77, 82, 85, 90, 115, 116, 117, 121, 128, 131
transmission, 31, 34, 121
transparency, 60
transport, 13, 15, 19, 34, 115, 157, 159, 162, 173, 192
transportation, 4, 13, 14, 15, 18, 68, 115, 116, 158, 159, 160, 161, 162, 163, 165, 166, 189
treaties, 33
treatment, 39, 50, 64, 67, 68, 70, 71, 72, 75, 123, 126
trial, 70
truck drivers, 118, 163
tuition, 52, 56, 57, 58, 61, 103, 122, 123
turbulence, 43
Turkey, 55, 101, 148
type 2 diabetes, 67

U

U.S. Bureau of Labor Statistics, 173, 177
U.S. Department of Commerce, 2, 9, 12, 37, 46, 71, 85, 93, 95, 97, 101, 103, 104, 108, 113, 127, 135, 136, 137, 186, 188
U.S. Department of Labor, 2, 95, 97, 101, 114, 116, 118, 120, 130, 143, 148, 154, 171, 175, 184, 186, 187, 188
U.S. economy, 2, 11, 21, 52, 165, 171

U.S. immigration law, 35
UK, 41, 53, 55, 56, 70, 74, 75, 79, 80, 82, 104, 129, 146, 151
Ukraine, 10, 127
UN, 2, 37, 68, 71, 72, 73, 74, 108, 113, 126, 127
underwriting, 189
unemployed individuals, 124
unemployment rate, 66
UNESCO, 2, 30, 31, 54, 97, 103
uniform, 34, 119, 164
uninsured, 66, 68, 73, 76, 126
United Nations, 2, 31, 50, 54, 71, 73, 97, 100, 103, 108, 113, 120, 127, 185, 190
universe, 150, 157
universities, 7, 51, 52, 53, 54, 55, 56, 57, 58, 60, 61, 123
urban, 64, 76
Uruguay, 91
Uruguay Round, 91
USA, 69, 102, 103, 104, 106, 125, 126

V

valuation, 127
variables, 138, 139, 189
vehicles, 162
Venezuela, 38, 127
Vice President, 92, 93
videos, 28, 31
Vietnam, 55
visa system, 55
voting, 188
vulnerability, 21

W

wages, 4, 9, 11, 18, 23, 24, 49, 69, 83, 90, 91, 92, 137, 138, 139, 146, 148, 149, 156, 164, 189, 190
Washington, 93, 94, 95, 96, 97, 98, 100, 102, 105, 108, 110, 113, 114, 119, 181, 187, 188, 190, 192, 193

waste, 135, 136
waste management, 135, 136
water, 159
wealth, 123
web, 93, 120, 185, 190
websites, 146
welfare, 5, 9, 19, 90
Western Europe, 6, 40, 43, 51, 76, 169
white-collar workers, 21
WHO, 2, 63, 65, 109, 123, 124, 125, 127
wholesale, 17, 18, 46, 157, 173, 189
wind turbines, 175
Wisconsin, 113, 174
wood, 96, 119
work environment, 164
workers, 4, 5, 8, 11, 18, 19, 20, 21, 22, 23, 24, 42, 49, 50, 61, 66, 69, 75, 91, 117, 118, 122, 126, 138, 143, 149, 153, 154, 156, 157, 158, 159, 161, 164, 165, 167, 171, 175, 189
workforce, 2, 9, 69, 76, 84, 146, 154, 159, 163, 164, 171, 184
workload, 82
workplace, 164
World Bank, 15, 63, 65, 93, 94, 98, 100, 105, 108, 110, 111, 124, 144, 146, 181, 182, 190
World Health Organization(WHO), 2, 69, 106, 108, 124
World Trade Organization, 2, 49, 60, 94, 97, 101, 104, 115, 183
worldwide, 11, 14, 30, 34, 52, 67, 96, 118, 145
WTO, 2, 10, 12, 14, 15, 31, 37, 39, 49, 50, 94, 97, 101, 102, 104, 115, 117, 118, 119, 120, 121, 122, 123, 126

Y

Yale University, 53
yield, 189
yuan, 39